ES
JL2611

new
arcadians

new arcadians

EMERGING UK ARCHITECTS

Lucy Bullivant

MERRELL
LONDON · NEW YORK

Introduction

The exquisite propositions and projects in this book combine to provide a wealth of profound architectural scrutiny responding to the United Kingdom's programmatic needs in the twenty-first century. Architecture remains a meaningful cultural synthesis, if it is any good. Carefully assembled, these proposals would make an interesting fictional city. That is easily done in digital space, but *New Arcadians* is far better off elaborated as an illustrated book of stories – stories about the capacity to invent, and reinvent, through architecture.

It is seven years since I wrote *Anglo Files: UK Architecture's Rising Generation* (2005, published in the United States as *British Built*),[1] and a follow-up is well overdue. Since then the political, economic, cultural and social landscape of the United Kingdom has changed dramatically. Ecological and economic pressures mean that it is highly desirable to reassess, reuse and extend existing buildings, but new facilities are just as badly needed because social patterns are changing. This book celebrates the re-emergence of socially engaged architecture by young architects. It might not make front-page news that often, but actually it has never gone away. It was a force I analysed in great detail in *Space Invaders* (a touring exhibition for the British Council, curated with Pedro Gadanho, 2001–2003),[2] *Anglo Files* and many articles.

New Arcadians includes profiles of practices as well as their fascinating responses to a list of questions ranging from childhood memories, challenges, technical advances, communication tactics, and positions on making, thinking and the bespoke, to theories, typologies, good client relationships, participation and views on how to improve the procurement of architecture. Everyone answered in full with huge good will, spending time explaining things one would otherwise have to visit their studios to find out.

In essence, *New Arcadians* collects new evidence of the deep enthusiasm and commitment of emerging practices to devise affordable, robust solutions that respond imaginatively both to voiced wishes and to unspoken desires, not only in the United Kingdom but also across the world. These practices are part of the dynamic and entrepreneurial business community that exists in the United Kingdom, but they also work in a unique way: all those competitions, the long hours, the site research, the mix of teaching and practice, the speculative capacities, the energy, the optimistic gene that stays with them. You really need to love architecture to surf the waves of globalized practice, and they do. They and their peers use digital and social media in a myriad of ways as an innate part of their research and testing, gauging and gathering information and feedback, and responding to the needs of the community with maturity, generosity, intuition, playfulness, ingenuity and innovation.

Following on from *Anglo Files* and *Space Invaders*, *New Arcadians* considers anew the emerging languages and tactics of a purely personal selection of young, socially engaged architects. Most of the featured practitioners are in their thirties or early forties, since 'under forty' does not capture the full richness of emerging talent. We do not need to know how old everyone is, as though biological age were a badge of acceptability; rather, we need their readings of, and strategies for, society. We needed them a decade ago, and we need them just as much now, if not more, and not only because the affordability of projects is a big issue. It seemed useful to collect some clearly highly gifted practices in one book so that the overlaps and differences could be considered in clearer focus; although making just a small selection from the large number of talented emerging practitioners was a difficult task in itself.

Architecture is one of the very few generalist professions; medicine is another. I hesitate to say that both these will save us, because we all know that is not exactly true. But the presence of engaged architectural generalists at a time of economic crisis and the current government's localism agenda means that work of value to our cultural, social, ecological and economic future is taking place. It may not be because of a huge flow of funds, but is rather caused by the shared search for something better, with collaboration and commitment from all concerned, responding to and interpreting society's changing needs. Because good architects pay attention.

Rainham Marshes Nature Reserve, Essex, Peter Beard_LANDROOM (2011)

Kunsthülle Liverpool, OSA (2006)

London's Largest Living Room, Studio Weave (2008)

Why the title *New Arcadians*? Arcadia is for me simultaneously an idealized pastoral landscape and a poetic utopian idyll with some degree of mystique. A proverbial rustic paradise in the Renaissance, the Greek region of Arcadia was hit many times by population loss and natural disaster. The word stands for values that prioritize the integration between human activity and the environment, between dwelling places and nature. It stands for a public place in which people can feel engaged, one that has a conscious, responsible approach to natural cycles and energies, instead of ignoring their potential. The United Kingdom is waking up to new realities: what do we want from our land, our space, our architecture? With imagination and skill, what more can be done? *New Arcadians* is concerned with the aspiration for a new relationship between architecture and landscape, building and context, ecology and culture.

For good measure, I also throw into the associative pot Tom Stoppard's play *Arcadia* (1993), which explores the relationship between past and present and between order and disorder, and the certainty of knowledge. To make something meaningful, the utopia of the everyday makes the most of what there is – nature and landscape, for example; reuses what is there; builds on ecological knowledge; does not waste resources or regard climate change as something that industry alone has to face; engages in poetic narratives and with metaphor; and takes on such dichotomies as the ugly–beautiful conditions of society.

Testing and prototyping the future

The partners in many young practices teach alongside running their offices. The advantages for practising architects of developing academic programmes lie in their innate interdependency, reinforcing the opportunities to develop and refine methods and techniques. Keen to find fresh solutions, these architects make the most of limited means through lateral thinking. Testing and prototyping are an important part of their work, producing innovative fabrication techniques through heuristic processes.

The energy invested in the creative speculation that is the stock-in-trade of young architects helps them to envision a different, better, more thoughtfully arranged and, in many cases, more interactive future. Sometimes they must adjust reality to let that future in. This is not something to be nervous or self-conscious about; it is simply that designing the future involves far more than the next social media upgrade. Testing, prototyping and creative laboratories put speculative architecture on a par with best practice in science. The ethic of a dynamic relationship with one's civic environment is also put into motion, born not out of sheer necessity (as when brushes and brooms were brandished in the aftermath of the British riots in 2011) but out of the mindset that something greater will come if one is more than just a passive recipient or consumer.

I do not make a qualitative distinction between architects who adhere to parametric, software-enabled approaches to architecture and those with more analogue inspiration and tactics; I admire both methods. The question is whether dedication and skill are being applied through testing and prototyping to demonstrate valuable results in specific contexts. Does this project engage with the cultural lives of communities? Does it encourage the client to strive for higher standards in programme and design in the future? Does it maintain the necessary level of idealism about objectives, in spite of many difficulties? Is it a micro-arcadia? Does it reveal a magic quality in the everyday? And if not, why not? Zeal at too high a price is not fun or sensible for anyone, while restless innovation can move mountains. The art is in finding a balance between the two.

There is an innate playfulness about emerging architecture and the way it engages with its language. This phenomenon is not new; I charted it in *Space Invaders*, flagging up the communicative power of architecture through an informality of means, and examples in the present book include AOC's Lift – A New Parliament (pp. 34–35). There are various strands to this cultural approach. One is sampling and synthesizing, as AOC defines it, and

Rainham Marshes Nature Reserve, Essex, Peter Beard_LANDROOM (2011)

Martello Tower Y, Suffolk, Piercy Conner Architects (2010)

this is shared by such practices as David Kohn Architects (with the temporary restaurant Flash, for example, and more generally in the mixing of narratives). Concerned more with effect than with expense, this creative tactic is increasingly acknowledged by architecture in alignment with other art forms, such as music, film and fashion. Fundamentally, architecture is a social field in which art and science are mixed.

Bricks with everything?

There is a great deal of brick in the United Kingdom, and, depressingly, much of it has been put into service in a bland and uninspiring way, both historically and more recently. There is nothing innately bad about the material, and the New Arcadians show its varied potential, whether it is co-opted into reworking old building stock or applied to new buildings. Beyond that, materials are creative and affordable, ranging from David Kohn Architects' ETFE roof for Skyroom (pp. 56–57) and Studio Weave's scavenged hardwood bars for the Longest Bench (pp. 11 and 239) to AOC's off-the-shelf spindles at Hearth House (pp. 38–39), NORD's use of tarred shingles in Dungeness (pp. 162–65) and 6a Architects' burnt timbers treated in a traditional Japanese way for Raven Row (pp. 22–25). They are idiosyncratic, of course, but such hybrid, bespoke languages can make a space feel rich and multi-sensory.

Creating bespoke spaces is a matter not merely of the imaginative use of materials but also of taking spatial qualities away from the realms of repetition, pastiche and generic, undifferentiated environments. Plasma Studio and IJP (George L. Legendre), for example, create forms and spaces that express the many aspects of the contemporary world; in Plasma's case, in a way that is free of old linguistic and historic codings.

Creative reuse and ecological edutainment

Creative reuse has great ecological value, and is exemplified by Piercy Conner Architects' Martello Tower Y in Suffolk, a conversion of a Napoleonic defence tower dating from 1808 (above and pp. 190–91). At Rainham Marshes Nature Reserve in Essex, a post-industrial arcadia rescued from development more than a decade ago, Peter Beard_LANDROOM's rusted-steel shipping containers rendered as birdwatching hides (above, left, and p. 7) create a peaceful fusion of artificial nature and history. The apparent dichotomy of ugly–beautiful is not to be shied away from, but can be accepted as unavoidable, and the two reconciled by being given a dovetailed sense of purpose.

Another strand of this is architectural activism. EcoLogicStudio applies innovative techniques and technology to its research-based prototyping strategies. But the practice also encourages public involvement through interactive exhibitions and personal engagement with issues that affect society. It does this with appealing edutainment tools that break down perceived boundaries between research, tourism, agri-business and other newer industries, and citizens' ecological consciousness. IJP's installation PV [Photovoltaic] Dust in Abu Dhabi, for example, harnesses renewable energy, converts it into electrical power and distributes it to the city's grid. Such experimental concepts could have real agency without the need to wear a hair shirt (as many eco-activists focus on); many are conceived with a sense of exploratory play and an engaging grasp of the contemporary relevance of cybernetics. English cybernetician Gordon Pask, admired by such architects as EcoLogicStudio, did not strive in vain!

The rich spaces of the digital–physical threshold

Another aspect of this prototyping and testing is that, with the help of digital technology, architecture is forging a new relationship with nature. Through parametric modelling and the considered application of typologies to different contexts around the world, a hybrid architecture has emerged that can emulate the generative effects of nature. Serie's projects, for example – from the variegated branching structure of the Tote in Mumbai (p. 229) to the undulating web of hedges and various types of villa in the Bohacky-

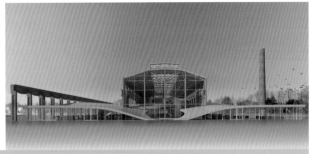

XianTian Di Factory H, Hangzhou, China, Serie (2010–)

Zahorska Bystrica masterplan in Bratislava (opposite and p. 228) – have a contextual sensitivity that engages the user.

Design strategies that produce a mix of programmes rather than compartmentalizing functions, and challenge the opposition between building and landscape, are central to GroundLab's work. These are coupled at the Xi'an International Horticultural Expo 2011 (pp. 204–207) with a landscape strategy conceiving green spaces and the river as one interactive, interconnected system, generating a coherent ecological strategy. The adaptable parametric architectural and urban design models GroundLab, Serie, MÆ and others adopt are relational in their urbanistic intentions. This means using new technology to spur new social organizations, environmental sustainability and economic development logic across sectors, and engaging multiple disciplines, allowing negotiation and the non-linear transfer of knowledge. The process entails the generation of typologies and a database-controlled distribution of components. The architects test massing, spatial qualities, the performance of infrastructure and alternative scenarios through three-dimensional models, making it easier for stakeholders, clients, developers and architects to communicate about a scheme. Relational urbanism enables a range of urban patterns and their effects to be evaluated, and means that the decision-making process can be inclusive, and the plans easily modifiable.

Robust proposals do not arise from cut-and-paste urban design. Past forms, ideas and processes may still carry weight, as the answers in the interviews about precedents attest, but this is allied with a desire to reinvent urban relationships. Younger architects research patterns as well as empirical givens, and find creative ways to rework them, even at a very small scale, applying them with a deft mix of intuition and scientific rigour.

Working in the negotiated system

While the Dutch talk about the 'makeable' society, the United Kingdom's fabric is malleable and open to reinterpretation, if only it could be persuaded away from the perils of excessive codification by planners. One young planner, the architect Finn Williams, for example, calls the English system 'arcane' and 'negotiated', less a scenario of strict zoning laws than in the United States or elsewhere in Europe: 'There are few clear-cut rules but plenty of guidance to interpret and bend … [This] allows for eccentricity and the unexpected.' This is an advantage in a country with so many layers of history and old ways of doing things, some of which remain valid. Planners now even consider well-thought-out projects of certain kinds for the once sacrosanct territory of the green belt; the edge of Letchworth Garden City is the site of MÆ's non-denominational chapel, mausoleum and cemetery, in a parkland setting that provides a transition between the city and the countryside (pp. 154–55).

When it comes to a vision of housing, the proliferating sensibility is one of affordability and the achievement of maximum value through the shrewd use of means and techniques. As MÆ attests, based on extensive research into present housing needs carried out by everyone in this book, housing models for the twenty-first century should be flexible enough to adapt to various locations and types of inhabitant. Not a catalogue style, not a low space standard, not hemmed in by planning codification, but working adeptly within restrictions of budget, location and legislation.

Well-being can be promoted by architecture through design that responds to climate change with permeable building envelopes and passive techniques of lighting and temperature control, etc., that allows access to landscape for psychological reasons, and in which due attention is given to light and to legible, non-cellular circulation. At this juncture, making long-lasting, low-carbon buildings with a loose fit, but which are non-generic in spatial language, is both ecologically sound and stimulating. One suitable approach, the pavilion, is exemplified by Duggan Morris Architects' (DMA) proposal for the South London and Maudsley Hospital's New Learning Centre (pp. 76–77), which aims to challenge preconceptions of mental illness, and is also strongly connected to the surrounding landscape.

Bohacky-Zahorska Bystrica masterplan, Bratislava, Slovakia, Serie (2009–)

The Longest Bench, Littlehampton, Studio Weave (2010)

The New Arcadians' organizational and networking strategies enable framework planning to work with, not against, communities, furthering a vision of creative collaboration on urban projects, rather than one of lone developments put into place unilaterally. The urban strategies of the former Regional Development Agencies, sadly closed down by the present coalition government, drawing on the impulses of 'urban renaissance' advocated by Richard Rogers in 2000, are still present. Young architects are deeply involved in community activism contributing to this, from the Centre for Community Practice jointly set up in Glasgow by Alan Pert of NORD, and MÆ's and Gort Scott's work with Design for London (now part of the Greater London Authority), to such collaborative ventures as 6a Architects' Offley Works in south London.

Amelioratory strategies evolved with strong stakeholder involvement – such as East's work on the Uxbridge Road Public Realm or Studio Egret West's masterplan for East Croydon – can involve social enterprise (as with the revival of Brixton Village) or public artworks that draw attention to local priorities of all kinds (as the Liverpool Biennale has done by involving such polemical practices as Gross.Max and the American avant-gardists Diller Scofidio + Renfro). Even the 'worst' can be seen as an opportunity, as with the Denny: Future Town scheme by Architecture + Design Scotland with Denny High School, for a degenerated town centre in Stirlingshire.

Reclaiming spaces: Cedric's cultural cues

In focusing on urban-design plans and proposals, temporary projects and exhibition design, I am taking my cue from the radical English architect Cedric Price (1934–2003), who remains a strong inspiration for British architects. He is known for having said that sometimes the best solution is not a building at all. Many of our emerging architects are natural collaborators and excellent framework planners: a valuable asset at a time when communities need help steering towards localized solutions, as the present government appears

to want. The field of urban design has long been concerned with drawing out a fresh sense of potential from communities, rather than with cultural imposition. This requires extensive research as the first step in any project – information must be up-to-date and site-specific, not generic and third-hand – and the careful matching of means to the required ends.

Taking a microplanning approach to the high street, for example – as Gort Scott was invited to do with the Bartlett, University College London, in 2009 for the London Development Agency's High Street London agenda – to understand better the function of high streets as it relates to a city or town's sustainable growth and development, requires the neglect of their latent value to be overcome. This takes them out of the abstract categories of retail hierarchy or transit corridors, as they have usually been regarded in terms of planning and transportation. It entails thorough research into oral and written memories, exploring the notion of the street as a place for markets and social exchange, as Architecture + Design Scotland has also been doing.

Public spaces remain a key part of a city's identity, and in them is developing a sense of domestic intimacy that goes far beyond the modern identikit cappuccino street culture of our cities and towns. Going into the realms of the custom-designed and embedded in idiosyncratic contexts, such architecture and design (Studio Weave's Longest Bench in Littlehampton, West Sussex, for instance; above and p. 239) skirts or enters the territory of public art. While most installations are part of existing programmes, the capacity of younger architects (OSA is a good example) to reclaim abandoned spaces in an ad hoc way is laudable; it is mirrored by community groups in cities, for example in London with Vacant Lot (an allotment scheme in Shoreditch, 2007) or Ben Faga's biodynamic apiaries at King's Cross and Dalston (If You Build It, They Will Come, 2010). There is also the practice 00:/, which transformed an unoccupied residential building in a post-industrial suburb in the West Midlands into a community 'living room'. Young architects enjoy the idiosyncrasy of infill or making something work in unprepossessing

South London Gallery, 6a Architects (2010)

Frieze Art Fair, London, Carmody Groarke (2011)

urban scenarios with innumerable layers of history: for example, the urban garden setting of Kings Grove in Peckham (pp. 70–71) by DMA, or 6a Architects' Raven Row and South London Gallery (opposite and pp. 20–25).

This impulse is not part of 'the experience economy', as Hal Foster puts it in his recent book *The Art-Architecture Complex* (2011), fuelling 'banal cosmopolitanism', but rather illustrates the wish to explore the creative potential of urban voids, and mirrors similar global activities. In the early twenty-first century British cities became 'laboratories of the new enterprise economy', as Owen Hatherley wrote in *A Guide to the New Ruins of Great Britain* (2010). He described the country's relative dereliction as an expression of 'a failed politics'. By contrast, and in an era of economic crisis, bottom-up creative reuse is authentic and focused.

New Arcadians are empiricists. 00:/, for example, wants to create 'genuinely sustainable places founded on evidenced social, economic and environmental principles'. Principles: now those will take architecture forward in a way that the tired polarization of traditionalism and modernism never will.

Public consultation

This book advocates further investment in a lucid set of public consultation techniques and participatory methods, to allow diverse groups to establish shared priorities for local development. I understand the cynicism and negativity that exist in the United Kingdom concerning this field: failure burdens the soul, and in the 1970s and 1980s many community plans were squashed by much more powerful business interests. It is still valid to ask people why places are significant to them and what they would like, and to show them alternatives to doing nothing or choosing conservative approaches.

A strong sense of local ownership has accrued from Making Space in Dalston, for example (an initiative of Design for London, designed by J. & L. Gibbons and MUF Architecture/Art; p. 14), which consists of seventy-six small-scale public-realm proposals. Its most recent project is the Eastern Curve Garden, which hosts community activities and is staffed by the campaign group Open Dalston. Moreover, the borough's masterplan benefits from the testing of proposals within the community, a type of collaborative research.

Fast-track and low-carbon opportunities

With reduced budgets and improvisatory means to the fore in many cases, a new gestation period for architectural projects is emerging with full force. The pop-up, the agitprop, the functioning 'found object' installation that can be disassembled and moved, the near-spontaneous happening (crowd-sourced or otherwise) are all facets of a phenomenon that includes such movements as guerrilla gardening. Mobile and temporary structures, from AOC's Lift – A New Parliament to Carmody Groarke's pavilions, create new, interactive cultural opportunities without the time or investment conventionally required by permanent buildings. While the solidity and enduring nature of tectonics and materials can produce glorious and fitting landmarks for the twenty-first century, the rise of fast-track and/or reusable, recyclable architecture, nimbly responding to changing social needs, has the power to bring fresh narratives. It would be cynical to call the ephemeral side of architecture – the more immediately delivered architectural projects – doomed performances.

Fast-track, medium-term and long-range plans all need to promote the minimum use of carbon as a high priority if we are ever to shift from a fossil-fuel economy to a renewable one, in which resources are managed in cycles and nothing is lost as waste. Architecture, with its combination of science and art, and its interpretative and collaborative skills, is perfectly placed to help effect the transformation. Various schemes in this book, from MÆ's Clay Country Eco-House in Cornwall (p. 148) and 6a Architects' Mines Farm in Cambridgeshire (p. 18) to EcoLogicStudio's villa conversion at Ciriè in Italy (p. 92) and Algae Farm masterplan on the coast of Sweden (p. 87), and Piercy Conner Architects' 'Restello' housing for Kolkata (pp. 188–89), show that a modest budget is no obstacle to effective and imaginative ends.

Making Space, Dalston, London, J. & L. Gibbons and MUF Architecture/Art (2009–)

Evelyn Grace Academy, Brixton, London, Zaha Hadid Architects (2010)

Passivhaus principles are increasingly followed, for example in the award-winning houses by Justin Bere of Bere Architects.

Landscape: a vital connective tissue

Urban agriculture, green roofs, recycling schemes, pocket parks and green lungs are all proliferating. But there are as many areas of difficulty. Playing fields are being sold off and youth clubs closed down, and new green-space projects are just as likely to be shelved as shopping centres, if not more so. Natural landscape as a public amenity is an important part of cities and towns, and needs to be preserved and used in a myriad of ways.

While this book is not about young landscape architects per se – they deserve a book in their own right – the featured practices all embrace the synergy of building and landscape in their own way. This has political overtones at a time when public-realm schemes in which landscape design is used to soften the impact – such as the exemplary work by Design for London – have faced financial cuts. Finding a way of integrating a vision for landscape into a project, as Gort Scott's Finding Flotmyr proposal (pp. 112–13), GroundLab's Xi'an scheme (pp. 204–207) and AOC's Spa School (p. 31) exemplify, helps to give a context character and ambition.

Related to this is the growing awareness of the need to nurture rural contexts. The Planning Policy Statement 7 system introduced in 2004 by the Department for Communities and Local Government allows exemplar schemes to be built in rural areas, and Featherstone Young's Ty Hedfan house near Brecon in Powys is a convincing example of how hard the planning authorities are trying to encourage outstanding projects, not merely to prove they can be done, but also to enhance the fabric in all territories, urban and rural, without discriminating against place.

There was a time in the United Kingdom when landscaping was invariably commissioned late in a project, as an embellishment that was peripheral to formal tectonics. This is fortunately no longer the case: the landscape architect is a more prominent figure, and works very closely with architects, taking on urbanism with a long-term vision. Three examples are J. & L. Gibbons' work across the United Kingdom and its ongoing collaboration with MUF Architecture/Art on Making Space in Dalston; Gross.Max's work with Zaha Hadid Architects (most recently at the Riverside Museum in Glasgow); and the Jubilee Gardens scheme by Dutch practice West 8 on London's South Bank, due to be finished in time for the Queen's Diamond Jubilee and the Olympic Games in 2012.

The field is full of inspirational young practitioners, including the founder of the architectural practice Exploration, Michael Pawlyn, a young architect who takes his cue from nature via biomimicry, and who was for a decade part of the core team at Grimshaw behind the Eden Project in Cornwall. Pawlyn's first book, *Biomimicry in Architecture* (2011), focuses on nature as the inspiration for building forms.

Client bodies

New forms of client body have appeared in the new century, for example the international charity ARK (founded in 2002), with a philanthropic investment programme that includes ARK Schools (2004–), an initiative that aims to close the achievement gap between pupils from disadvantaged and affluent backgrounds. The charity's Evelyn Grace Academy in Brixton, south London (above), was confidently designed by Zaha Hadid Architects to a complex brief, and won the Royal Institute of British Architects' Stirling Prize in 2011, to some controversy. (We need more awards; one major prize is not enough in such a varied field.) The rise of the ethical marketplace via private philanthropic giving is something 00:/ has speculated on, using the term 'pro-social neighbourhoods'. The vision and commitment of such clients should be cherished and emulated.

A vast amount has been done since *Anglo Files* came out in 2005. Going through a severe economic crisis in an increasingly economically polarized society

The Guts, New Islington Millennium Village, Manchester, MÆ (2009–)

Janet Summers Early Years Centre, London, AOC (2006)

points to the value of new institutional forms of social outreach: campaigning groups, social entrepreneurship, mentoring programmes and so on. These should not be substitutes for the support of central and local government, but may constitute another layer of procurement that deserves to flower.

Health and happiness

MÆ has consistently carried out research into the way health can be improved through good design of the built environment, in response to the Marmot review (*Fair Society, Healthy Lives: A Strategic Review of Health Inequalities in England Post-2010*, 2011). MÆ's shortlisted project for the Deansgate Exchange area of Salford, Greater Manchester, for example, focuses on four core values: fair employment and social inclusion; life-cycle design (reducing the environmental impact of architecture, its systems and materials through strategies for recyclability, reusability and ecological management and their performance); health, happiness and nature; and the benefits of environmental sustainability. It goes far beyond a 'that would be nice' conversation into concrete design proposals that have long-term effects, but to straddle the two is fundamental. Talking about the practice's housing scheme at New Islington in Manchester (above), MÆ partner Michael Howe recently said, 'We want this to be a happy and sociable place', adding: 'Give a man a balcony and he eats on his own. Give a man a garden and he barbecues for life – with all his mates.'

Many aspects of society need creative input from architecture, and health and learning are two critical areas. Emerging patterns of activity – life-long use of schools and colleges, a more holistic approach to health – necessitate responsive architecture and call for discussion with the public, hence the desirability of informal design charrettes. One such, Green [in] the Suburbs (2008), staged by the young architects' collective Departure Lounge in Bristol (one of three such bodies in south-west England), was a mix of discussion, design, urban exploration, art, model-making and fun, with the participation of professionals, students, locals and visitors.

The flexible modernism that has evolved on the British architectural scene since the 1980s and is visible in most award-winning schemes has been joined by other currencies, which – although modernist at root – engage with very specific alternative practices through fresh design languages, hybrid strategies and rigorous methodologies. This book is not about 'isms' but rather about valid architectural approaches in contemporary society. That our emerging architects may include an arcadian architectural sensibility in their kitbag of creative ways and means can only be a bonus.

1 *Anglo Files* discussed the work of Adams Kara Taylor (structural engineer); Adjaye Associates; Alison Brooks Architects; Allford Hall Monaghan Morris; AOC; Ash Sakula; Atopia; Caruso St John Architects; de Rijke Marsh Morgan Architects; DSDHA; Bill Dunster; East; FAT; Field Operations; Kathryn Findlay; Fluid Architecture; Foreign Office Architects; General Public Agency (curators/facilitators)/Nils Norman (artist); Gollifer Langston Architects; Gross.Max; Michael Hadi (structural engineer); Hudson Architects; Jamie Fobert Architects; Sebastian Khourian and Ciro Najle; Klein Dytham architecture; McDowell + Benedetti; MUF Architecture/Art; Niall McLaughlin Architects; OSA; Plasma Studio; Annalie Riches, Silvia Ullmayer and Barti Garibaldo; S333; Sarah Wigglesworth Architects; Sergison Bates; ShedKM; Softroom Architects; Surface Architects; Tonkin Liu; Charles Walker (structural engineer); Dominic Williams; Witherford Watson Mann; and ZM Architecture.

2 *Space Invaders* discussed the work of Adjaye Associates; Atopia; Block Architecture; de Rijke Marsh Morgan Architects; dECOi; East; FAT; Foreign Office Architects; General Lighting and Power; Klein Dytham architecture; MUF Architecture/Art; Piercy Conner Architects; S333; Softroom Architects; and Urban Salon.

6a Architects

'Our aim is to ensure that contemporary spaces are enlivened by their relationship and contact with history, and that existing heritage is also enhanced by the new buildings', say 6a Architects, whose best-known realized projects are subtle experiences. The practice favours a mix of the new and innumerable layers of the old – especially borne out by interventions in east, south and central London (the last within a Regency terrace designed by John Nash) – as a means of evolving a lightly but thoroughly contemporary spatial feel, fundamentally wedded to its architectural and social context.

The extension and restoration by 6a of the Grade I-listed Raven Row (2009) in Spitalfields, east London, as a new centre for contemporary art for Alex Sainsbury, and of the South London Gallery (2010), a Grade II-listed building in Peckham, south London, received excellent reviews and feedback from visitors.

Raven Row sits on a former weapons practice ground on Artillery Row, subsequently occupied by a monastery, then by luxury shops for Huguenot silk merchants, before the buildings were modernized in the nineteenth century, and housed market workers in the early twentieth century. The new art exhibition centre, in what is now a hugely gentrified area, involved the addition, to the existing warren of rooms, of two gallery rooms sunk below street level, building on this raw wealth of history with the help of a historic-building consultant, Nick Tyson. The difference between the older fabric and 6a's intervention is blurred by the merging of design language, including shared construction and ironmongery details (such as sand-cast bronze doorknobs), lighting and materials, including cast-iron panels based on Georgian timber mouldings and burnt timber fabricated in a traditional Japanese way. The unfolding sequence of rooms and offices with their exposed concrete floors, below a flat for a guest curator or artist, is in keeping with 6a's idiosyncratic melding of narratives, evoking the historical spirit of Spitalfields without copying the past.

The practice's scheme for extending the South London Gallery, which has a longstanding history (Edward Burne-Jones and

A Rococo room in the historically hybrid Raven Row art gallery in Spitalfields, east London (consisting of two eighteenth-century silk mercers' houses and a concrete-framed office building dating from 1972, reworked in 2009). In 6a's narrative design a mix of spaces, surfaces and textures connects old with new.

William Morris were associates) and international reputation, and is set in wooded parkland bordered by a housing estate, elegantly reworks the identity of the gallery, expanding from its Victorian house on to the footprint of its original lecture hall. The main features are a double-height building with a cafe (called No67) and function room overlooking the garden, and the Clore Studio, a second, larger education and events studio with a skylight and fully pivoting doors below walls of art, opening into the garden. There is also a flat for artists. While the original gallery, which opened in 1891, is of Portland stone with handmade pressed bricks, the two 'boxes' are soberly clad in brown Eternit cement board composed in a bespoke pattern with brass clips designed by 6a. 'Very similar tones are mixed randomly to get a slightly textured overall colour', explains 6a director Tom Emerson. These are key elements in a loose ensemble incorporating well-managed shifts in scale.

In 2011, 6a won a planning appeal to design Mines Farm, a zero-carbon five-bedroom house on 39 hectares of arable land in Weston Green, Cambridgeshire, an exception allowed to the rule of not developing rural contexts, provided the project is truly outstanding. The planning inspector said the design fitted this criterion of significantly and sensitively enhancing its setting through its innovative use of materials and construction method (a two-layer exposed-concrete-and-timber frame with Hemcrete infill), and would act as a local landmark of considerable interest.

The practice's approach to the recent invitation for proposals for the Nash-designed home of the Institute of Contemporary Arts (ICA) on the Mall in central London is in line with Cedric Price's much-quoted comment that, sometimes, one may not actually need a building. Instead of inserting a lot of new design, 6a has fundamentally decluttered the existing fabric, reinventing its identity, but not in a facadist way. The practice has stripped back the Nash Regency building's entrance hall, at which it was initially asked to look, taking out the bookshop so visitors can see the gallery and cinema, uncovering windows and giving the ICA a sense of openness and freshness.

The building no longer matched the ways in which departments wanted to work, but – rather than giving it a major redesign – 6a chose to instigate a process-led renewal, investigating how an intervention could better reflect the way the organization was changing. By stripping out layers of fit-out, the existing building was rediscovered and redeployed, and the circulation improved. 'We wanted to find the qualities of the space', says 6a co-director Stephanie Macdonald.

The original building read as a hidden white box, but 6a made opening it up a key principle of the work. After discussing with the client how to meet the needs of the ICA's members, 6a chose not to make a members' room, but instead created the ICA Studio, a multipurpose room for members above one of the cinemas, in a space that had served as a workshop and delivery depot for more than forty years. The practice replaced the old, yellowed roof lights, creating a new sliding version in clear glass so that neighbouring buildings are clearly visible. The Studio houses the ICA archive (until now stored in different locations around London), but is versatile in use, and kitted out with bespoke, reconfigurable and easily stored furniture by the designer Simon Jones, who also designed the folding seats for Studio Weave's Floating Cinema (see p. 237).

Since 2007, 6a has been working on Offley Works, now in planning, in Kennington, south London. Built about 1899 for the manufacture of pickles and chutney, and sold by Lambeth Council in 2004 to the London Development Agency (LDA), the dilapidated complex is being regenerated by developer Matching Green into houses, flats and workspaces in which apprentice schemes can also be run. Six deep-plan warehouses with a total area of 6000 square metres, close to neighbouring buildings, are being transformed through an 'explicitly low-key approach', says Emerson. By cutting a section through the buildings connecting east and west courtyards, 6a's design opens them up and adds a new access route for the public, while instituting a full range of sustainable principles on the innovative mixed-use site, a policy of Matching Green. Design for London, working with the LDA Land and Development Team and the Architecture Foundation, ran a limited design competition, as a result of which 6a was selected for its sensitive approach to the reuse of existing buildings.

6a excels at hardworking spaces: a studio for the photographer Juergen Teller and a house for the artist Richard Wentworth are now on site, as are the refurbishment and extension of the Grade I-listed Romney Studio in Hampstead, north London, and the refurbishment of Gallery 40 as the Fashion Gallery at the Victoria and Albert Museum. 6a's DNA is, however, more than merely modest; it is exploratory, restorative, capable of plumbing the depths of history and embedding and/or coming up with viable new meaning. Viable means many things: the calm spaces for the South London Gallery have more than doubled attendance; and the engaging fusion of rooms and layered domestic aura, ideal for improvisatory use, has enabled the not-for-profit Raven Row to realize a fine addition to the East End art scene.

The South London Gallery in Peckham (2010) holds breakthrough shows by young artists alongside installations by internationally established artists. It is based in a refurbished, formerly derelict Victorian house that was used as a working-men's college in the mid-nineteenth century. The wall drawing is by Dan Perjovschi.

Interview with Tom Emerson and Stephanie Macdonald

Can you recount a few architectural memories from childhood?
SM When I was a child my family would go on long walks on the Downs and in the woods south of London, and I'd find amazing spaces that became great halls, houses and castles. My dad could never extract me from the family sack of wooden bricks. We would make epic structures taller than ourselves.
TE Making tree houses.

How would you describe your architectural background?
Unconventional in parts, but privileged in the brilliant and passionate teachers we have been fortunate enough to have met in both art and architecture schools.

What are your greatest influences, architectural or otherwise?
Lina Bo Bardi and João Batista Vilanova Artigas are currently to the fore; the artist Richard Wentworth, the illustrator Sempé and the writer Georges Perec have always been there, too.

Give one example of the way in which your architecture communicates effectively with people.
The South London Gallery has provoked very warm responses from artists, critics and visitors. There is something about its character that makes it a powerful place for art, yet also intimate and social, and which seems to draw people to it.

Are you a maker or a thinker?
We work very hard to avoid that opposition. Making is a form of thinking and thinking is a form of making.

Do you prefer bespoke or standardized?
The world needs both.

What theories lie behind your design methods and practice?
Raven Row, our new contemporary art gallery in Spitalfields, and the South London Gallery, for example, represent an approach that tries to remove the opposition in architectural discourse between tradition and the contemporary. Theories were necessary

South London Gallery

The three-storey extension behind the house contains double-height, 6-metre-high space – part gallery, part garden room – with views of the sky and surrounding buildings (opposite). A wall painting by Ernst Caramelle (far left, top) dominates one of the first-floor galleries in the original house, 67 Peckham Road (far left), where irregular floorboards and empty fireplaces contrast with the flush white surfaces of the contemporary gallery. The new stair (left) replaces a traditional Victorian staircase but retains a domestic feel. Its supporting steel stringers, which brace the original brick facade like a vertical truss, merge with painted timber. The wall drawing is by Gary Woodley.

a hundred years ago to clear away the muddle between the repressive morality of Victorian values and the emancipation promised of technology (and the future). Today theory only deepens outdated dichotomies between tradition (conservatism) and technology (avant garde), or between nature and culture. In these projects, we have tried to find an approach where history and the contemporary form a single body in which all experience, whether embedded in history or anticipated, exists in the present.

We are more interested in the ideas within contemporary art and literature, where narrative plays a more inclusive role to reconcile differences, than in the rhetoric of rival architectural styles. Special attention to materiality helps embody these narratives in architecture. History does not begin here and end there: it is always going on – as is the contemporary. Environments and buildings are never complete but are continuously under construction directed by the users as well as the architects.

Do you strive to create new architectural typologies? If so, please give an example.
Typologies are not so relevant any more. Every type has been overwritten by another at some point. More interesting is to find ways of making space that respond specifically to contemporary life, which is fluid and changing all the time, rather than establishing a new typology.

What are the most challenging aspects of your architectural practice today?
Finding clients who share our architectural values, and holding on to them in the face of economics to make meaningful work.

What impact do you hope your architecture has on the public realm?
To be inclusive, adaptable, beautiful, challenging.

What personal significance do you give to architectural precedent?
Precedent taken in broad terms is extremely important. It can be a building that inspires you, but more often it is a combination of things one has experienced that can stimulate the design process; a film combined with photography, a conversation and a walk all form a background from which new ideas are developed.

Raven Row

6a's contemporary art galleries within a new semi-basement in eighteenth-century houses represent its latest venture into spaces that bind past and present (opposite). The practice lowered the floors by 1.5 metres to increase the useable wall space. The first-floor plan (below, top, with ground-floor and basement plans below) shows the charred roof lights on the green roof above one of the galleries. Pictured right is a first-floor room in 56 Artillery Lane in 1972.

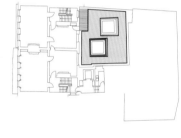

Which technical advances excite you the most for exploitation?

Communication and the ease with which one can cross-fertilize different media.

Do you practise a transdisciplinary approach to architecture, and if so, what is especially important to you right now?

Always; no architect works alone. We have collaborated with many fashion designers, artists, engineers, scientists and historians. The most important thing is to synthesize all this available knowledge in a creative way, and not just apply it.

How do you go about generating the best possible relationship with your clients?

By listening to them always, and challenging them sometimes. Important clues can be found in the most ordinary observation. The relationship develops over time, and one has to balance provocation with accommodation.

Can you give an example of your participatory methods?

Genuine participation requires time and sound choices. We involve our clients in architectural decisions through detailed material models and drawings, and the work is developed with their engagement.

How do you communicate your architecture?

With models, photographs, prototypes, drawings and text.

What do you aim to achieve with your practice (in a single sentence)?

To make places that are beautiful and useful, support civic life, encourage social life and sustain private life.

What advice would you give to a young architect embarking on their career?

Look hard at the world that surrounds you: that's where ideas are found, but they are often well hidden. Don't compromise.

What single improvement to the procurement of architecture in the United Kingdom would you recommend? More competitions, different planning system, legislation affecting developers, etc.?

More planners with a knowledge of and passion for architecture.

Raven Row

A tough urban language is conveyed by the cast-iron facade on Frying Pan Alley at the rear of the building. It is fabricated in a traditional Japanese way and bears the texture of its burnt timber mould (opposite, top left).

AOC

AOC stands for Agents of Change, and, since 2003, when the practice was founded, this versatile, agile group of 'architects, urbanists and interpreters' has propelled into motion its compelling grasp of the forces and factors – besides architects and architecture – that shape spaces. Complementing the practice's built work, AOC Participation, an in-house unit, specializes in consultation and participation, working to allow diverse groups to establish shared priorities concerning local development, a much-needed specialist field in which to develop a clear and engaging approach. The team also places individuals in organizations – as project managers, advisers and teachers – to help with the exchange of knowledge and ideas, and to build communities.

Sampling and synthesizing are techniques that AOC likes to apply to its design work. It is clear about the reason why, too: 'If this were to feel like the invention of one designer it could be too claustrophobic, suffocating the potential for the family to create their own associations and narratives for the space', explains Geoff Shearcroft in his essay 'Domestic Discovery or Sampling & Synthesizing with Daft Punk', published in the architectural fanzine *PEAR* (*Paper for Emerging Architectural Research*, no. 3, 'Sample & Synthesis', guest-edited by Tom Coward, 2011).

Giving an insight into how far this could be taken with the public realm – in which the same problems recur, but in different ways – incisive rigour and democracy are always beneficial. That issue of *PEAR* also includes Vincent Lacovara's amusingly telling 'Note of Meeting' of a Public Realm Workshop (set in 2011, but really timeless) that could be of great use to so many towns. In considering the transformation of a town's public realm from a 'corporate concrete graveyard', a 'mini-Manhattan', why not synthesize ambitions and sample the myriad visions and views by letting your fellow stakeholders speak without interruption, and now, and for all time, use PESTLE cues (Political, Economic, Social, Technical, Legal and Environmental) to help develop a SWOT (Strengths, Weaknesses, Opportunities and

The civic nature of the Spa School's facade (Bermondsey, London, 2011) harmonizes the street elevation, bringing together disparate elements of the school estate and signalling a fitting image to the wider community. WIth its red English-bond brickwork with matching mortar, the east elevation complements the existing Victorian building. AOC has reinterpreted the depth of the original facade, with protruding brickwork framing significant windows and recessed bricks forming a pattern of crosses.

Threats) analysis, and positively engage with the process by duly recording your thoughts as spider diagrams on large sheets of paper?

The Janet Summers Early Years Centre in Southwark, south London (2006), part of a strategic framework for the long-term development of its site, and the Lift – A New Parliament mobile performance space (2008–) put AOC on the map, two projects born of modest means but which have had a major impact. Potentially a theatre, concert hall, open-air stage, cinema, gallery or public meeting space, the Lift, an arts venue commissioned by the London International Festival of Theatre (LIFT) group and the London Thames Gateway Development Corporation, has travelled to numerous locations in London. A kind of reconfigurable village hall, it transforms the city square, playing field or housing estate in which it is installed into something immediately interesting through the play between its monumental scale and the translucent patterned facade, inspired by the personalized intricacy of the hand-sewn quilt. A flexible membrane based on a tent with a huge retractable front window, it was designed to be installed in different locations, with scope for other structures with their own lighting to be built inside it, and for the internal space to be adapted.

At Hearth House (2008) in Golders Green, north London, a semi-detached Edwardian house for a family of five, AOC created a space that, Shearcroft explains, 'would feel instantly familiar, loaded with past stories … combining the qualities of the eighteenth-century country house, the 1960s communal loft and the twenty-first-century media hub'. The new triple-height central space employs a mix of architectural styles, sampled and synthesized in response to different functions and symbolic associations. Ascending alongside a mock-Georgian balustrade to a landing that divides in two, the visitor notices the classic Modern open-tread steel stair to the attic. Planks of jarrah wood (a type of eucalyptus) from a demolished hospital were co-opted for the striking chevron parquet floor, a pattern that recurs in the hearth shuttering; £3.50 off-the-shelf spindles were used for the balustrade.

Longstanding tactics in art and architecture (seen in the work of John Soane, Edwin Lutyens, Robert Venturi and James Stirling), sampling and synthesizing in AOC's hands are about valuing 'hobbyism' ('do-it-yourself') and effect, rather than expense. The practice enjoys every aspect of the everyday and the lessons that can be learned from radical, affordable innovation: at Levittown on Long Island, for example – the archetypal, first mass-produced post-war American suburb, organically clustered with curved streets developed from the late 1940s – the houses are a blend of economical means and the promise of appropriate living space,

child-centred and with a common area, and expandable enough to accommodate growth in family and in wealth.

Realized projects that build on AOC's early success include an ingenious reworking of the Street, the public ground-floor atrium running through the Royal Armouries museum in Leeds (2008), conceived as an 'instant ruin' with new decorative appliqués; and, more recently, the Spa School, a new teaching block for secondary pupils with autistic-spectrum disorders, in Bermondsey, south London (2011). A school conceived as 'the best vision of a home', the latter has a garden treated as external classrooms, 'rehearsing the children for life', as part of AOC's long-term masterplan for the campus.

The principle of good, affordable domestic architecture is important to AOC. The practice admires Le Corbusier's Pessac experimental worker housing near Bordeaux (1920s): homogeneous, cubist and low-cost, adapted by its owners, and discussed by Philippe Boudon in *Lived-in Architecture: Le Corbusier's Pessac Revisited* (1972). Crown Terrace courtyard housing, for the Wandle Housing Association at Elephant & Castle in south London (2008), has the brick wrap associated with the London terraced house but evolves the typology to give the family-house scheme the adaptive potential and amenity more usually associated with the English 'semi'. The quality of the private space is increased by an accessible roof terrace behind two-storey timber boxes, clad to the residents' requirements in gold shingles (actually a copper–aluminium alloy), asphalt, timber, render or rubber, and an internal courtyard, a solution that is geared to the myriad tastes of inhabitants and engages with many different concerns relating to public housing.

AOC's language aims to change the feel of a space, to make it feel richer. The practice likes designing projects with immediate impact, triggered by multiple sensory memories of spaces. That makes its work linguistically diverse: from the subtle gestures of Hearth House to the playful propaganda of No. 1 Carbon Drive, a touring exhibition about reducing carbon dioxide emissions in residential buildings, in a structure similar to a Victorian terraced house in London's Trafalgar Square in 2007, to the interactive Polyopoly game, an exhibit in the Experimental Architecture section of the Venice International Architecture Biennale in 2008. One of its most expressive proposals to date, though, is the biomorphically shaped 'all-star' hotel and park with a restored 'pier' on Birnbeck Island off Weston-super-Mare in Somerset, AOC's entry to a competition staged by developer Urban Splash. 'Rupert Bear' picturesque, and reminiscent in an Anglicized way of Coney Island, it explores 'made nature'. If realized, it might even prompt another strand to the versatile AOC repertoire: that of home-grown magic realism.

AOC was placed second in Urban Splash's competition for Birnbeck Island, a 1.2-hectare island linked to the town of Weston-super-Mare by a pier. The firm's design (2008) for a new all-star hotel, holiday homes and a rooftop park creates a publicly accessible destination that would be a unique, natural–artificial inhabited mini-mountain.

Interview with Tom Coward, Daisy Froud, Vincent Lacovara and Geoff Shearcroft

Can you recount a few architectural memories from childhood?

The damp, dusty smell of building sites in the aftermath of demolition as I accompanied my parents to projects. The shock and awe of being confronted by Diplodocus on entering the Natural History Museum (Londoner). Visiting Bekonscot model village in Buckinghamshire or the De La Warr Pavilion in East Sussex while on caravan holidays to Bexhill (Suburbanites). The sound of thunderstorms on polycarbonate lean-to extensions. The composite formed by my family's farming cottage and the adjacent ancient ruins of an Anne Boleyn manor house (Country Boy).

How would you describe your architectural background?

It's mixed: we guess that is a consequence of a shared understanding of architecture as something that is not limited to, or owned by, architects; something that is implicitly, intricately and intimately bound up with social and political life.

In terms of our ages, we are postmodern children; our practice enjoys exploring the ambiguities of the multivalent contexts in which we live and work, specifically in London. Studying in Nottingham, Cambridge and the Royal College of Art in London encouraged certain sensibilities, as did the people we grew up with: art teacher Dad looked at architecture in the context of art and craft practice; farmer Mum instilled a bricolage approach. Overall, a rich mix of urban encounters, a commitment to the bodily experience and a delight in every aspect of the everyday – high, low and all the bits in between.

What are your greatest influences, architectural or otherwise?

Architecturally, Robert Venturi and Sigurd Lewerentz, Cedric Price and Adolf Loos, but the most consistent thread within our collective education is probably somewhere between Henri Lefebvre, Guy Debord and the Situationists. Tempered with an element of *Through the Looking-Glass* surrealism, hence storytelling and the importance of humour in our work, and

No. 1 Carbon Drive   Trafalgar Square, London | 2007

An exhibition pavilion for the Building Centre and London Development Agency is rendered as a typical Victorian house intriguingly fronted by a glazed shop window. It launched the Mayor of London's Green Homes concierge service, helping homeowners to lower their carbon dioxide emissions, and went on tour nationally from 2008. The exhibition explored energy saving, with interactive displays showing low-cost solutions and giving advice on technology and lifestyle changes.

This new teaching block (below) for secondary pupils with autistic-spectrum disorders is part of Phase 2 of Southwark's Schools for the Future initiative. The estate's disparate elements are unified in the new building, which has two floors of four teaching spaces around a top-lit, double-height staircase (far left). Every classroom is double-aspect to provide views, good light and maximum ventilation (left).

coincidence and collaboration, where various intentions and motivations come together to make something shared. Celebrating good moments of space that are worth replicating and studying; rituals of use, everyday misuse and evolution triggered by social and technological change.

Give one example of the way in which your architecture communicates effectively with people.

We like to think our work is mutually inclusive, encouraging interpretation and sparking off memories and connections; it aims to be culturally open. The Lift in east London was a building with this open intention at its heart, and the pattern and scale of its skin – akin to rustic quilts and geometric tiling – were, we hope, broadly appealing.

Are you a maker or a thinker?

Together, more likely a draughtsman, a modeller, a debater, an administrator, an arbitrator and an artist. We are a collection of people purposefully brought together for our range of skills, attitudes and characters.

Do you prefer bespoke or standardized?

What we like best is the re-appropriated or misused ready-made: when a standardized product is tweaked or customized to become bespoke. Or when a standardized product is refound and reimagined many decades later. This applies equally to our favourite items of clothing and to our architecture.

What theories lie behind your design methods and practice?

We practise an empirical approach to design, sampling and synthesizing from appropriate sources to create new combinations. We look to learn from other mix-masters – from James Joyce to James Stirling, Allan D'Arcangelo to Daft Punk – rather than from theorists. Plagiarizing Venturi Scott Brown initiated a productive reappraisal of our architectural concerns and subsequent approach. Lefebvre, Michel Foucault and Bruno Latour have always been useful for better understanding both the structures within which we operate and our capacity to act.

Do you strive to create new architectural typologies? If so, please give an example.

Not really; when people try to, their response is usually very suggestive of something they really already like. We love the

The Janet Summers Early Years Centre

AOC worked with the school community to develop a strategic framework for the long-term development of the Friars Foundation Primary School site. The first phase includes an Early Years Centre, a role-play space extension opening on to an outdoor classroom (opposite, top) and an external canopy (above), creating a covered learning landscape from natural and artificial materials, with a blackboard-paint-clad customizable playhouse (right).

blunt truth of Joyce: 'Have you ever noticed, when you get an idea, how much I can make of it?' A type needs to be copied to exist, otherwise it is simply unique.

What are the most challenging aspects of your architectural practice today?
Finding the right tactics for the procurement, budget and programme of each project, setting up the right process for building the best brief and creating the right forum for collaborative engagement. Creating enough time; time for the fullness of design and time for the appropriate politics to manipulate circumstances for all that is needed.

What impact do you hope your architecture has on the public realm?
A positive, appropriate and generous one. Sometimes that might be about being a polite background; sometimes it might be about making space where things can happen – making room for public life. Sometimes it might be about standing out. Each project is considered in isolation from its initial purpose and solely in terms of its generosity, its contribution towards making a little bit more of a place.

What personal significance do you give to architectural precedent?
'Immature poets imitate; mature poets steal; bad poets deface what they take, and good poets make it into something better, or at least something different', wrote the poet T.S. Eliot. Within the architectural world precedent is the mainstay: if you trade on your uniqueness you end up copying yourself; if you are busy, you will duplicate what you did last time; if you have aspirations to be 'better' you will copy your heroes. But to look at only the most academically profound pieces of our culture is to miss the point. A lot of culture that exists is actually through informal methods and relatively frugal means.

Which technical advances excite you the most for exploitation?
We still think it is brilliant what a group of people with pens and paper, and some prior thought, can do if they get in a room together, and we have yet to see that replicated in any kind of online forum. I suppose the one technology that does excite us is the potential of maps as a collective research and recording tool

Lift – A New Parliament

An example of AOC's 'suggestive spaces' – useable in many different ways, like Cedric Price's Fun Palace for theatre-maker Joan Littlewood in the 1960s – this mobile structure for up to 200 people hosts performances, workshops, talks and exhibitions by day, and by night transmits films and radio broadcasts.

This flexible four-storey tent can be a single open space (right) or inhabited with additional structures, some of them inflatable (above). It is easily demountable and has toured to Stratford Park, the Southbank Centre, Shoreditch Park, Canning Town and Abbey Green.

– people being able to lay down stories, memories and aspirations in a shared space, which can be easily accessed by others. This opens up a useful multi-dimensional space that can't easily be produced another way. So we like it for its potential ways of understanding or sensing more about a place.

Do you practise a transdisciplinary approach to architecture, and if so, what is especially important to you right now?
Collaborating with complex stakeholders, users and a wide range of consultants invariably means yes.

How do you go about generating the best possible relationship with your clients?
We give time to listening to people and to getting to know them and their lives at the start: a process of total immersion. With an organization, that is about understanding the intricacy of their internal culture and practice, in the same way that we strive to understand the way in which a private client aspires or needs to live. And we genuinely listen to the answers.

Can you give an example of your participatory methods?
In terms of brief-building, where much of our participatory focus to date lies, the Building Futures Game epitomizes the following principles:
• treating everyone, adult or child, as an intelligent person with something to contribute
• giving people the information and materials they need to make an informed and well-considered contribution
• asking people the right questions: ones that really get them thinking, that make them aware of their responsibility towards the outcome in addition to their 'rights', and where the answers can have some genuine influence on the architectural outcome
• seeing the decision-making process as agonistic, meaning accepting conflict as inevitable and looking for ways to harness the energy of that conflict and to produce interesting syntheses. The important thing is to make space for positive conflict, and to ensure that the debate itself and the decision-making are accountable and clearly explained
• offering people a clearly structured narrative journey through a process. This relates to appropriately equipping people, but also to …
• making it enjoyable, fun and interesting: if people are going to give up their time to participate, you need to give them something

Crown Terrace

AOC's winning design for a competition staged by Elephant & Castle Regeneration with the Wandle Housing Association (for which the architect is also designing Rodney Road, a mixed-use block in Southwark), Crown Terrace comprises five family homes in terraced courtyard housing. Brick unifies the low-level facade, retaining the robust appearance of the two-storey terrace. Behind, two-storey timber boxes are clad according to the residents' requirements.

back. We love it when people say, smiling, that we have made them work hard and think about something differently.

How do you communicate your architecture?
Slowly. It's not predetermined; it does not lead logically from one thing to another – it is a collective endeavour. At its best it is a series of stories, an evolution with all its human ups and downs, as well as a design process. Probably not well enough, sometimes with a lack of focus, but with a lot of exploration. We teach and slowly work it out that way.

What do you aim to achieve with your practice (in a single sentence)?
To be a practice that people feel respects them and understands the way they live their lives, yet looks for opportunities to challenge them positively and to open up new ways of doing or looking at things.

What advice would you give to a young architect embarking on their career?
Take a little advice and a lot of optimism.

What single improvement to the procurement of architecture in the United Kingdom would you recommend? More competitions, different planning system, legislation affecting developers, etc.?
Anything that would challenge the perception of risk. A clever way of pooling risk, such as a risk cooperative.

Hearth House

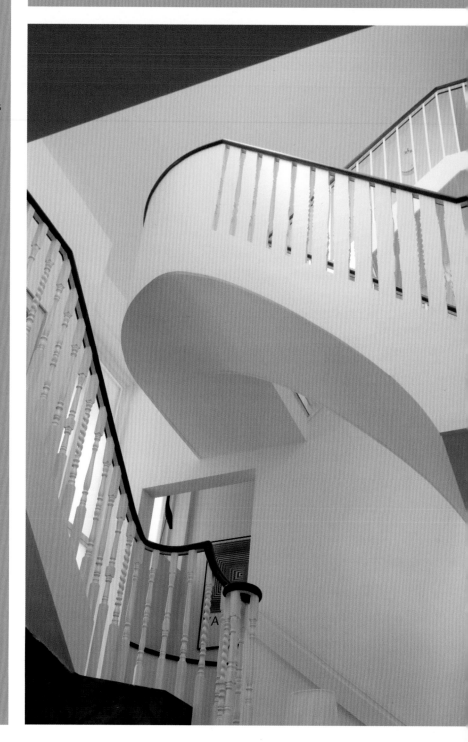

This redeveloped Edwardian semi-detached house for a family of five has at its heart a poured-concrete stair (opposite) and hearth, the surface of which repeats the chevron pattern of the reclaimed parquet flooring (left). Various elements define the quality of individual spaces, which are accentuated and made porous by nooks, internal windows and other openings.

AOC

Carmody Groarke

Kevin Carmody and Andrew Groarke, who had been working for David Chipperfield Architects, set up Carmody Groarke in London in 2006 as a result of winning a competition staged by the Van Alen Institute to design the Coney Island Parachute Pavilion in New York. The year before they had picked up the Burnham Award for a river transit system in Chicago. They breezed on to win four out of the five competitions they entered, including the Regent's Place Pavilion in London (organized by the Architecture Foundation), and eventually to win the commission for the 7 July Memorial in Hyde Park, London. 'We saw this as an opportunity to test ourselves as an architectural practice', says Groarke, and to work with a public client, in that case the Royal Parks and the Department for Culture, Media and Sport.

The success of Carmody Groarke's proposals is clearly largely because they are fresh, extremely logical and based on a critical design process. Groarke explains: 'We resist predetermining architectural solutions to a client's brief prior to a thorough investigation of each project's unique situation.' All designs are also backed up by thorough research. The Coney Island submission was accompanied by a research paper considering how pavilion architecture could work in a seaside context. More recently, in 2007, the firm won a competition to design the Sheffield Festival Centre, which aims to be a vibrant new cultural hub, and will be one of the practice's first buildings in the United Kingdom. In all cases Carmody Groarke's new ideas and materiality are grounded in place, with temporary structures used as a test bed for further architectural schemes.

Carmody Groarke's design strategy for the fit-out of the Architecture Foundation's London headquarters, in an Edwardian warehouse in Tooley Street, Bermondsey, responded to a modest budget. For its ground-floor exhibition and events space and offices (see also p. 18), the firm created an open-plan interior that is constructed entirely from plywood, and adaptable and authentic in character. The practice's ingenuity was tested by a commission for the Portland House Spa (2008), a 450-square-metre suite for exercise and relaxation beneath a mansion in Limerick on the west coast of Ireland. A cavernous space in chalky white limestone, the open-plan environment is punctuated with individual rooms with monolithic limestone blocks to give scale and order. At the centre, a 17-metre-long pool lined in textured black basaltina limestone contrasts dramatically with the white stone of the main space, and has a mirror effect, amplifying the apparent volume. It has a moving floor for varying the depth, but visible technology is minimized, preserving the clarity of the space and the tactility of its materials. All the artificial lighting is indirect, washing light over the stone, and can be adjusted and blended with daylight.

Carmody Groarke's London pavilions, in particular, have marked out the practice. In 2009 its 7 July Memorial was unveiled in Hyde Park, a permanent installation honouring the fifty-two victims of the four terrorist bombings in London on 7 July 2005. It was intended to offer a sense of closure to the bereaved families as well as a public place of remembrance for all who were affected. Commissioned by the Royal Parks and the Department for Culture, Media and Sport on behalf of the families, the project was given an open international competition, and the winning team, including structural engineer Arup, graphic designer Phil Baines and landscape architect Colvin & Moggridge, worked closely with representatives of the bereaved families.

They first found a site at the south-east corner of the park, and then the design evolved through collaboration and consultation, with the team ensuring that the feelings and needs of the bereaved families were met while sensitively and powerfully representing their loved ones in collective remembrance. Humane, non-monumental, not prescriptive but simply encouraging visitors to meander through, and with a compelling materiality, the memorial draws on both architecture and sculpture to create presence and meaning.

Solid-cast, long-lasting 3.5-metre-high stainless-steel stelae (columns), each one commemorating a life lost, are arranged in

The entrance to Portland House Spa (2008) in Limerick. Individual rooms are contained in monolithic basaltina limestone blocks, and the dark colour of the stone creates a double mirror effect in the water of the pool, amplifying the volume of the space (which has bianco neve limestone walls). An undulating ceiling cast in 9-millimetre-thick glass-reinforced gypsum, containing the hotel's air plenums, heightens its dramatic impact.

Carmody Groarke

four interlinking clusters reflecting the four separate locations of the tragic incidents. Each column has a unique finish produced by the casting process, and will stand for many generations to come. Inscriptions marking the date, times and locations of the bombings can be read by walking around the memorial, and the names of the victims are listed on a steel plaque on a grassy bank at the east end of the memorial, lending a further sense of quiet contemplation. In 2011 the practice completed another memorial within walking distance of Hyde Park, the Indian Ocean Tsunami Memorial outside the Natural History Museum in South Kensington, a single 120-tonne granite form quarried in France.

The practice's ornamental pavilion (2010) in Regent's Place, London, north of Euston Road, within a masterplan by Terry Farrell for the real-estate investment trust British Land, defines the public space at the entrance from Osnaburgh Street without enclosing it. The structure already contains many public artworks and installations, including pieces by Antony Gormley, Langlands & Bell (Ben Langlands and Nikki Bell), Liam Gillick and Edward Hodges Baily. Won in another competition, this time staged by the Architecture Foundation in 2007, it is an open field of very slender columns supporting a canopy that appears to float 8 metres above street level.

'The craft of things is very important', says Carmody. Carmody Groarke carried out extensive testing of full-size prototypes at the Building Research Establishment as part of the development of the complex engineered design, which was a collaboration with Arup and controls vibration and resonance. Its dramatic form, shimmering in the sun by day and glinting with projected 'gold' light by night, produces a moiré effect, and with its lack of cross-bracing creates a lightweight counterpoint to the public colonnades flanking the street. By turning the grain of the pavilion by 45 degrees the architect has set up a dynamic relationship between the pavilion, its historical backdrop and the street.

The same summer, one of the most distinguished pop-up restaurants launched itself on to the London skyline: Studio East Dining opened in a car park overlooking the Olympics site in Stratford, to the east of the city. An 800-square-metre 'solitaire', as the architect terms it – a gem set alone, with no front or back – it revealed shadows and silhouettes of the events within. Since the budget was tight, the architect opted for a fast build, with 70 tonnes of material hired from the existing construction site: scaffolding boards and poles, reclaimed timber and a cladding of polyethylene. All were returned to the site afterwards. With 'flying' roofs tilting towards the scenery, seven dining spaces radiated from the central area, a room pattern reflected in the herringbone lines of floorboard. 'We didn't want it to be too precious', says Carmody. Simply lined with scaffolding planks proportioned to the scale of each of the communal dining tables, Studio East Dining has been recycled, but it fulfilled the brief set by Pablo Flack, co-owner of the popular East End restaurant Bistrotheque, who remarked that 'this is the Rolls Royce of pop-ups!'

The Surreal House exhibition at the Barbican Art Gallery in London (2010) explored the power and mystery of the house in our collective imagination, in a labyrinthine journey through intimate chambers of varying scales. These evoke the different rooms of an imaginary house encompassing overlapping concepts (the House of Freud, the Portable House, for example) and alternating dark and light, sound and silence, compression and expansion. The metaphorical rooftops of the house lay above in eight individual bays focused on a dialogue between surrealist objects, contemporary art and architecture. The display was punctuated by cinematic images of houses under attack or magically transformed as if part of a dream. The graphic design by Angus Hyland, a partner at Pentagram, included a series of entertaining typographic illustrations used to identify areas of the exhibition and demarcate chapters of the catalogue.

This kind of immersive design is also demonstrated by the practice's collaboration with the Fondazione Prada and the artist Carsten Höller on the hybrid space of the Double Club, Islington, London (2008, for three months); also the nightclub space of the *Postmodernism* exhibition for the Victoria and Albert Museum (2011–12), as well as the *Drawing Fashion* exhibition for the Design Museum (2010–11), both collaborations with graphic designer APFEL, the latter with curved, softly back-lit paper lantern forms. This will be followed by a design for *Bauhaus: Art as Life* at the Barbican Art Gallery in summer 2012.

Carmody Groarke's commission for the Frieze Art Fair, Regent's Park, London (2011), returns in part to the approach of Studio East Dining, but with a series of irregular, bespoke pavilions, each with a tree at its centre, accommodating externally some of the functions that were previously arranged alongside the display areas. The pavilions create a new identity for this annual event. With timber I-beams and polycarbonate cladding, the structures are designed with an adaptability typical of this architect, to be demountable so that they can be used again in 2012. The practice's design for the Sheffield Festival Centre, won in a competition staged by the Royal Institute of British Architects (RIBA), is still at model stage, but the array of meticulously conceptualized and realized memorials, pavilions and exhibitions represents a vivid sense of the rich things to come.

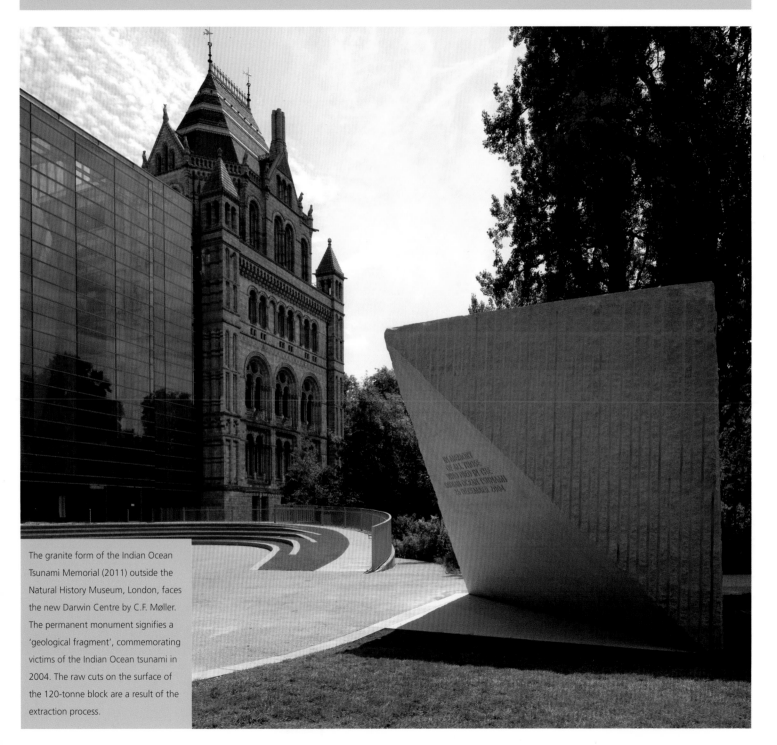

The granite form of the Indian Ocean Tsunami Memorial (2011) outside the Natural History Museum, London, faces the new Darwin Centre by C.F. Møller. The permanent monument signifies a 'geological fragment', commemorating victims of the Indian Ocean tsunami in 2004. The raw cuts on the surface of the 120-tonne block are a result of the extraction process.

Carmody Groarke

Interview with Kevin Carmody and Andrew Groarke

How would you describe your architectural background?

Kevin Carmody grew up in Australia and Andrew Groarke in the United Kingdom, so we have very different cultural, environmental and climatological backgrounds, giving us very divergent experiences of architecture. This has been an important influence in forcing us to compare approaches and consider that there is not necessarily a single starting point to each project.

What are your greatest influences, architectural or otherwise?

Art and architecture that link ideas to context and to the selection of materials and the craft of making things. Chance encounters and the experience of the everyday.

Give one example of the way in which your architecture communicates effectively with people.

Buildings do not come with an instruction manual about how to experience them. The ability for a building to communicate is limited, and so ideas about the project must be direct and unambiguous. At the same time, people have very particular and individual emotional responses to places and spaces, and we cannot always predict or determine what those will be.

We are interested in the potential of architecture to become a framework for experience through the manipulation of straightforward ingredients that we are in control of: space, light and materials. After that, as in the case of our project for the 7 July Memorial, we think it is more relevant for the experience to be interpretive rather than instructive.

Are you a maker or a thinker?

For us theory results from practice.

Do you prefer bespoke or standardized?

Each project is a result of its own situation of client and context. Our Studio East Dining project resulted from a very specific spatial idea relating to context: aligning dining rooms to specific views of the London Olympic site and the panorama of the skyline. We resolved this spatial idea by using a standardized construction technique for temporary buildings: scaffolding.

Studio East Dining

This temporary restaurant operated for three weeks in collaboration with Bistrotheque, and was constructed from 70 tonnes of scaffolding boards and poles from the London Olympic Games construction site. An overhead view of the completed project (left) shows the recyclable polyethylene cladding and seven spaces radiating from the centre (also seen in site plan, right). The interior view (below) of the dining area lined with scaffolding planks shows the transparent sections of the building envelope, opening up an array of different views of London.

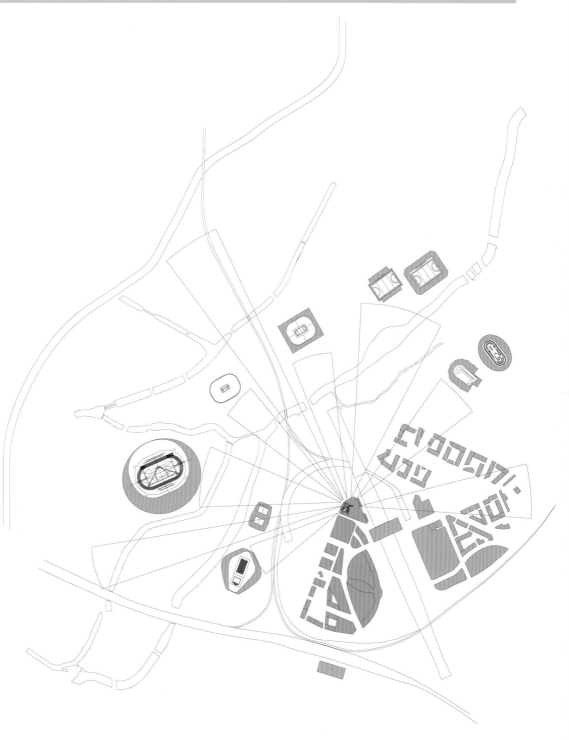

What theories lie behind your design methods and practice?

As much as possible our method is concerned with researching and designing through making things. Designing with physical materials and models allows a direct relationship between how ideas are developed and the experience of completed architecture. Equally, our projects result from a thorough investigation of each context – physical, cultural, social, environmental – and the purpose (not just the function) for which they are intended. We believe that it is necessary for projects to forge a strong synthesis between their situations, their constructive ideas and how people use them.

Do you strive to create new architectural typologies? If so, please give an example.

Although we often find opportunities to work on projects that explore the boundaries of conventional architecture – memorials, temporary pavilions and exhibitions – we would not say that this is an attempt to create new architectural typologies. These projects provide vital research opportunities for our studio to develop architectural ideas, which in turn influence the design of more conventional projects: places to live in, work in and visit.

What are the most challenging aspects of your architectural practice today?

Overcoming the bureaucracy of applying for public architectural contracts in the United Kingdom.

What impact do you hope your architecture has on the public realm?

We have already been fortunate enough to be able to test our architectural ideas at a range of timescales within the public realm, from temporary three-day event pavilions to memorials that are intended to last for hundreds of years. What interests us is how visitors react to these projects in the here and now.

What personal significance do you give to architectural precedent?

We are conscious that any new building should be grounded in an understanding of the fundamental experiences of places and spaces. These experiences are often the product of familiar associations.

7 July Memorial

Hyde Park, London | 2009

This sensitively conceived gesture marks the fifty-two lives lost in the four terrorist bombings in London in 2005. The stainless-steel stelae are 3.5 metres high, and bear individual characteristic finishes from the sand-casting process, with lettering (date, time and location of each life lost) designed by the typographer Phil Baines inscribed at eye level. The layout is of a collective whole, with a path leading up to and through the four clusters, and the faces of the stelae are rotated to encourage exploration.

The exhibition space is made up of interlinked, curved 'lantern' forms of back-lit paper. The sensuality of the ambient lighting helps to define the silhouettes of the display structures.

Which technical advances excite you the most for exploitation?

We are more interested in how people are engaged with the substance of the architecture than in its technology.

Do you practise a transdisciplinary approach to architecture, and if so, what is especially important to you right now?

It has always been interesting for us to collaborate with other creative disciplines on buildings and environments. However, it is important for us to remind ourselves of the limits of architecture as a discipline. Some of our projects, such as the 7 July Memorial, although dealing with the language of abstract architecture, can reveal solutions that are close to art practice, inasmuch as we have been closely involved with the sculptural qualities and substance of the work. It is nevertheless important to us that the projects deal with architectural ingredients – space, light and materials – and that they are designed so that people enjoy using them.

How do you go about generating the best possible relationship with your clients?

By investing a great deal of time in getting to understand what is absolutely necessary for a client before we embark on designing with them.

Can you give an example of your participatory methods?

Although we accept that the architect may be in a position to give creative identity to a project, we also recognize that his or her role is a small part of a greater team that works together to make a building, from brief to construction. For the 7 July Memorial, we were selected as designers from an open competition because we proposed a process of collaborative working with the client to generate a design, rather than offering a completed project on day one. We proposed this approach because we thought it necessary first to understand the complex emotional needs of the bereaved families as our clients for the design of a memorial to commemorate their loved ones. At the same time we realized that the project – in one of the busiest public parks in London – had a wider responsibility to the context of the city as a whole. As a result the project engaged us in a consultation process that lasted from first briefing to when the families publicly unveiled the memorial on the fourth anniversary of the bombings.

Regent's Place Pavilion

London | 2010

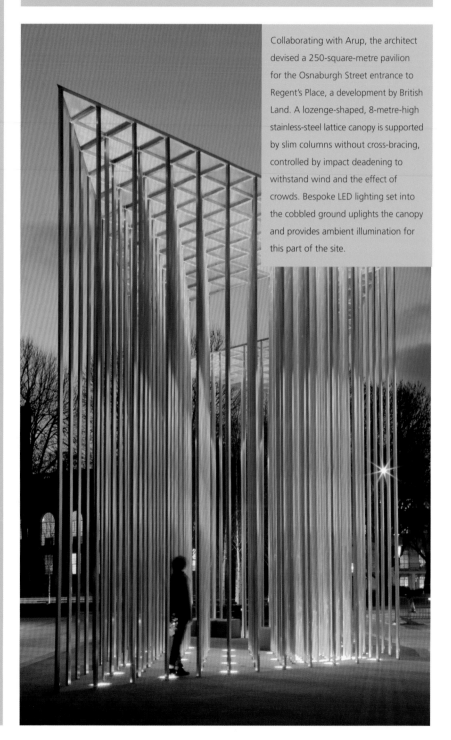

Collaborating with Arup, the architect devised a 250-square-metre pavilion for the Osnaburgh Street entrance to Regent's Place, a development by British Land. A lozenge-shaped, 8-metre-high stainless-steel lattice canopy is supported by slim columns without cross-bracing, controlled by impact deadening to withstand wind and the effect of crowds. Bespoke LED lighting set into the cobbled ground uplights the canopy and provides ambient illumination for this part of the site.

An Edwardian warehouse contains the Project Space, for events and exhibitions (right), and offices (below). Plywood throughout – textured Douglas fir ply for the walls, and birch-faced ply for desks – gives a robust, sustainable and warm materiality. Spaces are demarcated by furniture rather than walls, for greater connection and future adaptation.

How do you communicate your architecture?
We have always been interested in making architecture. On every project, this begins with testing ideas in physical architectural models and large-scale mock-ups – not only for designing with, and for testing spatial, lighting and material ideas, but also to use as a tool for dialogue with others involved in the process.

What do you aim to achieve with your practice (in a single sentence)?
To stay close to the craft of making buildings and spaces.

What advice would you give to a young architect embarking on their career?
Make sure that you enjoy what you do, and never be complacent about opportunity.

What single improvement to the procurement of architecture in the United Kingdom would you recommend? More competitions, different planning system, legislation affecting developers, etc.?
Increasing opportunities for clients to be professionally advised on how to select architects through competition.

Portland House Spa
Limerick, Republic of Ireland | 2008

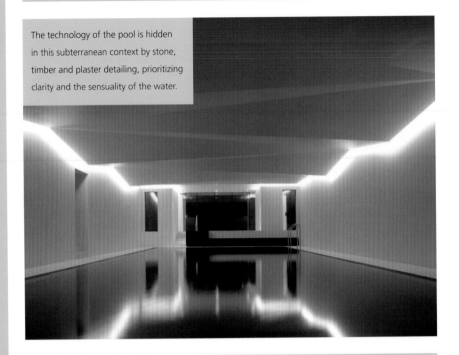

The technology of the pool is hidden in this subterranean context by stone, timber and plaster detailing, prioritizing clarity and the sensuality of the water.

Sheffield Festival Centre
Sheffield | 2007–

Exterior view of the model.

The Frieze Art Fair, held on the edge of Regent's Park, has a history of commissioning excellent architects. To leave more room for art, Carmody Groarke moved some of the social spaces outside the tented exhibition areas. The practice created an entrance area (above, left) and invented a new part of the fair, a series of interlinked, translucent pavilions surrounding the tents. The recyclable timber-lined spaces – 'rooms within a park' – are arranged around existing trees.

David Kohn Architects

David Kohn's œuvre, not yet very extensive, has a distinction that underlines his exacting research into the cultural and physical context of each situation, and his unerring ability to extract an imaginative solution based on narratives drawn from different sources that nonetheless suit the times very well. In 'Heterotopia', his entry (placed second) for the Arts Space of the Future competition held in 2007–2008 by the Arts Council and the Royal Institute of British Architects, Kohn envisioned a park in the Thames Gateway, to the east of London, fuelled by wood from new forests, as a place of utility and pleasure. It calls on the long-lost memory of the area's pre-industrial roots and popularity as a place to hunt, shoot, fish, boat and make merry.

Kohn's first work after setting up in practice in 2007 was the Modern Art Gallery, north of Oxford Street, for Stuart Shave, a central London branch of the original gallery to the east of the city. Kohn's design exploited the positive qualities of a 1950s building in a context that was gradually shifting from rag trade to encompass more art galleries. More akin to a house than a gallery, it prioritizes comfort as much as appearance, and led to a commission for a house for Shave in Norfolk: a modest design, but based on a mix of eclectic influences. Stable Acre (2010), a new house in brick with oak, glass and metal overcladding, contains spaces at a variety of scales; one has a wall of Crittall windows, culminating in the living room. Its landscape plan echoes the plan of the house with 'rooms' of wild grasses, flowers and trees. Kohn calls it 'a fictional ruin', a project in which 'the seemingly familiar image of an agricultural barn gives way to a more complex proposition concerned with growth of the house over time'.

Kohn's astute sense of urbanism is good at making the best use of interstitial or otherwise unusual sites. At Carrer Avinyó (2011), a *piano nobile* apartment for two brothers in the Barrio Gótico, Barcelona, by revealing the corner, he reconnects the triangular space to the city so that it registers the major crossroads beyond.

The Skyroom rooftop pavilion (2010) sits above the offices of the Architecture Foundation on Tooley Street, Bermondsey, south London. A central courtyard open to the sky and rooms covered in ETFE (ethylene tetrafluoroethylene) cater for public and private activities from lectures, debates and performances to dinner parties and meetings. The balcony cantilevered over the street has views over the More London development, the River Thames and the Tower of London.

David Kohn Architects

In Bermondsey, London, Skyroom (2010), a 140-square-metre rooftop pavilion for the Architecture Foundation, more than fulfilled the brief for a place for events and contemplation costing £150,000. With four small spaces topped by an ETFE (ethylene tetrafluoroethylene) roof, and a central courtyard open to the sky, it frames the Shard (Renzo Piano's London Bridge Tower, which rises high above London Bridge station) and has a balcony cantilevered over Tooley Street with views of the More London development, the River Thames and the Tower of London.

Kohn also brings together solidity and lightness of mood in a way he acknowledges to be somewhat contradictory. For Flash (2008–2009), a pop-up restaurant that was dismantled and recycled at the end of its three-month reign in London's Royal Academy of Arts, he created a playful reimagining of the garden of Burlington House (home of the Academy). Forging his design in a hybrid fashion in collaboration with restaurateurs Pablo Flack and David Waddington of Bistrotheque, fashion designer Giles Deacon and illustrator Rory Crichton, Kohn stacked art crates between the room's cast-iron columns. The crates constituted a new structure framing the windows, while walls were divided on classical lines, with Pompeiian murals showing figures dancing, and animals and plants writhing, and canted mirrors to 'allow spying'.

Kohn evokes eclectic memories and allusions, but he gets away with it. On the site of the Festival of Britain of 1951, but specifically inspired by Joseph Conrad's novella Heart of Darkness (1902), a story that begins by the River Thames, is A Room for London, a boat designed with artist Fiona Banner, intended to sit on the roof of the Queen Elizabeth Hall and be unveiled for the London 2012 Festival. Originating as a competition win for Living Architecture and Artangel, the project will create a small room for 'thinkers-in-residence' at one of the most visible sites in London. Given Kohn's capacity to look through history for references and to translate and mobilize them to thoughtful effect, his workstation Jerome – named after the fifteenth-century painting of the saint by Antonello da Messina – for Wallpaper* magazine and the furniture maker Porro (2011), a domestic room within a larger office, comes as no surprise.

Faced by the challenge of cohering the myriad shortlisted designs of the Brit Insurance Designs of the Year at the Design Museum (2011), Kohn created undulating plinths that helped the visitor navigate around the space. Consisting of modular frames made of strong, slender, carbon-fibre rods, the plinths can easily be reconfigured and slotted together like tent poles. Above, an array of colourful canvas banners and bunting by graphic designer Multistorey gives the gallery the atmosphere of a street festival. The frames, explains Kohn, 'allow the exhibits to be viewed as objects in the round, enabling a multitude of relationships with neighbouring exhibits to emerge'. This matches the curators' aspirations to display projects from the fields of architecture, fashion, and transport, product, graphic, furniture and interactive design in constellations – for example, Home, City, Play, Share and Learn – that accentuate their cross-disciplinary cultural and physical links.

With all Kohn's myriad references, he appears not to have a house style, a refreshing stance since his perception of ways and means also has much to do with ends, to enable 'other things to take place'. He is as adept at industrial design as he is at architecture, and has produced a range of light-fittings: the Gas Light series, with a simple formal language inspired by historic gas-powered street lamps, is used in the Skyroom. He is an admirer of the Austrian architect Hermann Czech, whose coffee houses – memorable for their lighting and mirrors and intended to feel familiar rather than be solely novel – are echoed by the sensibility of Kohn's own architectural interventions. 'Architecture should value inhabitation over the panacea of technological progress', Kohn said shortly after being awarded Building Design's Young Architect of the Year Award in 2009.

SHARE

Many designs and products are only achieved through collaboration and the sharing of information. Working with others can drive the creative process and introduce designers to new ways of thinking and working. This is evident when designers work together on large ensemble projects that reflect their individual skills and sensibilities, but also in similar scale partnerships between designers, suppliers and manufacturers.

Other designs encourage shared user experience, either via traditional printed media or interactive digital networks.

LEARN

HOME

COALITION OF THE WILLING

The design concept of the Brit Insurance *Designs of the Year* exhibition at the Design Museum in London (February – August 2011) accentuates the cultural and physical relationships between exhibits, transcending their disciplines. Modular frames made of carbon-fibre rods form undulating plinths, creating a landscape for exploration, and canvas banners and bunting add a street-festival atmosphere.

Interview with David Kohn

Skyroom

Can you recount a few architectural memories from childhood?

When asked to bring a drawing of a favourite space to my first day at university, I arrived with an inky view of the inside of a tent. Throughout my childhood I spent weekends and holidays walking with friends across the United Kingdom: the Brecon Beacons, the North York Moors, the Pennines. It was more often wet than not but we were pretty good at getting by, priding ourselves on our camp-craft so that, come what might, we were comfortable and had a hot meal and a good time.

How would you describe your architectural background?

Diverse. The first public exhibition of the practice's work was entitled *The Hedgehog and the Fox*. The Greek poet Archilochus once said: 'While the fox knows many things, the hedgehog knows one big thing.' We promoted a fox-like approach to creativity that draws on diverse interests and influences, seeing projects as momentary coagulations rather than convergent endgames.

What are your greatest influences, architectural or otherwise?

Chicago, Achille Castiglioni, Cedric Price, John Coltrane, Richard Serra, Isaiah Berlin, Hermann Czech, Fiona Banner, Piero Portaluppi, Cosmati pavements, Josep Antoni Coderch, Pierre Chareau, *Heavenly Mansions, and Other Essays on Architecture* by John Summerson (1949), Richard Buckminster Fuller, Sicily, petrol stations, Lina Bo Bardi, Roberto Burle Marx, Italo Calvino, Michel Foucault, Saul Bellow, James Stirling, James Gowan, Sigurd Lewerentz, Gio Ponti and London.

Give one example of the way in which your architecture communicates effectively with people.

The Skyroom is a rooftop pavilion standing above the Architecture Foundation near London Bridge. Taking advantage of its location, a courtyard frames a view of the Shard [London Bridge Tower by Renzo Piano], rising overhead, while covered balconies frame views of the River Thames and south London. The space is intended to be a celebration of being on a rooftop

The walls of the Skyroom are clad with mesh, and the floors are of larch decking. It was designed as a light, durable and affordable structure to be used for events both public and private. In order to limit the pavilion's visual impact on Magdalen House, the building in which the Foundation is housed, the perimeter walls are set back from the existing parapet.

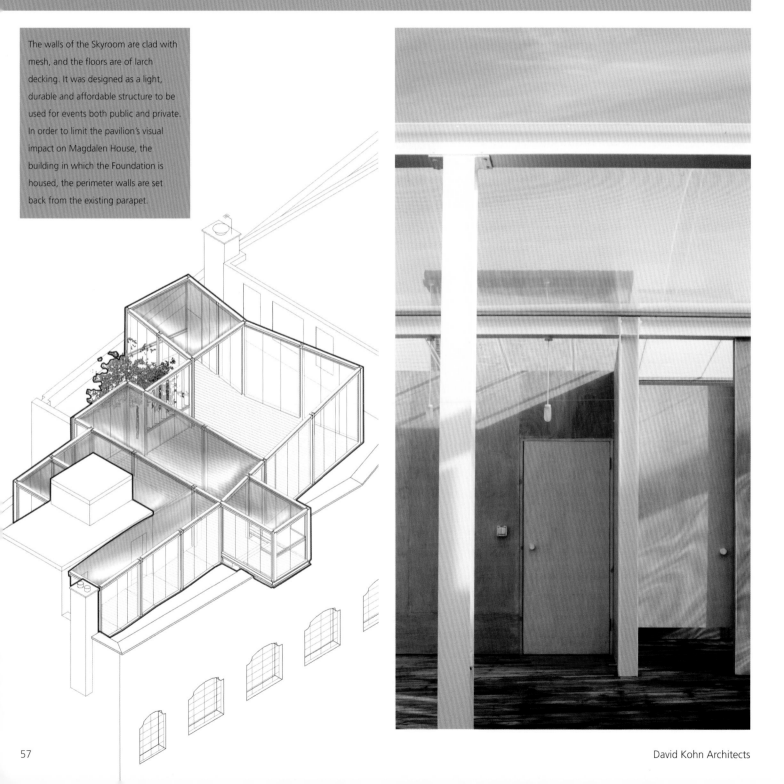

David Kohn Architects

in this remarkable city, and has hosted parties, lectures, film viewings, exhibitions and sunbathing. The architecture does enough to let people know they are invited to take their time and enjoy the situation. They do the rest.

Are you a maker or a thinker?

Quite possibly we are all more one than the other. For my part, I began making things before I wanted to, or could explain why. Architecture, however, requires a kind of practical knowledge that is predicated on an understanding of the relationship between thinking and making. They are inseparable.

Do you prefer bespoke or standardized?

We like both and sometimes together, as in bespoke assemblages of standardized components. We often try to find standard products, materials or production methods that we can bring into unfamiliar contexts, so shifting perceptions, such as using packing crates to build the temporary restaurant Flash at the Royal Academy of Arts, London.

What theories lie behind your design methods and practice?

The office is influenced by a number of philosophical positions concerning the relationship of society to spaces. In particular, the philosopher Michel Foucault's idea of heterotopia as set out in his essay 'Of Other Spaces' (1967) has helped us understand those real spaces – such as gardens, museums and ships – that nonetheless operate as utopias. Also, the Austrian architect Hermann Czech's conception of comfort has helped us clarify how architecture can be both rich and a background to life by inviting use: for example, good acoustics allowing an intimate conversation to take place in a crowded space.

Do you strive to create new architectural typologies? If so, please give an example.

Our prize-winning entry for the Arts Council's Arts Space of the Future competition was entitled 'Heterotopia'. We proposed that, in the future, arts and energy production facilities would be combined. A network of gardens in the East Thames region would provide energy crops that would be cut down in crop circles that became arts venues. A willow-fuelled power station would ensure the venues were comfortable all year round.

Carrer Avinyó

The architect stripped back internal partitions in the *piano nobile* apartment to reveal the major crossroads on which the building is situated, reconnecting it with the city beyond. With just under 100 square metres of space, the apartment has new bedrooms inside large pieces of furniture, like buildings in their own right. The mosaic pattern of the floor echoes the plan, which is graded from green to red to differentiate the two owners' private spaces.

David Kohn Architects

What are the most challenging aspects of your architectural practice today?

Projects are no longer continuous, but rather stop and start as funding dries up or becomes available. The challenge is always to be ready to move on to other work, to make sure the work is there to pick up, and then to jump back on to projects when they restart.

What impact do you hope your architecture has on the public realm?

We are working with Harrow Council on improvements to its town-centre streets. We see ourselves as identifying where and how the existing context can provide pleasurable use – making the most of the sunny side of the street, gathering planting into legible urban events or making cycle routes as simple to navigate as possible.

What personal significance do you give to architectural precedent?

Many of our projects have explicit relationships to architectural precedent. In our apartment on Carrer Avinyó in Barcelona's Barrio Gótico (Gothic Quarter), we have inserted a scaled-down version of Coderch's apartment block La Barceloneta, one of my favourite projects in the city. The playful strategy complements our approach to turn the interior of the apartment into a piece of the city, and the furniture into its monuments.

Which technical advances excite you the most for exploitation?

We are interested in materials that challenge one's perception. At the Design Museum in London we used carbon fibre to make an exhibition display system that was so fine, it gave the exhibits the appearance of floating.

Do you practise a transdisciplinary approach to architecture, and if so, what is especially important to you right now?

We are working with the artist Fiona Banner on an installation for Living Architecture and Artangel. The proposal is for a boat perched on the roof of the Queen Elizabeth Hall, overlooking the River Thames and the city, and containing all you might need to survive indefinitely: sleeping quarters, kitchen, library, wind turbine. We took inspiration from Joseph Conrad's novella

Flash restaurant

A collaboration with the restaurant Bistrotheque, illustrator Rory Crichton (for the carpet) and fashion designer Giles Deacon (who designed the chandelier), Kohn's design for the pop-up restaurant Flash in the former Museum of Mankind owned by the Royal Academy is a playfully hybrid design drawing fully on its decorative means. A timber structure of stacked art crates was set up between the cast-iron columns of the ground-floor room, creating a room within a room. Crockery by Will Broome and *tromp l'œil* and Pompeiian wall paintings add to the fantastical, other-worldly narrative mix.

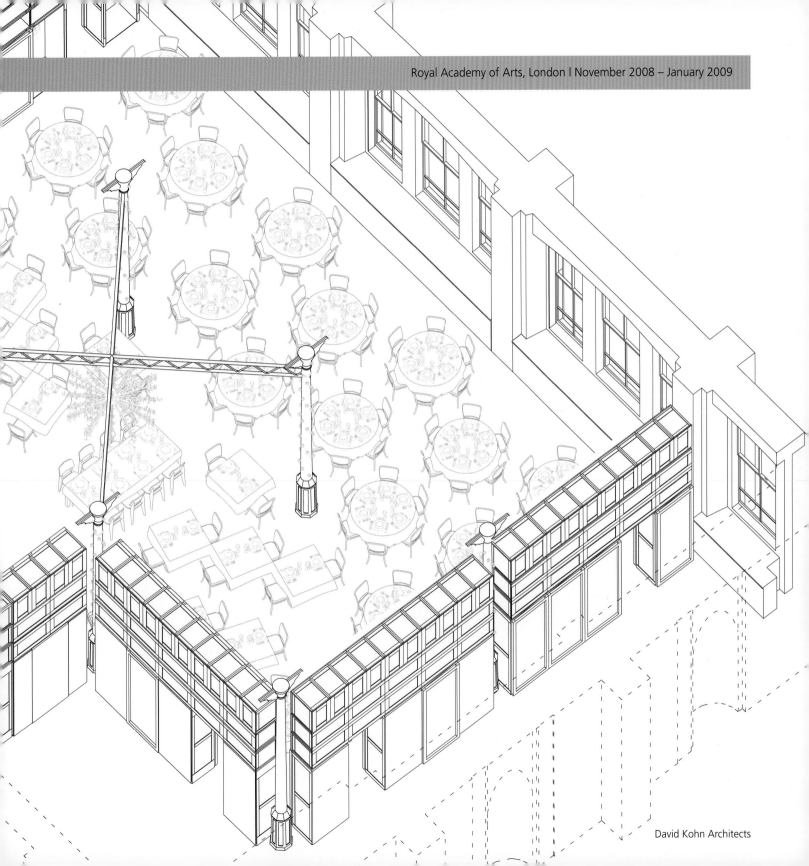

David Kohn Architects

Heart of Darkness (1902), a story told on the banks of the Thames of travels to distant places.

How do you go about generating the best possible relationship with your clients?

As a practice, we carry out ongoing research into certain cultural and typological issues, for example the future of spaces for art in the city. This is supported by our involvement in teaching architecture at London Metropolitan University, where we set up related research programmes. We often involve clients in the research process, inviting them to be critics for our students, for example, which gives them insight into a much broader range of possibilities than the brief might at first suggest, and which further informs our research. Beyond this, we always make design decisions jointly with our clients, believing that we can synthesize all possibilities into our proposals if we remain sufficiently open-minded and flexible.

Can you give an example of your participatory methods?

We are currently working on a new arts centre, to open in 2012 adjacent to the London Olympics site. The project is being funded by LOCOG [the London Organizing Committee of the Olympic and Paralympic Games] and will be run as a not-for-profit venture by Space Studios. We won the project in competition with a proposal to work with local artists and makers – Space Studios' future constituency – to deliver it. Rather than simply canvassing local opinion, we will undertake the project in collaboration with local businesses.

How do you communicate your architecture?

In as many different ways as possible, from site meetings reviewing mock-ups one-to-one to public lectures, from sketches in front of a client to live building projects with students.

What do you aim to achieve with your practice (in a single sentence)?

To work with others to bring about enduring and beautiful backgrounds for social interaction.

What advice would you give to a young architect embarking on their career?

Enjoy the variety that the work brings while being both flexible and tenacious.

Heterotopia

London I competition entry, 2008

Kohn's entry for an open competition staged by the Arts Council and the Royal Institute of British Architects, calling for an arts space of the future, proposes an art park in the Thames Gateway, an agglomeration of different spaces. This gallery structure, with its light timber truss, has flexible exhibition space and is set in a clearing in the coppice.

This barn-like house grows in scale through the interior. The largest space is the living room, which has views across the garden and a new orchard. The chief construction materials are brick for the perimeter walls, Crittall glazing, oak for cladding and a profiled metal roof.

What single improvement to the procurement of architecture in the United Kingdom would you recommend? More competitions, different planning system, legislation affecting developers, etc.?
That architects learn how to communicate clearly the multitude of skills they offer, so that they can charge fees appropriately.

Working with the artist Fiona Banner, David Kohn Architects won a design competition staged by Living Architecture and Artangel in association with the Southbank Centre to create a temporary installation on top of the Queen Elizabeth Hall. Playfully conceived as a timber boat with many nooks and crannies, the space was designed to be bookable for overnight stays (Living Architecture sold all its tickets), and has a single bedroom. Perched above the city, the boat has panoramic views from its lower and upper decks.

A Room for London

David Kohn Architects

Duggan Morris Architects

The tailored building, one that respects the intricacy and idiosyncrasy of its context, does not stand alone but is fundamentally part of an urban continuum of enhancement for all. Mary Duggan and Joe Morris of Duggan Morris Architects (DMA), established in 2004 in London, have always been very interested in site conditions and how their buildings influence their sites, and enjoy taking responsibility for playing a proactive role in a city's cycle of growth and enhancement.

Since their early work testing ideas, Duggan and Morris have always driven their projects through a rigorous process of iteration, and are interested in a whole range of form-finding challenges, such as repetitive folding elements, for example, for the Waterworks Pavilion project on the Leeds–Liverpool canal. They have also pushed the boundaries of what might be expected in a certain context: for example, remodelling and extending an East Sussex oast house to create a bespoke building that convinced the planners, despite being in the green belt.

DMA has gradually widened into a global workforce, with projects encompassing an extensive range of locations, sectors and typologies: from house renovations and commercial retrofitting to the practice's largest scheme to date, a mixed-use project with more than 200 residential units and 1800 square metres of work space for a range of business types on the site of the old Neptune Chemical Works in Deptford, south London, working closely with the local authority. There it has created a new connected ground plane above the restricted-use land. Phase 1 of the Brentford Lock West mixed-use masterplan, with 500 homes beside the Grand Union Canal, is a collaboration with Karakusevic Carson Architects and Riches Hawley Mikhail Architects; and DMA is also working on the New Learning Centre at the South London and Maudsley Hospital campus in Denmark Hill, south London. In all it does, DMA engages and collaborates, using a deep understanding of the labyrinthine complexities of the United Kingdom's planning system.

In 2010 the practice applied its tailored approach to the refurbishment of a two-storey Modernist house dating from 1968 in Hampstead Lane, Highgate Village, designed in a Brutalist style by well-known local architects Stirling and Margaret Craig. The simple, cubic five-bedroom house was constructed from fair-faced concrete blocks with a silver sand and white cement mix. DMA collaborated with the clients, also architects – Graham Stirk of Rogers Stirk Harbour + Partners and Susie Le Good of Allford Hall Monaghan Morris – to renovate it and create a more fluid arrangement of internal spaces (there is a 200-square-metre gross floor area) than in the more cellular original. DMA has also made a greater connection between the living spaces and the gardens, which have been completely redesigned with ley lines of basalt extending from the gridlines of the original to create a series of strata. Birch trees were planted in a new wild-flower meadow at the rear, and the house has a new sedum roof. The house was awarded the Royal Institute of British Architects Manser Medal in 2011.

Faced with the option of renewal or replacement, owners out for financial gain often demolish even a fine example of a historic building and construct two new ones in its place, or make an ill-considered conversion into cramped flats. DMA's project for Derwent London focused instead on qualitative gain, and shows a shrewd sense of the ability of Brutalist design to be adapted through sensitive and intelligent means. Tackling the renovation of two buildings in Maple Place and Fitzroy Street (2010), DMA joined the 1950s concrete-frame buildings with a staircase to create 1880 square metres of work space, a project that belies its complexity and maintains the individual identities of the two buildings.

DMA is hugely gifted at drawing out the best from urban scenarios. It has won six awards for the sense of civic pride and related benefits it brought to Yew Tree Lodge, a sheltered-housing scheme – a particularly neglected sector – in Ruislip, Middlesex. At Kings Grove (2010) in Peckham, south London, DMA created

The robust interior of Kings Grove, a two-storey, four-bedroom house in Peckham, south London, is a mix of brick, oak joinery, concrete flooring and brass fittings, a contextual response to the site: a vacant plot between the gardens of two parallel streets of Victorian terraces.

Duggan Morris Architects

a family dwelling on a former industrial site, a casting workshop in the backlands between ten gardens of typical Victorian terraced houses. Both Yew Tree Lodge and Kings Grove were creative variations of designs by other architects, given planning approval. Setting the Kings Grove house at right angles gives it an unusual aspect over the gardens of its neighbours. DMA chose reddish-pink brick to respond discreetly to the context and almost to camouflage the building, and to form the transition from the raw surroundings to the polished surfaces of the interior, with its oak joinery, concrete floor and brass fittings. A unique glazing system covering the entire facade both front and back maximizes the light and views in this unusual setting.

A planned swimming pool extension to the Victorian private Alfriston School for girls in Buckinghamshire is intended to be a contemporary expression of the local 'pitched-roof' vernacular. What that actually means is a simple building reminiscent of the work of Pier Luigi Nervi, its timber hat articulated by three pitched-roof segments, which open out to the rear, inverting the pitch and evoking the ripples of the pool below. Reading internally as though it floats above the pool, the roof also serves as an acoustic baffle, reducing reverberation, a crucial requirement in the brief for this special-needs school.

In an initiative that would surely be close to the chef Jamie Oliver's heart, DMA recently obtained planning permission to develop proposals for new secondary schools in Croydon, south London, as part of the Cooking Spaces Project, related to a wider governmental focus on promoting health and well-being. This expands the experience of cooking by encouraging a 'seed to plate' approach in the teaching curriculum, involving allotments and culinary hospitality. Construction work will have to avoid disrupting teaching, so DMA has proposed fast-track assembly systems and dry construction methods for simply formed buildings of structurally insulated metal panels. Each has a metal profile deck roof, a system commonly used to construct cold stores, and is then wrapped in a simple decorative mesh.

A project heightening DMA's sense of collaboration still further, for the world-renowned South London and Maudsley NHS Foundation Trust, is the New Learning Centre under development at the hospital's campus in Denmark Hill, an overtly Georgian context. It will replace the old Training Centre, which is not suited to contemporary teaching and learning methods. The trust needed a centre for the teaching of the results of academic research into mental illness to clinical practitioners, with teaching and learning

facilities, a cafe, and exhibition, meeting and office spaces. Through networking and social media, each user will be able to tune their learning process to their needs for best results. The centre will challenge preconceptions of mental illness, says DMA. By promoting an integrated learning environment – learning for everyone, anywhere, at any time – the practice makes education accessible to everyone on the campus and in the community: doctors, nurses, teachers, service users and carers.

DMA's scheme has flexible, subdividable spaces around a void with a grand open staircase, with floorplates and stair in close alignment. Externally, the four-storey building complements the Georgian principles of its neighbours, with pre-cast concrete fins, and brick and glass. With terraces at ground level and inset balconies above, the centre is more of a pavilion with a central atrium, non-cellular and not driven by grid, closely connected to its surrounding landscape, with activities spilling out from the series of connected rooms. There is a rose-garden event space on the roof, and the ground-floor cafe is intended to be a marker along a permeable route forged within the masterplan by Emoli Petroschka Architects to open up the campus to the local and outlying neighbourhoods.

DMA's most radical project to date, requiring openness but an elegant method of creating a secure environment, the New Learning Centre shows how well the practice looks deeply at context, including the timeless, classic elements and engaging with Southwark brick. The aim is to make a building that introduces novelty to a domestic ambience, and connects it with the natural setting of the public spaces beyond.

The architect has retained and intervened in the Brutalist structure of the Hampstead Lane house (2010) in Highgate Village, north London, to create a contemporary dwelling. Two supporting cross walls were removed and replaced by a new arrangement of steel beams and columns, creating an open-plan, flexible living space with greater connection to the garden (seen here).

Duggan Morris Architects

Interview with Mary Duggan and Joe Morris

Kings Grove

Can you recount a few architectural memories from childhood?

MD A primary-school friend lived in a 1960s Eric Lyons-designed T8 Span house in Wimbledon. I remember thinking that it was fantastic to be able to run through the house from front to back, uninterrupted by the staircases and partitions of my Victorian family house. The accommodation was very easy and practical: it didn't need curtains to block the view of passers-by, and the free plan made it very sociable. I recall coming home after days spent there feeling that my house was very complicated and fussy. My single-form-entry primary school had a similar 1960s Modernist ethos; each classroom was a clear, simple block distinct from the next, and the classrooms ascended through a split-level site. In hindsight, this made the journey through infants and juniors, from four to eleven, unintimidating. The fear arrived when I moved to an institutional block.

JM My childhood memories are filled with images of suburbia. The Warwickshire village where I grew up was typified by rows of post-war houses with small back gardens, playing fields and local shops. It was neither extraordinary nor without event. What remains most vivid for me is the pride my parents and neighbours took in the ritual personalization and decoration of their homes, interpreted in a range of ages and styles – many of them garish. Against this backdrop of the seeming banal was a cast of unlikely characters, all of whom made the village memorable.

How would you describe your architectural background?

Both directors followed similar paths to professional practice, working through 'regional' universities at undergraduate level before completing Part II and Part III qualifications at the Bartlett School of Architecture [now part of University College London]; in this respect, a well-rounded and broadly based level of discipline, while also having studied at one of the leading universities of architecture in the world.

What are your greatest influences, architectural or otherwise?

The Great Mosque of Djenné in Mali, Africa, is the most wonderful example of how architecture can bring together many

The compact house (seen in model form opposite, top) is set in the back gardens of a Victorian terrace, echoing the materials of the older houses. The glazing system wraps the entire facade, front and rear, and is a unique, project-specific solution in timber edged with brass. Silicon-bonded low-emissivity double-glazed units allow the smallest possible transition between windows and bricks.

Duggan Morris Architects

aspects – communities, culture, local skills, ecology, materials and events – in one poetic piece. The building, made from sun-baked mud bricks, is eroded by the weather and reclad annually with the help of decorative rodier-palm sticks, which serve as scaffolding. The building is the event and the event is the building.

Give one example of the way in which your architecture communicates effectively with people.

Our project for a sports complex for Alfriston School in Buckinghamshire has a very simple design concept born out of the needs of the children. It is located in a school for children with learning difficulties. The roof is pitched to serve as an acoustic baffle. Little glass is used, to reduce temperature fluctuation, and it is kept low so that views out are possible only from the pool. The giant timber hat appears to float above the water.

Are you a maker or a thinker?

Both directors are thinkers and makers, communicating through differing means and methods with the excellent staff, who collaboratively interpret through making, drawing and rigorous analysis.

Do you prefer bespoke or standardized?

This is really a question of what is appropriate for a particular project; it's important to get the balance right. We rarely do one or the other singly.

What theories lie behind your design methods and practice?

Suggesting that the work of the practice is influenced by one or more theories of architecture would be misleading. However, we believe our work displays clarity in thought and execution; a rigorous approach in terms of both strategy and delivery; and abundant original 'site and programmatic' thinking.

Do you strive to create new architectural typologies? If so, please give an example.

In many cases, such as housing and the commercial sectors, 'typologies' tend to be fixed by market needs and trends. This is not to be dismissed: using existing typologies when appropriate is good practice. New typologies tend to arise from unusual settings, complicated or demanding briefs, and new programmes. For two projects in London, Curtain Road and Maple Place/Fitzroy Street – commercial schemes for different clients – our aim has been

Swimming Pool, Alfriston School

This extension to the sports department of a special-needs girls' school contains a swimming pool, a gym and an administration block. The scheme has three pitched roof segments in timber, which open out to the rear, inverting the pitch and evoking ripples in the pool. The form also serves as an acoustic baffle, preventing excessive reverberation of sound, a vital requirement in such a context.

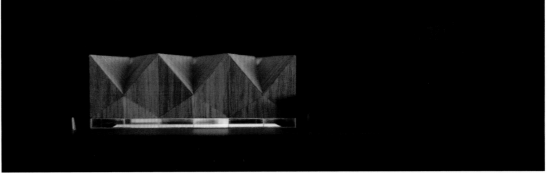

Duggan Morris Architects

to generate bespoke typologies within a fixed set of deliverable elements. While at face value these projects create industry-standard office space, on a conceptual level they are focused on the specifics of the site in order to express a unique building narrative, manifest in particular details of doors, signage and way-finding, lighting, cores and the floorplates themselves.

What are the most challenging aspects of your architectural practice today?

One of the greatest challenges in architectural practice is to remind the industry that architectural ambition once existed in this country and is growing exponentially in other countries. The skill of the architect, therefore, is to challenge preconceptions and extract greater value from both programme and site.

What impact do you hope your architecture has on the public realm?

The relationship of building to public realm cannot be overstated. We hope our work is considered to be joyful, appropriate and stimulating.

What personal significance do you give to architectural precedent?

It is important through first-hand experience, but should not be shorthand for actual design. Remaining critical and focused when considering architectural precedent is a sure-fire way of responding with original thought, instead of lazy plagiarism.

Which technical advances excite you the most for exploitation?

Our practice is influenced in equal measure by traditional techniques and technological advancement. Combining the traditional and the 'cutting edge' thus has a significant influence on our thinking, whether pre-fabrication on a huge scale, or the use of machinery and digital technology to carry out the simplest of tasks, such as laying a brick.

Do you practise a transdisciplinary approach to architecture, and if so, what is especially important to you right now?

Our design methods are inclusive, democratic and transparent. We actively encourage an interdisciplinary approach where all aspects of the project are given equal weight and importance. Equally, none of the participants in any of our workshops is

Maple Place/Fitzroy Street

The renovation for Derwent London of two very different buildings involved connecting them by a staircase. The detailing of lighting, balustrading, way-finding and structure has brought the scheme a consistent aesthetic, allowing the buildings to work as one, or to be divided.

Duggan Morris Architects

tied down to a single label or function, but all are required to think laterally across architecture, construction, structure, environment and cost.

How do you go about generating the best possible relationship with your clients?

The client–architect partnership is the central relationship in the delivery of high-quality architecture. It relies on nurturing deep trust in each other's ability; thinking through complex issues; striving for excellence where possible; and above all reflecting on each other's opinion and thoughts. Listening is the key in this respect, and we are great listeners.

Can you give an example of your participatory methods?

Over the years we have developed a number of sophisticated participatory methods, which are used at various stages during the evolution of a project. A preferred method is one of 'immersion', where fact-finding is a process of mutual exchange. During the conceptual development stages for our New Learning Centre on the South London and Maudsley Hospital campus in Denmark Hill, we embarked on a voyage of discovery and exploration with the client, including visits to see built examples both in the United Kingdom and abroad, workshops and presentations, and a blog. This digital platform is accessible by all members of the team, the campus and the wider community for posting updates as well as gauging opinion through an open forum. Our aim was to separate the low expectations associated with this sector from the brief, and introduce a new, higher aspiration.

How do you communicate your architecture?

Communicating our architecture is a constant need, whether to a design team during a workshop session; to a client as we seek approval, sign-off and instructions; to a contractor so that the ambition of the project is understood; or to a wider community of peers, patrons, critics and journalists. In every case we aim to be clear and concise and to utilize a vast variety of graphic and physical methods, as required.

What do you aim to achieve with your practice (in a single sentence)?

We aspire to a design legacy born out of delivering high-quality, stimulating buildings that go far beyond the client's expectations.

New Learning Centre

The centre (seen from Grove Lane opposite, bottom) is designed to be an integrated environment, accessible to all doctors, nurses, teachers, users and carers on the campus. It will house teaching and learning facilities, a cafe and flexible, subdividable exhibition and ancillary space positioned around a void negotiated via a big open staircase (see section, below). The ground-floor plan (opposite, top left) shows the abundant landscape around the project; learning activities will spill out when appropriate.

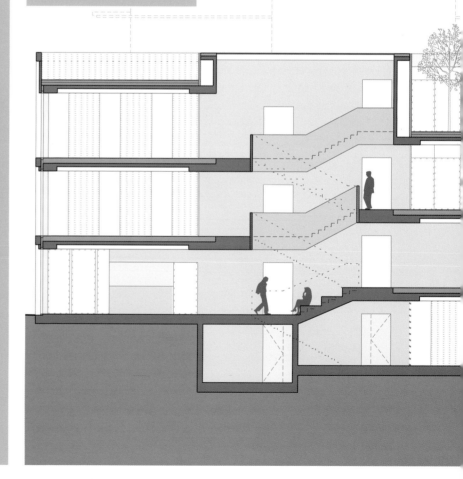

Duggan Morris Architects

What advice would you give to a young architect embarking on their career?

It is a misconception that setting up in practice is the only way to influence the design of buildings and create great architecture. Contemporary architectural practice relies to a greater and greater degree on collaboration between team members within the same practice and across disciplines. Working for an established practice has a significant part to play in moulding your architectural skill and experience.

What single improvement to the procurement of architecture in the United Kingdom would you recommend? More competitions, different planning system, legislation affecting developers, etc.?

Architectural education needs to broaden its remit to place greater emphasis on a skill base covering all aspects of design and construction. This must cover the conceptual, the urban, the technological and the environmental if architects are to wrest back the role of lead consultant in the delivery of high-quality architecture.

Hampstead Lane

A two-storey, late twentieth-century Brutalist home of cellular design was refurbished to give a fluid arrangement of spaces with a greater connection to the gardens, now also completely redesigned. Components were closely matched with contemporary versions for a seamless combination of old and new.

Duggan Morris Architects

EcoLogicStudio

EcoLogicStudio is a firm of highly astute, visionary systems thinkers concerned with the cybernetic relationship between architecture and its environment. They neither merely exploit new technology to create natural metaphors, nor reject or conceal them in a vernacular language. Over the seven years of their London-based practice, co-founders Claudia Pasquero and Marco Poletto have extended their work beyond the objectives of the first generation of architects wedded to parametricism, to create hybrid buildings and prototypes that are dynamic systems, responding to environmental and behavioural influences. Not just generating spatial and climatic effects, such buildings also trigger intense exchanges between the natural and the artificial, the designed and the accidental. In masterplanning, EcoLogicStudio's design programmes incubate new urban programmes with the agency of networks and natural processes. Its many responsive installations assign technology an edutainment role in demonstrating these instrumental aspects of their architectural work to visiting members of the public, drawn to the enjoyment of participating in the game.

Demonstrating its ability to attune buildings to their environment and reinvent conventional typologies, in 2009 EcoLogicStudio converted a large family villa dating from the 1970s at Ciriè, outside Turin, Italy, into flats. At the time of the villa's construction, concrete was a new material that was widely used to copy styles in a way that was wasteful of energy, for example with thick walls, redundant in a location where temperatures can reach 40°C in summer and -10°C in winter. The villa was given a 'lightwall' envelope, a solid but permeable 'sponge' with 'pores' able to absorb and filter heat, light and views to and from the surrounding garden. Meanwhile, for the local library, in an existing warehouse with a shed roof, EcoLogicStudio conceived a new 'forest of culture' inhabiting its container, with a custom-designed system of shelving and desks, as a means to be free from traditional typological constraints and segregation.

The Algae Hanging Garden at Simrishamn Marine Centre, Sweden (2011), showcases the architect's masterplan to engage with small local producers through regenerative prototypes, shown in a networked plan. Visitors are invited to walk over the plan and blow into photo-bioreactors suspended above it, activating oxygen production and letting them view the colours and ecology of algae at close range.

The practice's scheme for North Side Copse House in Haslemere, Surrey, is one of a new generation of wooden-framed houses responding to Planning Policy Statement 7 (2004), which stipulates design excellence in sustainable development in rural areas. The design, now in planning, creates a synergy between the outstanding natural beauty of the site and the formal nature and construction logic of the house. Its diagram was generated by the landscape of the wooded setting, and EcoLogicStudio plans to have the parametric design – which bifurcates along flow lines and responds to the density of tree canopies, allowing views of the valley – realized by an innovative wood-processing facility near by, using local wood. Inwood Developments can take wood from the site and process it with a laminating technique in a way that makes it usable for both structure and the patterned cladding, thereby producing architectonic beauty from an ecological ethic. Passive design strategies give the house good natural ventilation, lighting, access to sunlight, thermal mass and insulation.

In 2010 the Swedish Municipality of Simrishamn invited EcoLogicStudio to design a masterplan for the coastal region of Skåne. Mapping its riverbed, lakesides, farms and woodland, villages, ports, deep sea and shallow waters, the practice devised an interface to help incubate new models for agri-tourism and new industry, involving farmers and fishermen in the production of algae. Both fields have huge potential but need testing and feedback so that the prototypes the architects present – multi-use educational resources related to context – can be usefully evolved. A large map of the region, mimicking its tourist map, shows a plan for collaborative action and six design prototypes (a tower, a museum, a garden, a greenhouse, and new circulation routes and networks) that harness the input of different local actors and agents in industry, tourism and research, reimagining old clusters of farms as hubs that are assigned specific roles in agri-tourism and the production of algae.

Crane Greenhouses, new symbiotic algae and seafood/fish farms in the form of crane-like structures at the region's underused ports and coastal areas, have ETFE (ethylene tetrafluoroethylene) canopies from which adaptive greenhouses are suspended. EcoLogic's edutainment installation in Simrishamn's Marine Centre in 2011 invited visitors to experience the photosynthesis of algae via a responsive memory system using LED lighting. With the gambit of a game, these imaginative design proposals, connected by a network of cycle paths and cross-country ski tracks, avoid the hermeticism of a purely technical research centre. Pasquero and Poletto argue that if

you do not connect with the user, the building will end up just being an out-of-town factory; their advocacy of working with nature allows people to be involved in a playful rather than bureaucratic way.

For STEMcloud v2.0, a prototype oxygen-making machine to help improve the micro-ecology of the Guadalquivir River in Seville, Spain, installed in a gallery in the city for the YOUniverse exhibition of 2008, visitors to the gallery became ecologists in a kind of playful laboratory. Not only the transparency and porosity of the project but also the growth process were further enhanced by patterns of interaction with the public, who could feed the system with nutrients, light and carbon dioxide. EcoLogic defines the starting point of each experiment, treating it as a primed condition necessary to promote interaction with visitors. The practice wants its extended models of systemic architecture to be understood in cybernetic terms, as a means of dealing with change and transformation.

'It is for architects to move beyond the self-conscious set pieces and to devise, as in the best music scores, gaps of uncertainty in which the individual can participate', wrote the visionary English architect Cedric Price in Re: C.P. (2002). While it was impossible to predict the kind of equilibrium that would emerge and what kind of algae ecosystem would grow from STEMcloud v2.0, or how visitors would interact with it, the architect could be sure that there would be communication between the three systems from which lessons could be learned.

In their generation of knowledge, EcoLogicStudio's playful and engaging laboratories recall the work of the English cybernetician and psychologist Gordon Pask (1928–1996), inventor of the conversation theory, who focused on the personal nature of reality and, like EcoLogic, had a preference for advocating open-ended and functional systems of value. The practice is also inspired by Price, who conceived the idea of using architecture and education as a way to drive economic redevelopment, most notably in his 'Thinkbelt' project of 1965 for the north Staffordshire Potteries area. This is what I would call an expressive, edutainment approach, which has huge potential in any neo-liberal society emerging from economic crisis and seeking new models of urbanism, agri-tourism and other light industry in which a new ecological culture can play a major role. Such a society is all the better equipped through the imaginative agency of such creative architects as EcoLogicStudio.

EcoLogicStudio invites people of all ages to participate in ecological research. In Seville it cultivated the STEMcloud cybernetic 'machine', supporting the growth of micro-ecologies from the local river. This is STEMcloud v2.0, the Guadalquivir experiment (2008).

Interview with Claudia Pasquero and Marco Poletto

Aqva Garden

Can you recount a few architectural memories from childhood?

MP When I was in kindergarten there was a little girl I fancied, so to attract her attention I drew a house with a large attic as a romantic gift.

CP No, as a kid I didn't like architecture!

How would you describe your architectural background?

The background of our team reflects our interest in a transdisciplinary approach to architecture. In particular, both directors of EcoLogicStudio, Claudia Pasquero and Marco Poletto, have always engaged in scientific and technological research, in the tradition of Turin Polytechnic, where they studied as undergraduates, as well as with artistic and theoretical research at the Architectural Association (AA) in London. This educational trajectory responds to our desire to create a design practice that is sensitive to contemporary society, and is able to establish a relevant line of design enquiry to influence the development of our cities. Studying in two radically different institutions and countries gave us the ability to hybridize methods and instruments, to synthesize what today appears as EcoLogicStudio's design style and our educational method in the Inter10 Unit at the AA and workshops we lead elsewhere in the world.

What are your greatest influences, architectural or otherwise?

Philosophically our agenda has been influenced by Gregory Bateson's book *Steps to an Ecology of Mind* (1972), and the name of our practice comes from the extended definition of ecology given in that book. Architecturally, we were first influenced by Renzo Piano's attitude towards the crafting of buildings – our first job was in one of his practice's most exciting Italian building projects, the reinvention of the old Fiat factory building, Lingotto, in Turin in 1983 – and by its conceptual counterpart found in the work of Andrea Branzi and other Italian radical groups.

Through our experience in London we have since been exposed to and influenced by English radicalism, Cedric Price in particular, as well as by the early digital work of the American

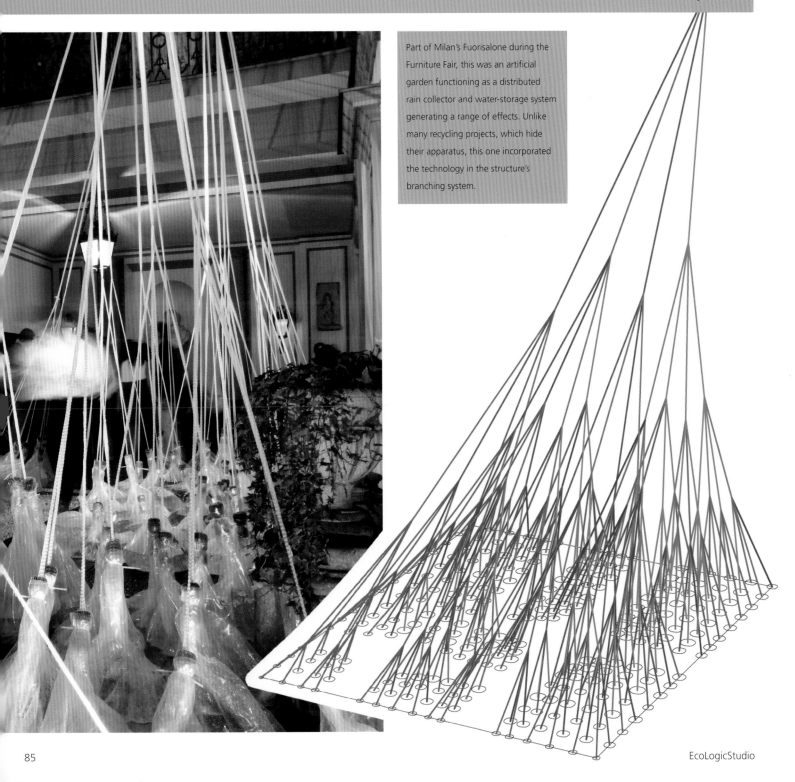

Part of Milan's Fuorisalone during the Furniture Fair, this was an artificial garden functioning as a distributed rain collector and water-storage system generating a range of effects. Unlike many recycling projects, which hide their apparatus, this one incorporated the technology in the structure's branching system.

EcoLogicStudio

avant garde, namely Greg Lynn and Reiser + Umemoto. Last but not least, our lives and the places where we grew up have been sources of inspiration: the incredibly diverse social network and natural environment found in the Piedmont countryside in north-western Italy. There we learned a form of embedded environmentalism that refuses political connotations and engages in a deep, systemic relationship with the social, economic and ecological context.

Give one example of the way in which your architecture communicates effectively with people.

Our projects work as experiments; they are truly experimental in their relationship with the context and with the users, who are asked to interact and interfere, thus eventually becoming co-designers. Communication is envisaged as an extended conversation, a form of cybernetic feedback among architectural machines, humans, environmental systems and back again, in the form proposed in the 1970s by Gordon Pask. It is not by chance that he, as a scientist, was not merely sitting in his lab but was constantly building artefacts or machines for interaction or conversation – real spatial machines. Digital technology does not suffice to develop truly innovative architecture: it must be embedded into material artefacts to operate in space and time and engage human and natural systems. It is the responsibility of the architect to develop spatial frameworks for a new ecological society, able to establish a deeper and more dynamic dialogue with its surroundings, whether those are natural, social or machinic.

Are you a maker or a thinker?

We prefer thinking through making.

Do you prefer bespoke or standardized?

There are certain degrees of standardization in our architectural prototypes, but each project is bespoke! We are interested in the repetition of architectural design protocols or algorithms that, when instantiated in a specific context, become bespoke prototypes.

What theories lie behind your design methods and practice?

Systems theory influenced by cybernetic culture, and cultural radicalism embedded with some degree of environmental activism. For us, digital design techniques become a means to develop the critical know-how to synthesize a new systemic architecture.

STEMcloud v2.0 — Guadalquivir River, Seville | 2008

This systemic architectural installation was conceived as a cybernetic machine in a laboratory for the *YOUniverse* exhibition commissioned by Fundación BIACS (curator: Marie-Ange Brayer). Visitors could take part in the breeding of micro-ecologies from the local river, feeding the colonies with nutrients, light and carbon dioxide in response to organic and electronic feedback.

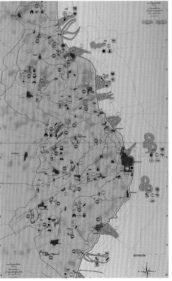

The architect analysed the topography of the Skåne region and created six prototypes, including the Crane Greenhouses for algae and seafood/fish farming (above), with their ETFE (ethylene tetrofluoroethylene) canopies, and an exhibition in the local Marine Centre (left), where visitors could blow their carbon dioxide into photo-bioreactors, and with lenses study the algae more closely. These facilities are part of the network of identified actors and agents across the fields of research, industry and tourism shown on the plan (above, right).

Do you strive to create new architectural typologies? If so, please give an example.

Yes, we design hybrid architectural–biological systems, such as the STEMcloud or the Cyber-Gardens series. But we don't think of them as new types. In fact, we are more interested in working with proto-typologies or prototypes; you can see them as pre-architectonic platforms of interaction and communication in space and time, which emerge from the indexing of the social and environmental context and landscape. In this sense, our projects overcome the definition of type and are instead part of a differentiated lineage of proto-architecture.

What are the most challenging aspects of your architectural practice today?

There is a tendency for architectural discourse to be compartmentalized, so that you find digital architects, designer-makers, environmental designers and media artists operating exclusively within their networks. We try to resist that: we do not brand ourselves as part of a single group or network. The advantage or reward is to be able to gain relevance transversally and have our say in many different circumstances. For instance, in recent months we have been keynote speakers in Copenhagen as digital craftsmen, at Cornell University in the United States as eco-cybernetic designers, and in Vienna as media architects.

What impact do you hope your architecture has on the public realm?

Generating a new urbanity and new models of urban dwelling based on a form of interactive learning about the surroundings. It is about stimulating the emergence of new communities or networks from the bottom up, and it is preoccupied with the tackling of common issues of the contemporary metropolis.

Our recent project in Trento, Italy, for the Museum of Science (MUSE), for instance, proposes an open biodiversity laboratory, a new urban prototype where research on the biodiversity of algae in the Alpine region is conducted with the participation of the public, who harvest and cultivate the organisms. In the library we designed in Ciriè, Turin, shelving prototypes were used to articulate the functions of the space without dividing it into rooms, thus encouraging group work as well as casual encounters and exchanges. And in our latest project, in Sweden, algae are used as a medium to engineer a hanging garden completed as part of a regional masterplan, tuned to stimulate

Il Bosco della Cultura

Il Bosco della Cultura ('forest of culture'), a public library housed in an old industrial building, was conceived as a field of prototype and parametric furniture responding to environmental and social conditions. The resulting differentiation contributed to the distinctive character of the individual programmatic intensities within a large, open plan.

interaction among members of the municipality, researchers at the local marine centre, locals and tourists.

What personal significance do you give to architectural precedent?

It is very important, as it helps you develop consciousness of things you have already been doing, so that you can keep evolving your agenda. Also, great precedents are extremely powerful, as they operate through a sort of snowball effect, which keeps increasing their relevance. Such projects as Cedric Price's Fun Palace [an unbuilt project in east London], for instance, inspired Renzo Piano and Richard Rogers's Pompidou Centre in Paris, which in turn keeps inspiring hundreds of architects worldwide. At the time we moved to London, Foreign Office Architects completed its first main project, the Yokohama International Port Terminal in Japan; that was a very powerful influence for us, most probably because it signalled a big shift in our architectural culture while we were absorbing the lessons of the AA. It is the same with songs: it does matter a lot what moment of your life they relate to.

Which technical advances excite you the most for exploitation?

We are excited by affordable open-source digital technology and the possibility it opens up for every person to be directly involved in the design and shaping of their city. Suddenly you have small companies and design start-ups delivering projects that can become more relevant than those delivered by big research institutions, such as the Massachusetts Institute of Technology.

Do you practise a transdisciplinary approach to architecture, and if so, what is especially important to you right now?

Yes, we do: in doing so it is very important to be able to set up a framework that supports the coherent transposition of information across disciplines and the incorporation of data from many sources.

How do you go about generating the best possible relationship with your clients?

We've worked mainly with clients who were particularly interested in our approach and way of working. We discussed the projects with them at length in order to produce a series of prototypes that engaged their curiosity and interest.

Eco Footprint Data Grotto Machine

2 The cell depth represents the country's ecologic **debt** or **credit**.

Based on research into fifty years of evolution in the world's ecological footprint, this installation is a 'grotto' of suspended cells relating to different nations, some more wrinkled and baggy than others according to levels of ecological 'debt'. Visitors can express their opinion by pushing a cell, causing the world's ecological footprint to reorganize.

EcoLogicStudio

Can you give an example of your participatory methods?

We use installations and models not as maquettes or sculptural pieces but rather as immersive spaces of playful interaction. That is why we call our installations 'apparatuses' or 'ecoMachines': they are mechanisms of communication.

How do you communicate your architecture?

We discuss it through lectures, seminars, blogs and books; we build installations for the most important architectural biennales; we run international students' workshops; and we teach at the AA.

What do you aim to achieve with your practice (in a single sentence)?

We aim to be recognized as an international practice for design innovation and ecological development; we wish to establish an atelier model that has a high-level workforce and can afford to remain small in size while developing research-quality work and delivering unique, bespoke design solutions for every project.

What advice would you give to a young architect embarking on their career?

You need to invent or craft your own way of thinking about architecture and being an architect. Develop your own idea of what architecture should do and craft the tools necessary to make it happen. The mainstream idea of what an architect does – designing buildings – is extremely limiting, so architecture has to evolve into something much higher-end, supported by the work of research-led design collectives.

What single improvement to the procurement of architecture in the United Kingdom would you recommend? More competitions, different planning system, legislation affecting developers, etc.?

CP More competitions, definitely, as we need to remember that young architects nowadays have not so much opportunity to promote their ideas in the United Kingdom. But also different types of competition, perhaps orientated to the distribution of research grants to develop and realize bold and innovative ideas for architectural prototypes, as is done in other fields, such as art, media technology or engineering.

Lightwall Villa
Ciriè, Turin, Italy | 2009

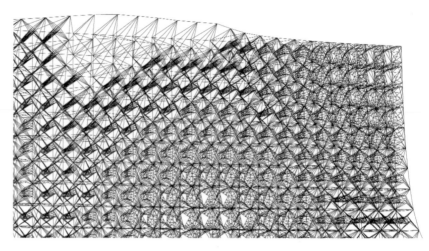

This villa conversion introduced the Lightwall concept, transforming the heavy concrete into a 'sponge' filtering heat and light and enabling views. The wall was modelled parametrically (top).

North Side Copse House

As with all the architect's projects, the design overcomes tension between technology and ecology. The house has a symbiotic relationship with its site, and employs local wood for both structure and cladding. It is formed of three interconnected structures (far right).

Glowacka Rennie Architects

Agnieszka Glowacka and Eleanor Rennie launched Glowacka Rennie Architects in London in 2004 after they won an East of England Development Agency (EEDA)/Royal Institute of British Architects (RIBA) design competition for their proposal for East Reef, a beach destination on the Essex coast, and what was to have been the United Kingdom's first offshore dive and aquarium centre.

East Reef was a proposal for the regeneration of the waterfront at Jaywick, Essex, a town that began life as a holiday village in the 1930s and became residential. It was once known as one of the happiest resorts on the Essex coast, and has been the subject of many revival efforts since social and economic conditions deteriorated in the 1980s. At the centre of a masterplan developed as an initial exercise by Llewelyn Davies Yeang, the East Reef Landmark Promenade, a 260-metre-long, 5-metre-wide pier with views out to sea and back over the town and surrounding area, would have been by day a beautiful 'stitch' between the sea and the sky, and at night a line of lanterns glowing on the water.

East Reef was one of a series of artistic proposals to assist regeneration, a number of which were regarded with enthusiasm by local residents, but there was understandable scepticism after many failed revival efforts in the past. Jaywick Tourist Board devised the Arcadia Revisited initiative to explore the essence of Jaywick, working with residents at its arts and heritage centre to develop a creative policy that established what an arcadian vision means to people in the United Kingdom today, a tough issue to crack in the face of very high local unemployment. Although the project has not been realized, Glowacka Rennie's practical designs enlivened the debate about the potential for integrated regenerative waterside programmes, and EEDA maintains its interest in supporting regeneration in the face of complex land purchase problems.

Some schemes bring a sense of arcadia relatively easily. The architect's conversion of the women's toilets at the Victoria and Albert Museum in London (2009) gives an everyday facility a

With the new, stone-clad interior and light, vaulted ceiling, the rippling lines of Felice Varini's geometric painting lend the women's toilets at the Victoria and Albert Museum, London (2009), a sense of spaciousness and relate them to the museum's tradition of fine and decorative arts.

95

Glowacka Rennie Architects

contemporary elegance that befits a museum designed to raise standards and promote the fine and decorative arts. The light, vaulted ceiling immediately reveals itself to visitors as they enter down the staircase, resonating with the rhythm of the existing windows. Emphasizing the generous height of the space, it is painted with an installation by Felice Varini (a Swiss artist known for his geometric, perspective-localized paintings), its hidden shape 'revealed' in the mirror as you wash your hands.

In February 2010 Glowacka Rennie opened a second office, in Beirut, Lebanon, and began work there on Yarze, a 6000-square-metre high-end residential development. Yarze is one of the most beautiful and serene areas of Beirut, in the hills east of the city centre, with lush vegetation and many secluded villas and diplomats' residences. The two buildings, each containing four 350-square-metre apartments, have panoramic views of the city from their upper levels, but are embedded in the forest. According to the architects, both have a textured, agate-like skin but each displays its own character, 'like a pair of couture garments from the same collection'.

This highly talented duo is slowly reaping the benefits of taking the time to respond to opportunities. They were notable runners-up in the New Islington Bridge competition for Urban Splash, for their footbridge design (2007). The intention was to respect the historic fabric of this area of Manchester with a versatile, sculptural bridge that acts as a welcoming gateway to New Islington from Ancoats Urban Village. Designed in the spirit of the masterplan – 'the Fish to Alsop's Chips!', say the architects, referring to Will Alsop's 100-metre-long apartment building, inspired by three chips piled on top of one another – the bridge is an elongated triangle that allows easy passage for flows of people coming from seven different directions. Like McDowell + Benedetti's award-winning bridge in Castleford, West Yorkshire, it has an intimacy to it, and serves as an extension of the public realm with scope for chance encounters: a place to sit, meet and take time out.

Invited to design the Rogerstown Visitor Centre scheme for the greening of a large landfill site on the Rogerstown Estuary north of Dublin, Glowacka Rennie proposed a striking but simple timber structure (2007). With its restaurant and community space, it is an expressive amenity in the landscape. The practice's competition entry for the Brockholes visitor centre for the Lancashire Wildlife Trust also demonstrates its ability to balance the needs of visitors and wildlife sensitively with its concept for a permeable threshold building or 'boundary'. This allows people to cross the site and view, unobserved,

while wildlife can enter the building, which is set on the side of the bowl formed by the bund of the new wetland and has entrances to the north and south. The first joins a walkway over water; the second creates a beacon for arriving car drivers, and its part of the building has spectacular views over the wetland from the cafe, meeting spaces and viewing gallery. This project was preceded by concept designs for what will be Norway's first wetland centre, the Dokka Delta on the banks of the Randsfjord, commissioned by the Wildfowl & Wetlands Trust. All Glowacka Rennie's designs demonstrate a strong aptitude for creating meaningfully connected spaces.

Sometimes commissions are just serendipitous. As part of the RIBA's Regent Street Windows Project in London in 2011, for which ten practices were invited to create shop-window installations on the theme of Cities of Tomorrow, the Spanish women's fashion retailer Hoss Intropia chose Glowacka Rennie to work with the window of its shop. As a result the firm commissioned the duo to develop their design for its Autumn/Winter 2011 collection, and it is now applied across its international stores. Glowacka Rennie's decorative screen can be configured in many different ways to display the collection. Its repeated geometric pattern, routed into PVC board, makes a flexible, fabric-like panel. A system of adjustable toggle hooks and steel cables hangs and gathers the 'fabric', transforming each panel into a complex, tailored three-dimensional display of clothing and accessories. Perforations in the joints and a golden iridescent finish transform the display from a shimmering surface during the day to a backlit silhouette at night. The play between geometry and place, fabric and light, two dimensions and three dimensions, building and nature in Glowacka Rennie's work is always a pleasure to experience, and articulates a well-considered and alluring functional language.

Rogerstown Visitor Centre on the Rogerstown Estuary, north of Dublin (2007), was an invited proposal that was part of a masterplan for the greening of a landfill site as a public park. The programme for the simple wooden structure included a restaurant serving food sourced from the estuary, a vantage point from which the river itself could be viewed, and a flexible community space.

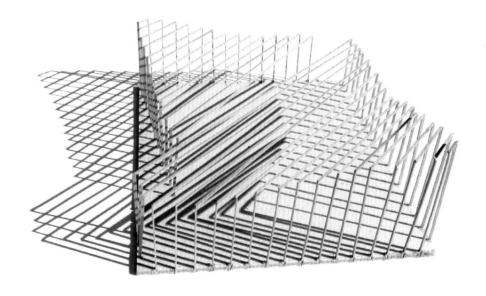

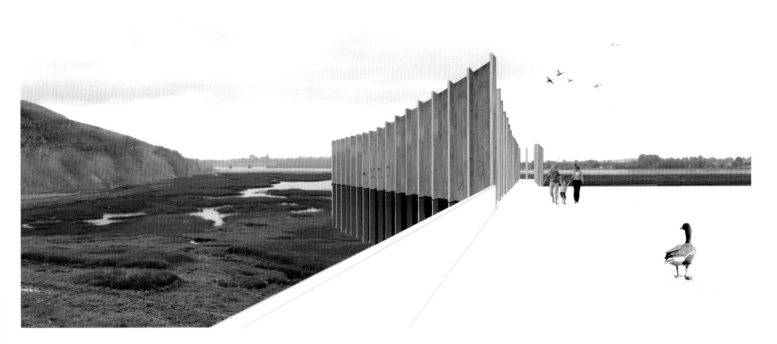

Glowacka Rennie Architects

Interview with Agnieszka Glowacka and Eleanor Rennie

East Reef Landmark Promenade

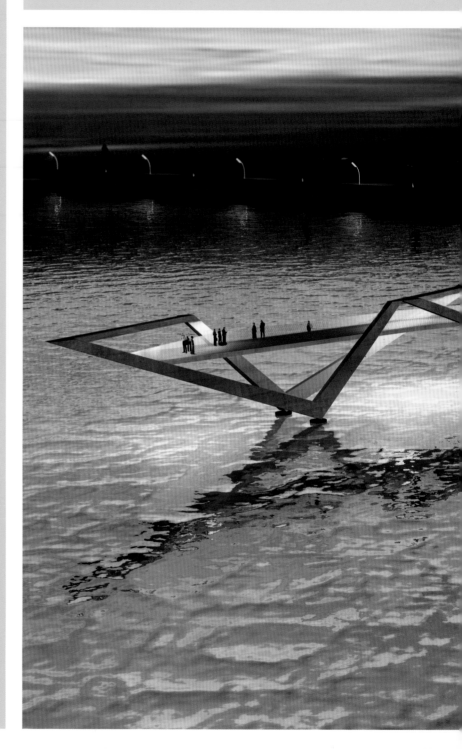

Can you recount a few architectural memories from childhood?

AG: Until the age of ten I lived in Poland. For me, a very powerful memory is of family summer holidays in rented tow-along caravans. I can palpably remember the excitement of inspecting the house on wheels outside our flat in the city, opening and closing the foldaway beds, table and drawers, before setting off on our holiday. I still love caravans – the ultimate compact, mobile architecture.

How would you describe your architectural background?

We share very similar architectural backgrounds. We both studied at the Bartlett School of Architecture, University College London, in Diploma Unit 17. This cultivated our love of landscape/architecture projects, interest in materiality and confidence in intuitive design. We then both worked for Buschow Henley Architects [now Henley Halebrown Rorrison] for several years before entering and winning the East Reef Landmark Promenade competition in 2004, when we set up on our own.

What are your greatest influences, architectural or otherwise?

For each project the site is generally our greatest influence and tends to be the root for all the branches of inspiration we follow.

Give one example of the way in which your architecture communicates effectively with people.

For the women's toilets commission at the Victoria and Albert Museum we set out to create a space that felt more like a new gallery than a toilet. We wanted people coming into the space to feel surprised and inspired – not the response one would normally anticipate when entering a toilet. Feedback from non-architectural reviewers seems to suggest that we have been successful.

Are you a maker or a thinker?

We are definitely both makers. That is how we generate our ideas – through making models, creating evocative images and taking photographs of the models we make. Our ideas are more often sparked by physical things we see than by things we read

This 260-metre-long, 5-metre-wide pier, a dynamic landmark for the community and for visitors, was intended to galvanize complementary development around the beach and waterfront of the coastal town, once a booming resort and the subject of many regeneration attempts.

Glowacka Rennie Architects

or hear. These visual prompts may range from a landscape experienced on holiday to an exquisite piece of antique jewellery seen in a museum.

Do you prefer bespoke or standardized?

Our overall approach is definitely bespoke. Each project is unique and requires a specific response.

What theories lie behind your design methods and practice?

There is no elaborate theory behind our work, but a strong desire to create architecture of experience, to craft spaces that are memorable and provoke a strong reaction. Our work is tested and shaped through physical models, as this gives us a visceral understanding of what the finished space or building might be like to inhabit or interact with.

Do you strive to create new architectural typologies? If so, please give an example.

As a practice we are not actively trying to create new typologies, as for us the beauty of being an architect is the variety of different project types one can work on. We love the fact that one day we could be designing a seaside pier and the next a window display. As a practice we are committed generalists.

What are the most challenging aspects of your architectural practice today?

Perhaps the pitfall of wanting to do lots of different types of project means that we are not seen as a specialist in any one type. Clients, particularly in the public sector, can be quite risk-averse and demand that you have built exactly the same type of project at least three times before. A fresh approach, unencumbered by years of churning out the same stuff, can be a benefit, but this is harder to sell even than badly executed experience.

What impact do you hope your architecture has on the public realm?

A positive one, of course. We want to produce architecture that makes the most of any given situation and that exceeds the expectations of those who use it. We want our projects to highlight the best and most exciting or beautiful things about their context, whether it is a visitor centre in a big, open landscape or a display screen in a shop window in a busy street.

New Islington Bridge

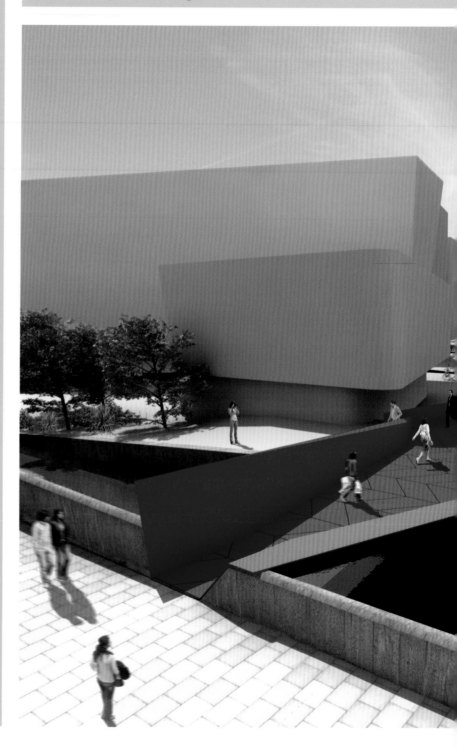

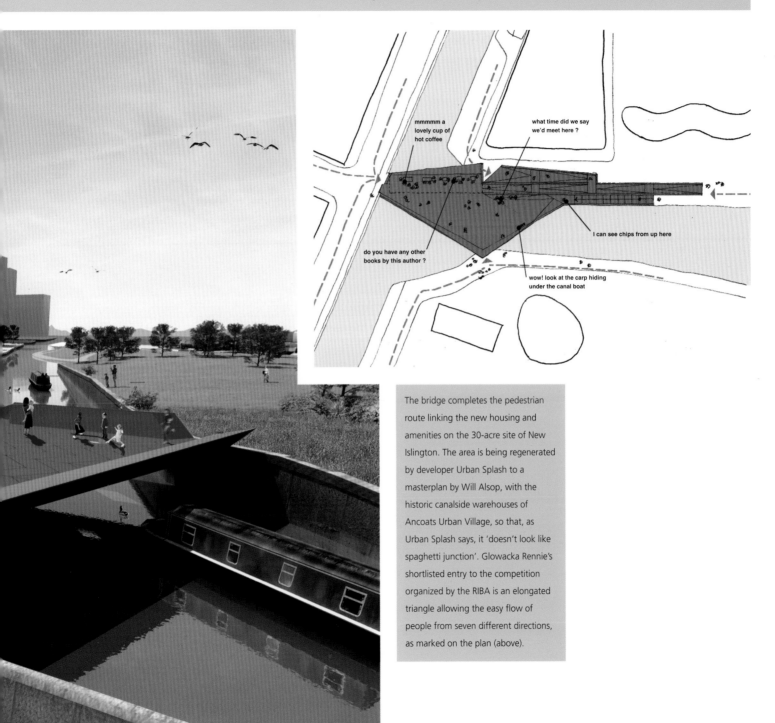

mmmmm a lovely cup of hot coffee

what time did we say we'd meet here ?

I can see chips from up here

do you have any other books by this author ?

wow! look at the carp hiding under the canal boat

The bridge completes the pedestrian route linking the new housing and amenities on the 30-acre site of New Islington. The area is being regenerated by developer Urban Splash to a masterplan by Will Alsop, with the historic canalside warehouses of Ancoats Urban Village, so that, as Urban Splash says, it 'doesn't look like spaghetti junction'. Glowacka Rennie's shortlisted entry to the competition organized by the RIBA is an elongated triangle allowing the easy flow of people from seven different directions, as marked on the plan (above).

Glowacka Rennie Architects

What personal significance do you give to architectural precedent?

We work in the context of countless incredible existing projects that both provide inspiration and are an enormous resource of information. If we were asked to design a concert hall we would of course look at precedent that we know and admire – it would be foolish not to. We would do this alongside thinking about the project as if it were the first concert hall ever built, since on the specific site, with the specific brief for the specific client, it would basically be different from any other.

Which technical advances excite you the most for exploitation?

Advances in building materials. We hoard samples of strange and wonderful materials that we hope to use in future projects. It is really exciting when materials cross over from other industries or from science into construction.

Do you practise a transdisciplinary approach to architecture, and if so, what is especially important to you right now?

We have always been really interested in the crossover between art, architecture and landscape and in blurring the boundaries between these disciplines. We also believe that there is real value in including other programmatic elements in basic infrastructure projects. That is something we started exploring with our scheme for East Reef in Essex, and will no doubt return to again and again.

How do you go about generating the best possible relationship with your clients?

We are not arrogant: we listen to our clients and are diplomatic and open-minded if we do not see eye to eye on any issues. This is pretty basic, but it's amazing how many architects don't follow it. We are also good at communicating our ideas to our clients, through sketches, drawings and physical models, so that they are kept informed and feel very much included in the design and decision-making process.

Can you give an example of your participatory methods?

We have carried out participatory workshops with schoolchildren and teachers, where we tried to stimulate a strong response and discussion through spatial 'games'. For example, we asked pupils to mark out with masking tape a familiar classroom, in the unfamiliar environment of an empty office floor in the Broadgate

Hoss Intropia

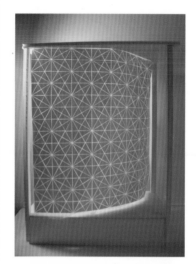

The RIBA's Regent Street Windows Project paired ten practices with ten retailers to generate shop-window installations. Glowacka Rennie's is a reconfigurable, decorative three-dimensional screen of panels, a versatile spatial tool on which clothing and accessories can be arrayed in various ways. Models of the screens are shown above.

Glowacka Rennie Architects

Tower [London], from memory and using only their bodies as rulers. This involved a lot of negotiation, pulling up of masking tape and pacing out of space, and it was interesting to see how the pupils remembered and thought about the spaces they inhabit every day.

How do you communicate your architecture?

At the concept stage and during the development of the project we communicate our architecture through models, drawings and visual material, as well as images of what inspired us in the first place. Once it is completed, we hope the project communicates itself through photographs and favourable reporting by those who visit.

What do you aim to achieve with your practice (in a single sentence)?

To be brave, to be bold, always to remain inventive and … to be asked to design the Serpentine Gallery's annual pavilion [in London].

What advice would you give to a young architect embarking on their career?

One word: opportunity. Seek it, follow it, don't be afraid to grab it. If opportunities don't seem to present themselves, try to create your own. If you are not working on interesting projects in your day job, do competitions in your spare time.

What single improvement to the procurement of architecture in the United Kingdom would you recommend? More competitions, different planning system, legislation affecting developers, etc.?

A public procurement system that placed less emphasis on identical previous experience and size of practice/turnover, and more on the quality of the ideas, would make it easier for smaller practices to compete for public projects. Reducing risk is understandable, but it seems we are trying to remove it altogether. There is no progress without an element of risk.

Women's Toilets, Victoria and Albert Museum

Glowacka Rennie Architects won an invited competition for the toilets off the Grand Entrance hall, used by visitors and guests at major events. A new staircase leading down to an interior refitted with a stone facade gives the facility its own grand entrance, and the elegant space has a new vaulted ceiling and a monochrome palette.

Glowacka Rennie Architects

Gort Scott

With an œuvre that ranges from furniture to urbanism, Gort Scott, founded in 2007 by Jay Gort and Fiona Scott, is a firm of young place-makers who have already been exposed to a variety of different contexts and challenges for local community projects, urban plans, private houses in rural settings and commercial developments. Their commitment to research and teaching gives them a propensity for the wider critical dissemination of well-judged ideas about the cultural role of architecture.

Balancing the need to retain a sense of the original proportions with the transformation of traditionally planned spaces into usable and welcoming environments, Gort Scott extended and completely remodelled a three-storey Georgian town house for the Swedish fashion brand Acne's first British store, on Dover Street in Mayfair, London (2010). The practice added two storeys – one on the roof and the other in the basement – and extended the space at the back of the building, which now has a new roof-lit staircase.

For Finding Flotmyr, a competition (2011) for a new mixed-use, high-density quarter of Haugesund, a town in western Norway, Gort Scott's response addressed the need to attract and retain a critical mass of young professionals, who currently leave the town for Bergen and Stavanger. The practice advocates realism: one site alone cannot miraculously fulfill Haugesund's wishes. But Flotmyr is 'a critical piece of the jigsaw', and can be regarded as a catalyst, expanding the offer of the town in both cultural and commercial terms. Gort Scott's proposition is accordingly flexible and sustainable, and that means defining the identity of Flotmyr's open spaces, in terms of their scale, layout, qualities and characteristics. Its design reinforces the existing green spine of Torggata and introduces a new pavement along Karmsundgata, linking to a new park and opening up routes to the wider landscape. This tactic makes the most of the topographical features of the surrounding area, as part of a fundamental rethinking of the cultural landscape in its totality, to draw out, rather than impose, fresh potential.

The design of the Acne store in Dover Street, London (2010), entailed the remodelling of a three-storey Georgian town house, traditionally planned and with split levels, into welcoming retail space. Gort Scott retained a sense of the original proportions of the rooms.

One of Gort Scott's key urban-design frameworks is for Blackhorse Lane (2010–) in north-east London, part of the borough of Waltham Forest's Area Action Plan (AAP), which is being developed by a multidisciplinary team including the architect Maccreanor Lavington. The area, next to the River Lea, will be transformed over the next decade: a number of key sites will be developed and there will be more than 2000 new homes and improved amenities and infrastructure, including a new waterfront park, a neighbourhood centre and a secondary school. The architects have undertaken extensive research and consultation with landowners, developers and other stakeholders, developing and testing a range of financially appraised options, and creating planning and design briefs for each site. As a result, evidence for the AAP will be created, providing the statutory basis for the council to achieve the regeneration, not just redevelopment, of the area. Gort Scott has also carried out research with University College London to help develop the London Development Agency's High Streets Agenda, which aims to evolve a further understanding of how high streets function in supporting London's sustainable growth and development. This work featured in the Technical University of Berlin's exhibition *City Visions 1910 | 2010* (2010).

The Living Screens (ongoing), in the centre of Cambridge, creates a new and significant edge to a large public square that was lacking character and ambition. It tackles the question of whether a private building can be perceived as public and civic. Gort Scott's ten-storey mixed-use building is fronted by a sculptural screen devised with the artist Michael Tuck, veiling the private and public spaces, which include an accessible, open-air terrace on the first floor. To disseminate information about the project and provoke a debate about contemporary architecture in the city, Gort Scott designed and built a mobile consultation stand, which was taken on tour to different public spaces: shopping centres, hospitals, schools and the square itself. The Cambridge Design and Conservation report (May 2008) called the Living Screens 'inspired': 'It could transform this part of Cambridge from a "non-place" into a public space of real quality.'

The multifunctionality of the George V Pavilion (2009), also in Cambridge and designed with the architect 5th Studio, includes a large motorized gate at the back to open up the interior to the recreation ground. Used by many different groups, from children to the elderly, this public hall replaces a burnt-out pavilion, and features external landscaping, lighting, spaces for bicycles, shelter and benches. It needed to be secure, and so Gort Scott gave it a robust, sophisticated aesthetic with steel mesh in front of glass and extruded plastic panels injected with gloss paint, by Michael Tuck.

Gort Scott's response to tight resources at Harlington Community School in west London is a series of exterior furniture pieces (2010): large benches made of recycled plastic planks on concrete bases, and translucent canopy shelters. These colourful, inventive elements make up for a lack of calm spaces for socializing. The firm staged a number of workshops with the pupils (who are of secondary-school age) to demystify the design process.

Underused areas of cities remain spaces of latent opportunity. Gort Scott won the Royal Institute of British Architects' Forgotten Spaces competition (2011) with a scheme for the quiet, glassy reservoirs of the Upper Lea Valley in north-east London. The two roofed structures – over-scaled, low-lidded and clay-tiled – are inspired by the work of William Morris and fit in effortlessly with the sublime location and their working infrastructure, opening them up to a wide range of users.

Another secluded location is Seamount, a house in Scarlett on the Isle of Man. The design is related to a series of connected outdoor landscaped spaces, including a swimming pool, an orchard, a barbecue and a drinks terrace. Inside the house are light scoops and roof lights, drawing illumination down into the centre of the house around a cantilevered stone staircase. At the high point of the garden site, sheltered by the wall, is a cottage with two flats for guests, a compact form clad in traditional Manx stone.

Gort and Scott complement each other very well. Their great experience in urban and rural contexts will serve them well in their varied activities.

At Harlington Community School in west London (2010), Gort Scott staged workshops with pupils to help advance their designs for an outdoor play area, with furniture made of recycled plastic planks on concrete bases, and translucent canopies. The school's resources were tight, but the lack of interior space for socializing motivated the staff to commission the project.

Gort Scott

Interview with Jay Gort and Fiona Scott

Can you recount a few architectural memories from childhood?

FS I remember, aged ten, being excited by the prospect of going to school in the Barbican in London: travelling into the City on the Tube, the aerial walkways leading to the school gates on the fourth floor, the playing field stacked on the gym, stacked on a pool, and overlooked by the hand-tooled concrete balconies of high-rise flats.
JG Making an ambitious, quite dangerous den in the back of an abandoned Swizzels Matlow lorry.

How would you describe your architectural background?

Our background stems from an inquisitive mind, a passion for understanding what makes spaces work, and an openness to dialogue. Both partners came to the discipline via art school, and were strongly influenced by the University of Cambridge architecture department in the 1990s. As a consequence, cultural context is very important to us, and we constantly have an eye on the bigger picture, on the things that exist around architecture.

What are your greatest influences, architectural or otherwise?

We are influenced by what we learn from the city around us, specifically London, which is an endless source of inspiration, but also other great cities, such as Istanbul and Berlin. At the same time, lurking in the background is a kind of dream of places with a powerful relationship between architecture and landscape: places like the Judd Foundation (for the artist Donald Judd) in Marfa, Texas, or the monastery at La Tourette near Lyon, France, designed by Le Corbusier and Iannis Xenakis [1956–60].

Give one example of the way in which your architecture communicates effectively with people.

Our George V Pavilion in Cambridge (2009), with the architect 5th Studio, is an informal, adaptable space, suggesting many different modes of use. The exterior is a robust mesh, which sits over cladding that was hand-decorated by an artist along with members of the community: the building can entirely close down, but it can also completely open up to the spaces around it. We think it communicates resourcefulness and community ownership.

Reservoir Roofs

An RIBA competition, Forgotten Spaces focused on ideas for underused space in London, and Gort Scott's winning entry celebrates but also respects the quiet monumentality of the working reservoirs in the Upper Lea Valley. Instead of a pub or sailing club, its design is for sheltered viewing points with clay-tiled roofs, inspired by the work of William Morris, a leading figure in the Arts and Crafts movement.

Finding Flotmyr

Are you a maker or a thinker?

Both. You have to be thoughtful to make things well.

Do you prefer bespoke or standardized?

We have no preference: it depends on the job in hand. Using standardized products, design methods and processes will often lead to a level of efficiency appropriate to the project. But the aim is for the result to be a specific response to the context.

What theories lie behind your design methods and practice?

We accept and embrace collision, and the multiple realities in which architecture has to sit. We aren't obsessed by single ideas or processes; architecture has the unique capacity to synthesize the many disparate inputs that make a building or piece of a city.

Do you strive to create new architectural typologies? If so, please give an example.

Not really. We are interested in contextual variations on existing tried-and-tested typologies, like the terraced house or the high street, for example, and in seeing how they evolve. We found ourselves making what we consider to be a new typology with the Acne store in London – a single shop that occupies all five floors of a Georgian town house in Mayfair – but it evolved quite naturally by adapting what had gone before.

What are the most challenging aspects of your architectural practice today?

Responding to the changing political and economic climate requires phenomenal agility. In the short lifespan of our practice much has changed, and this suggests that we must keep our ears to the ground. We have seen housing boom and bust, schools projects come and go, and now the near-collapse of the public sector. We must be Olympic gymnasts in that regard.

What impact do you hope your architecture has on the public realm?

We design with human situations in mind. This is equally the case within the rooms of a building as within the spaces the building forms in the public realm. We aim to produce architecture that offers a gift to its context. This might be an elegant elevation to a public space, a public route through the site or a generous room for the town.

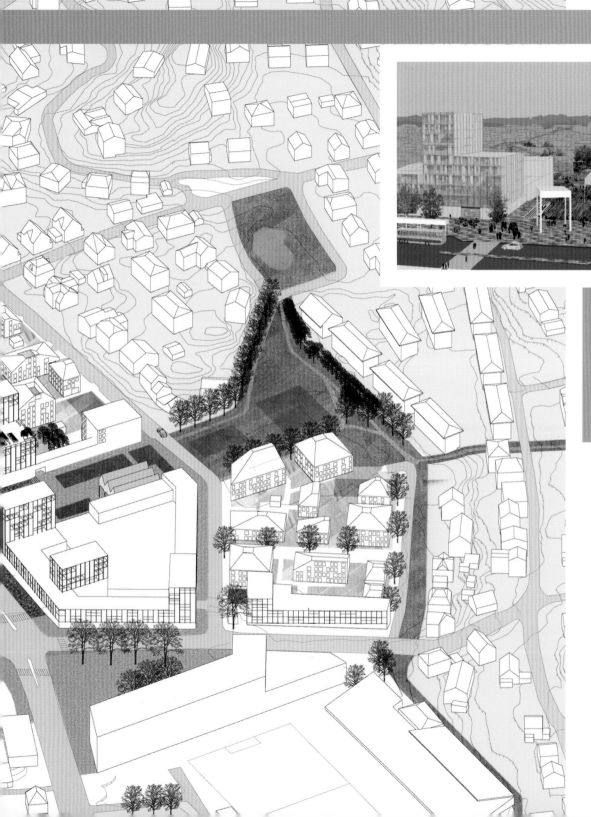

The design of this competition entry for a new mixed-use, high-density quarter of the town of Haugesund is defined by the scale, layout and characteristics of the quarter's open spaces. A reinforced green spine and a wide pavement link to a park that opens up connecting routes to the wider landscape.

Gort Scott

What personal significance do you give to architectural precedent?

We differ on this point:

FS I am ambivalent towards referencing architectural precedent if we are talking about architecture with a capital A. But in terms of understanding the evolution of certain types or understanding how things relate to a common architectural tradition, then I would say it has enormous significance.

JG Architectural precedent is very important. I am far more confident deploying tried-and-tested spaces, or pieces of city from both contemporary and historical precedents, while making them relevant for a particular situation. Precedent is important as a means of communicating ideas and aspirations with each other as well as with clients.

Which technical advances excite you the most for exploitation?

Our work doesn't typically hinge on technology: the tricky issues we face in our work at the moment are more likely to be solved by thinking creatively. That is partly to do with the scale and nature of our current projects. But we are excited by advances in materials technology, and by the transfer of materials into the construction industry from other sectors or industries.

Do you practise a transdisciplinary approach to architecture, and if so, what is especially important to you right now?

We work across architecture and urban design. Our interests, and the scales at which we work and think, are varied, and we see architecture and urban design as very different disciplines, despite the crossover of skills. At the moment we are focusing on building!

How do you go about generating the best possible relationship with your clients?

Being honest and straightforward, and involving them in a good level of dialogue that we all find interesting and engaging. We think it is important that client and architect should learn from each other, as much as from the process of designing and building.

Can you give an example of your participatory methods?

There are many, but one example is that we often work with a photography duo, Liz Lock and Mishka Henner, and carry out photography workshops in particular places. The purpose is to

Acne store

Planning permission was gained for the remodelling of a three-storey Georgian town house in Mayfair (a strict Conservation Area) into a five-storey development with four floors of retail by adding a full storey at roof level and an additional storey in the basement. The rear of the building was extended to create a top-lit staircase connecting all floors.

gain insight into the relationship between people and the places they know intimately, and this involves building relationships with people.

How do you communicate your architecture?

Communication is an essential part of the design process. We use handmade models, collages and sketches to test ideas and represent them to each other and to clients. In terms of communicating with a wider audience, we speak at events, from lectures at university schools of architecture to industry conferences. Teaching also provides a way of consolidating our ideas and communicating in perhaps a more theoretical way through the work of the studio.

What do you aim to achieve with your practice (in a single sentence)?

To make buildings and spaces through which people's daily experiences are improved in small but significant ways; to use resources efficiently; to work with people who share our values.

What advice would you give to a young architect embarking on their career?

Perhaps the old Cedric Price quotation holds the key: 'The solution to your problem may not be a building.' In other words, take a broad view of how you might be an architect without being an 'Architect'. You can influence architecture and the built environment creatively through politics, planning, development and art. Also widen your network, develop and nurture relationships: with other architects, consultants and anyone who might potentially be a collaborator, client or mentor. You need a lot of friends to support you in this game.

What single improvement to the procurement of architecture in the United Kingdom would you recommend? More competitions, different planning system, legislation affecting developers, etc.?

The Flemish Bouwmeester system, where a respected architect leads the procurement of public projects, seems to have raised the standard of public architecture and allowed 'new blood' into the system. The Bouwmeester's team monitors the quality of public projects, and advises clients through what seems to be a fair, competitive procurement process.

George V Pavilion

Cambridge I 2009

A derelict brick structure in a park is transformed into a new public amenity with a big hall and access to outdoor recreational space that everyone from the very young to the elderly can use. Gort Scott's security-conscious design for the city council is robust yet sophisticated in aesthetic.

A new predominantly private building on the edge of a large public square, lacking in character, brings a refreshed, civic ethos. An accessible open-air terrace on the first floor creates a sense of permeable urban grain, and a sculptural screen, devised with the artist Michael Tuck, sits like a punctuated veil in front of the building envelope.

Guarnieri Architects

Distilled in their formal and material resolution, Marco Guarnieri's projects have ranged from numerous residential refurbishments, production buildings and offices and a new building for a school of management, through a transport interchange and a train station prototype suitable for various semi-rural locations around Italy, to a high-rise tower open to the public.

After his studies at IUAV Venice (the University of Venice's architecture school), Guarnieri's further education at the Architectural Association, London, in Diploma Unit 5, run at the time by Alejandro Zaera-Polo and Farshid Moussavi of Foreign Office Architects (FOA),[1] enabled him to develop techniques for spatial and material organization: for example, devising programmes and geometries for architectural designs geared to specific conditions. Joining the FOA team in 2000 enabled him to develop some of these principles as he worked on its global schemes, including the Bluemoon Aparthotel, Groningen, The Netherlands (1999–2000), and the South-East Coastal Park and Auditoria, Barcelona (2004).

Guarnieri's first built scheme, designed with Lea Katz after they founded their own firm in 2003, was Pack Line's headquarters in Tel Aviv (2006). The production and office buildings sit side by side, connected by a glazed passage, and are both faced in aluminium in a large chequered pattern, which gives seamless aesthetic coherence across their envelopes. Guarnieri favours the abstract visual language and strong materiality of this 'veil' as a versatile way for the perforated panels to function also as a sunscreen over the windows on both floors. Corners and doors are also treated consistently, so that they appear to share a common DNA, in spite of the difference in their sizes.

A careful study of Pack Line's company logistics led to the design of a 30-metre-long service wall. Containing archives, air conditioning and lighting and with a cantilevered sequence of drawers and cupboards, it is punctuated with sliding doors with horizontal bands of opaque and clear glass. Dividing the building into formal and more

The offices and production unit (2500 square metres) of CMG, a hydraulic systems and maintenance company, in Trieste, Italy, were refurbished in 2007. Guarnieri created a new cladding of sandwiched aluminium panels filled with polyurethane for part of the building, to increase the thermal inertia. New continuous glazing with 25-metre-long steel plates screens the interiors from the sun and accommodates drainpipes. The entrance (right) is a free-standing element consisting of three glass panels.

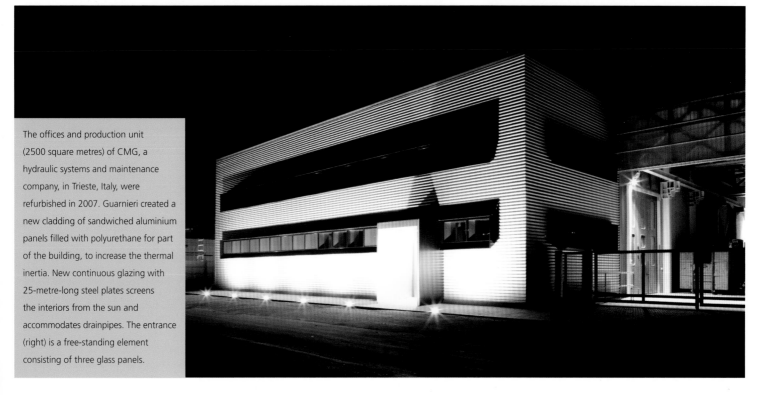

open spaces and serving both sides, this spine sits on a striking 'cracked-earth' floor pattern in white and green, created with layers of paint and epoxy resin. Outside, the firm's underlit iron-mesh perimeter fence, with vertical, wall-mounted planters with integrated lighting, also reflects the spine and facade patterns, and echoes, in alternately lit vertical strips on its street side, the new Pack Line design language.

The practice's ongoing investigation into natural systems and organisms also produced a design strategy for FM, a fashion retailer, realized in a boutique in the Givatayim Shopping Centre in Tel Aviv (2005). The visual and spatial language was based on the natural world, including the rippling of the surface of water and the cracked earth of the desert. The design employs faceted profiles of trees spatialized as tri-level display walls and changing rooms on a floor of natural green river stones.

Guarnieri is a pragmatist concerned with producing a close coincidence between the functional and the aesthetic. These first built works were not based on preconceived ideas but exploited the conditions of the site, and further projects have demonstrated his capacity to tackle design on a local basis, informed by streams of diverse information and integrating different systems. This capacity for multicultural solutions, robust in their setting yet born of diverse inputs stringently cohered, identifies him with the accomplished work of Zaera-Polo and Moussavi. Like them, he tempers design flair with great discipline. He reduces architectural elements not for the sake of it, but to find the least arbitrary decision.

Guarnieri is good at giving his projects a deceptively simple twist that distinguishes them from the work of other architects. His World Tower proposal for the Za'Beel Park in Dubai (2009) reinterprets the concept of the iconic building as a fresh way of thinking about programme, our relationship with natural species and their biodiversity. It is derived from a faceted map, with an observatory and a series of gardens at different levels. While images of cherry blossom inside laminated glass panels, cladding the facade of a new roof structure proposed for a penthouse flat above a warehouse in Whitechapel (2008–10), constituted a symbolic functionalist reading, his refurbishment – including an aluminium cladding system with elongated windows to assist solar screening and rainwater evacuation – of the CMG headquarters in Trieste, Italy (2007), enhances its identity, allowing the company to work in a new, more sustainable way. His competition scheme for the National Library of the Czech Republic (2006) with the Swiss architect A.A. Dunkel is a clear, effective and eye-catching solution (see interview, p. 126).

In an issue of the leading Italian architecture magazine *Parametro* on the Italian high-speed railway line, curated by Guarnieri in 2005, he discussed the processes of urbanization triggered by this major infrastructure project and its stations, some of them in degraded areas. His specialist research and informed approach helped him to make an excellent proposal in 2007 for a modular system in light wood for the Italian railway network's competition to design a station prototype adaptable to four different conditions, and which could grow in size as necessary and was minimally invasive of its natural environment. He drew on his work in the field of infrastructure for his proposal (with Arup Milan), conceived as an infrastructural landscape, for an international competition for the Oristano transport interchange, Sardinia (2009).

An early graphic logo for Guarnieri Architects was a mutation of the characters of its name into other alphabets, without losing their identity, in the manner of a transcultural code. The reality that there may be less difference between the specific cultural conditions of two cities in the world than between two in the same country motivates such architects as Guarnieri to advance each project with thorough local and global intelligence, with rigour, pragmatism and inventive capacities tailored to its specific conditions.

[1] In 2011 the co-founders of FOA demerged the practice into two legacy firms: AZPA, led by Alejandro Zaera-Polo (London and Barcelona), and Farshid Moussavi Architecture (London), led by Farshid Moussavi.

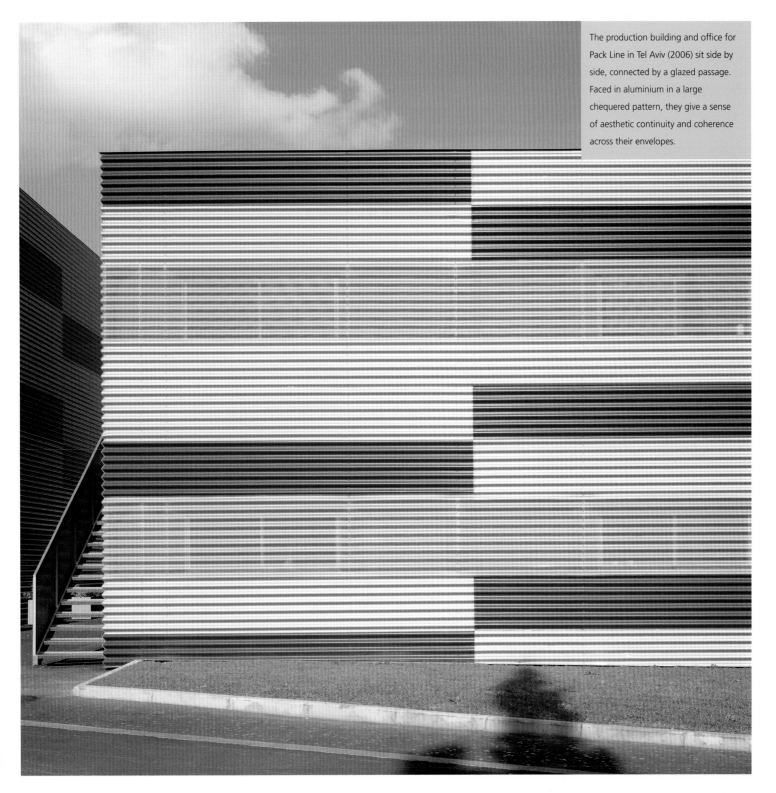

The production building and office for Pack Line in Tel Aviv (2006) sit side by side, connected by a glazed passage. Faced in aluminium in a large chequered pattern, they give a sense of aesthetic continuity and coherence across their envelopes.

Guarnieri Architects

Interview with Marco Guarnieri

Can you recount a few architectural memories from childhood?

I can't. I would divide my life into two periods: before and after engaging in architectural studies and practice.

How would you describe your architectural background?

I think it combines the desire to become an architect with good timing and a bit of luck. It was a combination of desire and luck that led me to study in two very different schools of architecture: the IUAV in Venice and the Architectural Association in London. The same applies to the two practices I worked for – Zaha Hadid Architects and Foreign Office Architects – and in very interesting times, as those practices were just about to emerge.

What are your greatest influences, architectural or otherwise?

We are influenced by many things both internal and external in the practice of architecture. I would not say I am influenced by one architect or one practice alone. I see two fundamental categories of practice: the 'dogmatics' and the 'pragmatics'. The 'dogmatics' work with a set of preconceived forms that are used across the field of projects the practice is developing: a sort of acquired and sedimented vocabulary of the practice. Foster + Partners and Zaha Hadid Architects, to give well-known examples, share this, even if their work is based on very different interests or criteria. Their work is the combination of a set of established forms. When you look at their buildings it is unmistakably the work of Foster + Partners or Zaha Hadid Architects.

The 'pragmatics' work with the conditions of the project to develop a uniquely appropriate solution to that particular architectural problem. When you look at the work of such practices as OMA and Herzog & de Meuron, each project is different from the other, although some common lineages can be derived. It is the result of the opportunity the conditions offer. I think I am more interested in this second approach to practice, and I would position the work of my office in this category.

National Library of the Czech Republic

The competition entry by Guarnieri in association with architect A.A. Dunkel is iconic yet highly energy efficient. The library stacks (which make up half of the 50,000-square-metre building) are devised in the form of a waffle above a transparent plinth housing the ground-floor public area, where the collections can be accessed. The inertia of the huge, thermo-technically insulated mass stabilizes the internal temperature all year round. Wrapped in different shades of rhomboid-shaped glass panels, which are translucent or reflective according to the weather, this audacious top layer is visible by the users below.

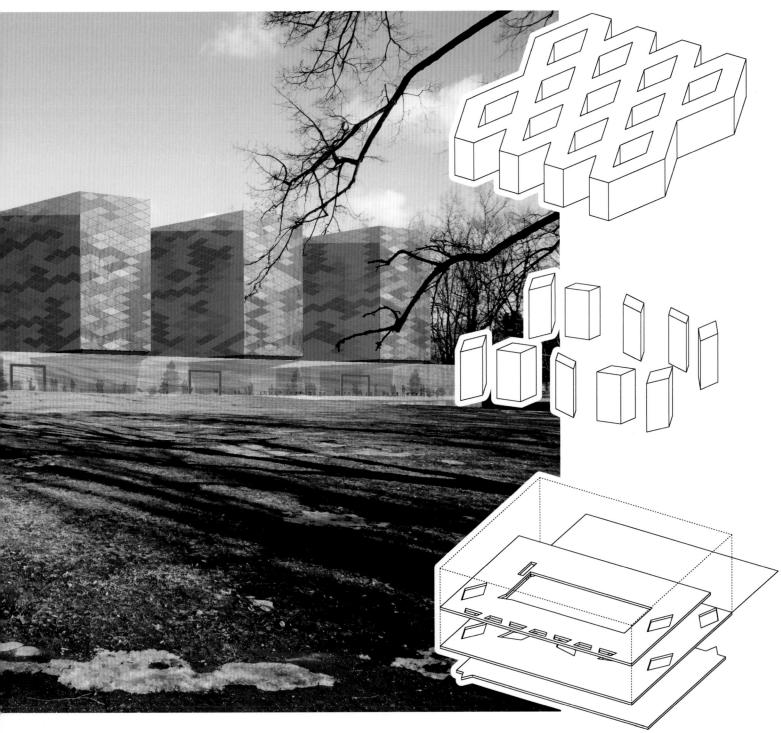

Give one example of the way in which your architecture communicates effectively with people.

Architectural work most likely communicates different things to different audiences: the client, the user, colleagues and the public at large. I think it is hard to give one straight answer. We work with one idea for one project that is specific to it and is not a priori, one consistent concept that drives the project throughout the design process. The idea we develop then comes through in a bold and uncompromised way, so that the comment, when looking at the final result, is often 'It is about that!', and the idea of the project is communicated.

Are you a maker or a thinker?

Well, this is an interesting question for me because I believe that ideas come by doing things. So, there is no thinking without making and there is no making without thinking.

Do you prefer bespoke or standardized?

It depends what is more appropriate for the success of the project. Standardization is an old concept. In large-scale construction, repetition, or a balance between difference and repetition, is crucial.

What theories lie behind your design methods and practice?

I am not sure the word 'theory' applies to all architectural practices. Perhaps only to those that base their work on a theory and are more attached to academia. I do not think we fall into this category, as my academic involvement and influences are limited. I would say that 'principles' is a more correct word to use to answer your question, and that, in current times, when there is a lot of emphasis on image and superficial appearance, rigour is one of the principles that distinguishes our work. We apply rigour at various levels in the project: analytical rigour, technical rigour, geometric rigour, and so on. We are also very pragmatic in our work and that is by definition antithetic to theory, although it does not exclude the possibility of deriving a theory in an empirical way. Even though our work is very creative, I would say that our approach to architectural practice is more scientific than artistic. When we start working on a project we look at material facts rather than ideological ones.

World Tower
Dubai I competition entry, 2009

A proposal for an ideas competition for Za'Beel Park, the World Tower reinterprets the iconic tower as a faceted form encompassing a map of the world, and housing an observatory, a cafe and a multi-level exhibition about bio-diversity with a range of species from all over the world.

FM Boutique
Tel Aviv I 2005

A playful design strategy based on landscapes for the youthful FM (Free Move) clothing brand evolved three alternatives: forest, ocean and desert. The forest concept was realized in plasterboard and Barrisol fabric, with fluorescent tube lights set in niches in each branch of the 'trees', giving warmth and depth to their geometric planes.

A side and rear extension of a house in Parsons Green, west London (2011; right), is conceived as a continuous system of glazing, differentiating it from the character of the house. Designs were invited for a 200-square-metre roof extension above a warehouse conversion in Whitechapel (2008–10); Guarnieri's (below) has a laminated-glass cladding system with a plant pattern. A render (below, right) shows the rear elevation of the refurbishment and extension of a house in west London (2010–; in planning).

Do you strive to create new architectural typologies? If so, please give an example.

Yes, I long to create new typologies. You need to be very analytical and rigorous to do this. For instance, with the National Library of the Czech Republic, we faced an extremely complex programme. We analysed it thoroughly and discovered that 50 per cent of the programme was archive stacks. This part did not need natural light and required different climatic conditions from the rest. Stacks are normally housed underground. We saw an opportunity and did the opposite. We put them on top of the public programme of the library. This gave us the opportunity to have a large consistent mass to work with that became the visible part of the project, and at the same time allowed us to develop a strong environmental strategy simply by using the mass of the stacks and its thermal inertia. I remember that the consultants were very excited working on this project, and we were too, because we were after a new building type, not only because of its appearance and organization but also because of the way the physics of the building was working. It was like a new scientific discovery.

What are the most challenging aspects of architectural practice today?

Keeping up to date with technological developments in the construction industry, and the tools we use – software, for example. Architects move at a very slow pace with work: even a small project takes at least a year from the first meeting to completion. During this time many things have already changed in the industry.

What impact do you hope your architecture has on the public realm?

Delivering exciting and enjoyable spaces to use and live in.

What personal significance do you give to architectural precedent?

It depends whether it helps to develop the project you are working on. Sometimes it is an advantage to know about precedents; sometimes it is an advantage not to be influenced by them and to develop something new.

Which technical advances excite you the most for exploitation?

Whatever helps to develop and implement a good project. For me it is always a matter of specificity and appropriateness.

Pack Line headquarters

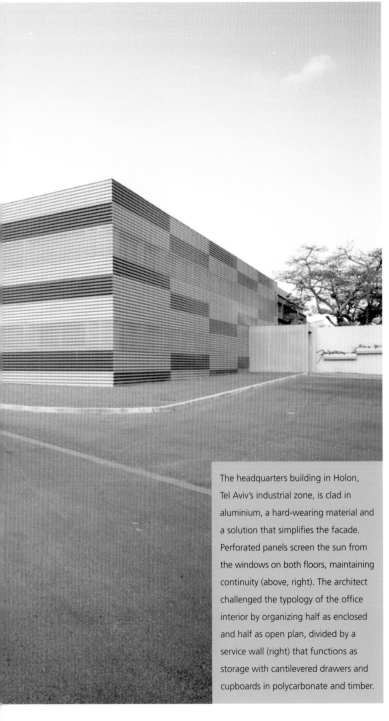

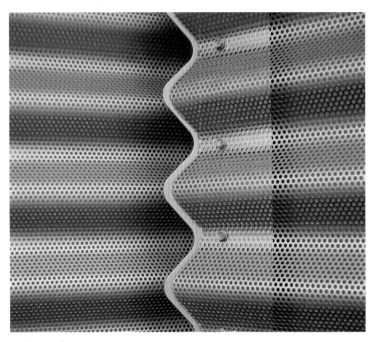

The headquarters building in Holon, Tel Aviv's industrial zone, is clad in aluminium, a hard-wearing material and a solution that simplifies the facade. Perforated panels screen the sun from the windows on both floors, maintaining continuity (above, right). The architect challenged the typology of the office interior by organizing half as enclosed and half as open plan, divided by a service wall (right) that functions as storage with cantilevered drawers and cupboards in polycarbonate and timber.

Guarnieri Architects

Do you practise a transdisciplinary approach to architecture, and if so, what is especially important to you right now?
Not as a principle. I believe in innovation from within the architectural practice, although you need other disciplines to develop particular types of project.

How do you go about generating the best possible relationship with your clients?
It really depends who is the client. However, I think it is about caring for their needs and understanding their aspirations.

Can you give me an example of your participatory methods?
When we meet to discuss a project I like everybody in the office to participate, and I like to hear everybody's opinion when we need to make decisions. We also like to have current work pinned up in the office so everybody can access the project and participate even if they are not working on it.

How do you communicate your architecture?
Images, models, videos: whatever helps communicate our architecture in the best way. I do not have a preferred medium.

What do you aim to achieve with your practice (in a single sentence)?
Innovative architecture!

What advice would you give to a young architect embarking on their career?
Good luck!

What single improvement to the procurement of architecture in the United Kingdom would you recommend? More competitions, different planning system, legislation affecting developers, etc.?
If you look at the numbers provided by the Royal Institute of British Architects' Practice Department, 50 per cent of British architects' fee income is from contractors. This suggests that contractors hold a lot of power. I wonder if there is a way of shifting power towards architects and design.

Markthalle
Basel, Switzerland I competition entry, 2006

A competition entry in association with the architect A.A. Dunkel strives to render this central site part of an urban pedestrian route linking the train station with the retail district. The circulation is placed on the main facade to increase the public character of the building.

Transport Interchange

In collaboration with Arup Milan, Guarnieri designed the interchange – which includes a bus terminal, a 250-space car park and a passenger terminal linked to the existing railway station – as an infrastructural landscape. The layout enabled the heat produced by vehicles to be reduced, and the canopies of the bus terminal, designed with an aerodynamic pattern, act as a passive extractor for fumes.

IJP

The architect George L. Legendre exhaustively explores the relationships between space, mathematics and computation, searching for a rigorous complexity belied by the elegant, sinuous forms of his realized projects. His unique work has been nourished by extensive research and development in parallel with, and related to, his teaching at Harvard Graduate School of Design (1995–2000) and Princeton University (2003–2005) and over the course of eight years as Unit Master of Diploma Unit 5 at the Architectural Association in London. Professor Peter Carl, head of the PhD programme in the Department of Architecture and Spatial Design at London Metropolitan University, points out in an article in 2003 (*ARQ*, vol. 7, no. 3/4) that Legendre, as a leading member of the younger global digital architectural fraternity, 'prefers his computing with as little interference as possible from pasteurized, off-the-shelf software', and the originality and richness of his forms bear this out.

An early project with long-time collaborator Adams Kara Taylor (now known as AKT II after a management buyout), a structural engineering company based in London, was a competition win for a roof to cover Glasshouse Street in central London with 1000 square metres of glass (2004–2005). While this ambitious little project, which employs surface mathematics to produce a sensuous, asymmetrical, Y-shaped woven form, extending the city's tradition of arcades, has not been advanced during the recession, London's cultural and social environment remains a place of compelling possibilities for Legendre.

Alongside his architectural projects and teaching, Legendre is an indefatigable writer, whose work includes *IJP: The Book of Surfaces* (2003), *Bodyline: The End of our Meta-Mechanical Body* (2006) and *The Mathematics of Sensible Things* (a guest-edited issue of *Architectural Design* magazine). His most recent publication, inspired by and evolved as an idea with another long-term collaborator, the Italian architect Marco Guarnieri (see pp. 118–29), over the course of innumerable meals, is *Pasta by Design* (2011), a pasta taxonomy in book form. Long before the ritual of eating is ever reached, in a magnification of the forming of pasta, Legendre painstakingly works out the mathematical formulae of pasta in all its incredible variety, from grooved and smooth shells (*conchiglie*) to cute racket-shaped *racchette*, to create an inventory that functions as a guide and culinary resource.

Henderson Waves (2008), IJP's first built project – won through international competition and realized in collaboration with RSP Consulting Engineers and AKT II – is Legendre's most significant realized work to date. It has been spectacularly successful, functioning as a popular destination for families, couples, joggers, cyclists and individuals in search of respite, and as an outdoor wedding venue and a unique location for photographs. A complex structure of wood and steel 300 metres long (forming a 1000-square-metre expanse of timber), it responded to a simple brief: to link via a continuous plane two ridge summits on the southern coast of Singapore. Some 36 metres above a six-lane motorway, it is the highest pedestrian bridge in the country, and takes about five minutes to walk across. Part of a plan to create a green pedestrian corridor linking the Southern Ridges to the waterfront in Bukit Chermin, the bridge provides spectacular views of the harbour by day and is a perfect observation point for the city lights by night.

The algebraic equation on which it is based was a direct application of Legendre's research on periodicity, and the design is an application of three-dimensional mathematical wave formulae to the bridge's structural requirements and the local topography. This process required the latest software (Mathcad) but also at least one sheet of paper at the outset to work out the basic parameters for the structure and design. The result is an exquisite bridge, elegant, flowing, organic and tactile. Its deck has a thin timber veneer stretched over steel members, 'peeling off' the structure to provide seating and spaces for play. The form of the veneer derives from IJP's mathematical equation, bending, undulating and ascending by 21 metres in one movement, deforming to enable pedestrians and

The flowing timber-veneer deck of Henderson Waves, Singapore (2008), a 1000-square-metre bridge spanning the city's Southern Ridges, incorporates seating and provides a vantage point for stunning views of Sentosa and the South China Sea.

cyclists full access in both directions, as well as providing shelter, relaxation and opportunities to view the scenery. Legendre chose steel for its structural properties and yellow balau (a tropical hardwood) to associate his bridge with, rather than fully emulate, natural forms – a highly appropriate choice, since the bridge is part of a nature walk through the Southern Ridges. The 24-metre-span members were fabricated, welded, galvanized and painted off-site and then craned into position.

Legendre applied lessons from earlier design experiments to his proposals for the National Museum of Art, Architecture and Design in Vestbanen, Oslo (2009) – interlocking the museum with an urban landscape in order to create a public piazza around 'an intimate museum experience' – and for the Art Fund Pavilion (2009). The latter was the subject of an open competition run by the Lightbox art gallery in Woking, Surrey, for a new temporary art space, a structure housing cultural seminars, exhibitions and fundraising events. Legendre has also always conducted experimental collaborations, for example with the sculptor John Pickering, for whom he reproduced his work using state-of-the-art software and numerically controlled fabrication techniques.

Other layers of research have also had a fruitful impact on IJP's work, for example the convergence of materials technology with functional requirements. Legendre used the new product Hemcrete for the Berkeley Bat House (2009), a high-tech, sustainable animal shelter at the London Wetland Centre in Barnes, to the west of the city, and for which the practice was delivery architect. The project was initiated by the artist Jeremy Deller and designed by Tandberg.Murata with the intention of creating a focal point for educating the public about the behaviour and habitat of bats. The planners were not convinced, and suggested timber as an alternative, but Legendre likes Hemcrete's mix of primitive and advanced qualities, and allied his focus on materials and form with extensive research on bats' patterns of roosting, breeding, hibernating and flying.

GhostHouse (2011), IJP's entry for an invited competition staged by the Museum of Modern Art's PS1 Young Architects Program, was realized in the courtyard of the museum's permanent space at Long Island City in Queens, New York. For the lightweight temporary installation, 5 kilometres of blue, white and red polypropylene rope (a material usually found in clothing and packaging, and the blue version of which the artists Christo and Jeanne-Claude used to tie up their wrapping of the Reichstag, Berlin, in 1995) are tensioned back to the bolt holes of the surrounding concrete walls to create a robust but light and counterintuitive structure with an aura of mystery and wonderment, like a ghostly presence haunting the courtyard.

With GhostHouse, Legendre wanted to express the tension between the 'bustling excitement' of today's spaces and the yearning most of us have for a timeless, simple house – a log cabin in the woods, for example. 'We simply strove to re-create what most visitors would readily recognize as a house', he says: one with fluidly conceived interconnected 'rooms'. Externally, 'our low-fidelity house offers only the minimum features of "house-ness": a pitched roof, eaves and a chimney'. It is free of windows and doors: visitors enter and exit through missing walls.

Legendre's Thematic Pavilion for the Yeosu 2012 World Expo in South Korea, dedicated to the sustainable future of the ocean, is a simple spherical form topped by a large circular opening, on the edge of the sea near six public access points. He also designed a Floating Island and Marine Life reef, applying the principle of seamless continuity between solid and reticulated forms, in which the same superficial geometry is given alternative material expressions above and below the flood line. Impressive, although as yet unrealized, schemes for improving transport infrastructure in the United Kingdom, for pleated roofs and double-curved bridges, use Legendre's profound grasp of mathematics as the raw material of computation, united with his innate sense of playfulness.

In *IJP: The Book of Surfaces*, Legendre wrote that 'seemingly, IJP is riding the fashionable wave of architecture's infatuation with curvature', explaining his love of such formal beauty, but that he wished to distance himself from the ideology that appeared to go with it. For he believes that curves are neither a fad nor something that can pretend to solve all the world's problems; he also disagrees that they are more desirable now that they can more easily be conceived and constructed. Legendre's position is that of an inspired instrumentalist, intrigued by questions that take architecture away from the thrall of existing figures and forms into fresh territory. It is to be hoped that in the process there will be further clients in the United Kingdom compelled into action by the obvious benefits of his structures.

center of circle of inversion:
INVx:=0 INVy:=5 INVz:=3

radius of circle of inversion:
INVR:=100

The top half of FO1B (2009), a model resulting from the experimental work by IJP with artist John Pickering, using state-of-the-art software and numerically controlled fabrication techniques.

Interview with George L. Legendre

Can you recount a few architectural memories from childhood?

We spent most summers in southern Greece. Our seaside house had marble kitchen worktops, mosaic floors and a concrete roof rendered with lime. To shield the interior from the noonday sun, the shutters were kept closed throughout the day, until a quiet coolness settled in its dark, cavernous corridors. I am forty-two now, and this exquisite sensation is totally gone. The air-conditioned interiors of modern-day Athens feel just like those of Miami, Tulane or Singapore.

How would you describe your architectural background?

Rich. When I graduated from Harvard, the Graduate School of Design was looking for someone straight out of university to teach design technology. The computer was taking over and the previous generation of teachers was overwhelmed by it. Based in Cambridge, Massachusetts, the Silicon Valley of the East Coast, I took time off from architecture to experiment with nascent technologies, often in the company of those who had invented them. In 1999 I released an interactive movie on the radical art group Fluxus at SIGGRAPH [Special Interest Group on Computer Graphics and Interactive Techniques] in Los Angeles. I took time off to write, think and enjoy, before starting my own architectural practice in 2004, with the benefit of having had a few years off.

What are your greatest influences, architectural or otherwise?

It is difficult to answer this question in earnest without sounding highbrow. I like all things quirky and do not take myself too seriously. I would, however, single out a 1970s group portrait of the Italian radical architects Superstudio, in which, inexplicably, the five blokes have chosen to don lab coats.

Give one example of the way in which your architecture communicates effectively with people.

Henderson Waves in Singapore, IJP's first built project, has received over a quarter of a million visitors since it opened in May 2008. Its 1000-square-metre timber expanse functions as

Berkeley Bat House

Barnes, London | 2009

IJP and Tandberg.Murata collaborated on a high-tech, sustainable animal shelter initiated by the artist Jeremy Deller, designed and realized in Hemcrete and sited next to the River Thames.

A close-up view of the bottom half of
the model (for the top half, see p. 133).

a suburban park, with stunning views of Sentosa and the South China Sea. It's now a favourite family destination, a romantic hideout for couples in the evenings and, on Sundays, an outdoor wedding venue of choice. According to a web page I recently came across, among nearly a million pages dedicated to the project, the giddy heights of Henderson Waves may be the safest venue to walk a cairn terrier, or any other small breed of dog – a lovely touch that I had not anticipated.

Are you a maker or a thinker?

I am a published author and a practising architect, so I would place myself somewhere in the middle. But I do not have much time for a distinction I feel is unkind to both ends. Dwelling too much on the opposition between thinking and making is typically the prerogative of those who do neither, says the philosopher Jacques Derrida.

Do you prefer bespoke or standardized?

In the future, those who can afford it will no doubt opt for bespoke. As many other practices have shown, building with off-the-shelf material can be intellectually and spiritually stimulating, but ultimately the development of non-standard, computer-aided manufacturing technology will see the affordable bespoke prevail.

What theories lie behind your design methods and practice?

The tenets of our practice were refined and formulated in my essay *IJP: The Book of Surfaces* (2003), after which our office is named. Henderson Waves exemplified this methodology literally. After winning the competition to design it, I gave a public lecture at Princeton University and made the argument that a bridge and a book could, through common references to mathematics, share an identical formal structure. Among many other spontaneous crossovers between theory and practice, the contractor of the project helped himself (without my knowledge) to the pagination principle of my essay, in order to label the project's steel beams and sort out the apparent complexity of the structure.

The Art Fund Pavilion   Woking, Surrey I competition entry, 2009

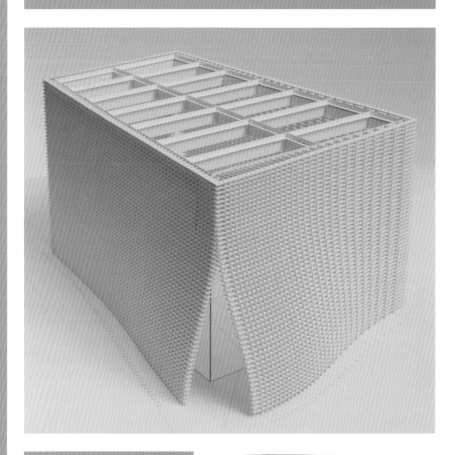

This proposal was submitted to an open international competition for a new temporary art structure for seminars, exhibitions and fundraising events next to the Lightbox art gallery in Woking. The model (above) shows the north-west corner with a zip-up entrance; the schematic plan is shown right.

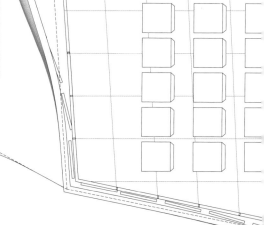

A render of IJP's proposal, which incorporated a public plaza around the museum.

Do you strive to create new architectural typologies? If so, please give an example.

Our work is a lot about novelty, as well as about typology understood in a traditional sense, that is, as a repository of ideas ordained by significant similarities and differences, eventually coalescing into accepted practice. Unlike the figurative and conspicuous types of the past, however, the new types are abstract and invisible. We do not recombine building parts and figures, as it were, to make new projects, but calibrate relationships, expressed for the sake of convenience in mathematical terms. Henderson Waves and Clydebank Canopy in Glasgow are mathematically defined by a similar mixture of periodic functions, for instance, despite looking utterly different.

What are the most challenging aspects of your architectural practice today?

To figure out for myself first – and then communicate to others – the net added value (if any) of patience, precision, rigour, solitude, earnestness and originality.

What impact do you hope your architecture has on the public realm?

Our project in Singapore has become a beloved popular venue, and even a monument, with its own postcards – and worldwide Flickr posts.

What personal significance do you give to architectural precedent?

Please refer to the answer about typology above.

Which technical advances excite you the most for exploitation?

Any manner of software, which for me is the new idiom of creativity. And Hemcrete, a new product we used for our Berkeley Bat House in the London Wetland Centre in 2009. As a building material, Hemcrete is both primitive and advanced: one person patting a mix of hemp and glue with a stick can build a two-storey-high load-bearing wall.

Do you practise a transdisciplinary approach to architecture, and if so, what is especially important to you right now?

All realized projects are the product of collaboration. Our work to date is based on an open dialogue with our closest-minded

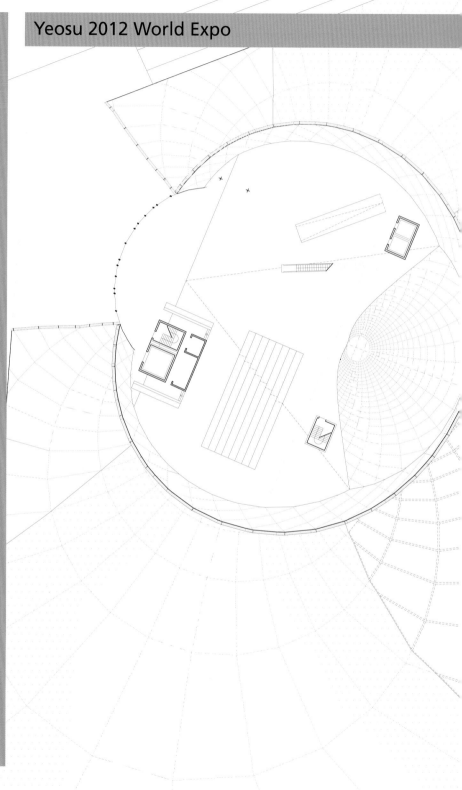

Yeosu 2012 World Expo

IJP's design for a Thematic Pavilion, Floating Island and Marine Life reef is seen left in plan. The model is seen right, from the south-east. The bird's-eye view (below, right) shows the simple spherical form of the Thematic Pavilion with its large circular opening, on the edge of the sea. It has six public access points.

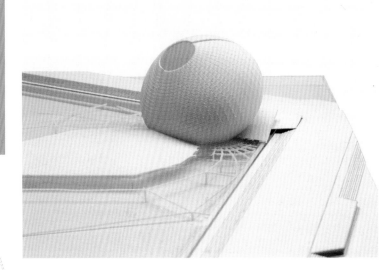

colleague, the structural engineer Adams Kara Taylor (AKT), which is based in London. When the engineer is a closet architect, and the architect a closet engineer, the dialogue can be open but tricky. Each has something the other clearly wants, but neither is willing to give up their priorities in the process. I have also enjoyed working with artists and local pasta manufacturers (we are developing new pasta, in tandem with the release of our art and design title *Pasta by Design*, 2011).

How do you go about generating the best possible relationship with your clients?

I listen to clients. I try to be well-spoken and urbane, punctilious yet considerate. I dress smartly for every meeting. I take the client's concerns deeply to heart: it's their time and money after all, they have a choice of architects, and I am not here to crucify anyone. I also reply to emails immediately.

Can you give me an example of your participatory methods?

While developing the Berkeley Bat House, a high-tech animal shelter commissioned by the London Wetland Centre, for which I acted as the executive architect of Tandberg.Murata, I sat down with and learned a great deal from Dr Peter Shepherd, a passionate expert in zoology. Understanding how bats fly and roost is the first step towards building a house for them to dwell in.

How do you communicate your architecture?

I publish the office's work, and give several lectures on the international lecture circuit every year. Teaching a Diploma Unit at the Architectural Association in London for eight years, and several studios at Harvard and Princeton, has forced me to articulate clearly an architectural position. The students demanded it.

What do you aim to achieve with your practice?

I had the good fortune of spending many early years exploring a wealth of new building concepts. I pray that in the future IJP gets the opportunity to realize – as an office or in partnership, and with our clients and trusted colleagues – as many projects as is humanly feasible.

Henderson Waves

IJP's first built project, in collaboration with RSP Consulting Engineers, is a complex, organic structure with a series of undulating curved ribs: a continuous plane linking two ridge summits on Singapore's southern coast (opposite). The flowing surface of the timber veneer deck (this page) is popular with a wide range of people.

What advice would you give to a young architect embarking on their career?

You should not embark on this without a sense of thorough enjoyment.

What single improvement to the procurement of architecture in the United Kingdom would you recommend? More competitions, different planning system, legislation affecting developers, etc.?

London offers a vibrant environment to practise in, much more so than Paris, my equally desirable but culturally saturated hometown. Practising in London has been immensely rewarding, but I hardly see the point of having to carry £10,000,000 of professional indemnity insurance to be eligible for a small public project. To our British friends, I say: such levels of risk aversion may stifle innovation. And while you are at it, do give us another break! We are ready for it.

GhostHouse

The winning entry in an invited competition, GhostHouse was a lightweight but robust temporary installation made with 5 kilometres of polypropylene rope and set up in the main courtyard of the museum's permanent PS1 space. Supported by ropes tensioned to the boltholes of the surrounding concrete walls, IJP's 'low-fidelity' house offers only minimal features of 'houseness': a pitched roof, eaves and a chimney.

MÆ

MÆ's co-founders, Alex Ely and Michael Howe, have actively built up an excellent reputation for sustainable urbanism and housing, working with a wide range of local authorities, public agencies and housing associations on housing regeneration and design, and masterplanning. Their projects demonstrate their belief that, while intelligent, clear design enables a collective urban identity and communal order, housing should also be loose enough to accommodate variation, adapt to place and respond to people's sense of individuality.

MÆ regularly gives policy guidance alongside its urban regeneration schemes. It works on sites of all kinds, including post-industrial and 1950s and 1960s housing estates. At the Colville Estate in Hackney, east London, for example, designed with Karakusevic Carson Architects, blocks dating from the 1950s are being replaced with 925 homes; the scheme was granted planning permission in August 2011.

Instead of trying to change people's preference for low-density living, MÆ prefers to focus on making sustainable communities with 'the optimum mix, density and quality of public realm, without compromising quality'. This, it believes, can happen through masterplans for every town or city that anticipates growth. A key part of these masterplans are strict guidelines for typologies, which MÆ regards as making 'the ground' of the city; it believes they should be supported by place-specific planning guidance that plans, rather than just controlling development in a limited way.

MÆ's Lift-up House, an extension on Hoxton Street in London (2006) providing a 100-square-metre flat on the roof above the owner's office, critiques the 'corporate glass city, visible from the roof terrace, with its pretence of transparency'. Reinterpreting the weavers' lofts in the area, it is a simple pavilion, classically proportioned, with a skin of Reglit U-profile glass that plays with light and transparency.

Under construction in 2011 were two key schemes that underline MÆ's capacity to evolve a new housing type within a wider urban context. The Guts (2009–), Phase 3 of the New Islington Millennium Village in Manchester for the Great Places Housing Group with Urban Splash, is a scheme of eighteen affordable semi-detached houses. So named by residents because it is in the middle of the plan, it is elevated from the ordinary through legibility, differentiation, play on scale and spareness of detail. A mix of terraced and semi-detached houses in two urban blocks were designed to supply the needs of new and returning residents to the area. Each achieves its own identity through variegated bricks on upper floors, but the houses are bound together as an urban whole by means of a ground-floor red-brick wall, which continues beyond the building envelope to become garden walls. Designed with generous space and height, the houses have oversized doors and windows, and MÆ sees them as a 'joyous and constructive response' to the requirements of the area.

At Hammond Court (2007–), a forty-three-unit residential scheme for East Thames Group in Waltham Forest, north-east London, the vernacular of the surrounding Warner Estate with its half-houses is neither ignored nor copied. Its qualities inspire three-storey town houses that sit with maisonettes and flats in five-storey buildings within a perimeter block. They enclose a quiet, south-facing courtyard with private gardens, and a landscaped communal garden, and have good proportions, clean lines and detailing, large picture windows and private amenity space. The local planning committee called it 'an exceptional design' and 'an opportunity not to be missed'.

Clay Country Eco-House (2010), a proposal for St Austell in mid-Cornwall for the developer Eco-Bos (which is planning one of the most sustainable integrated town developments in Europe: 5500 eco-homes, 40% of which will be affordable, and including live–work options, on 700 hectares of former china clay-mining land), is a terraced housing concept conforming to Passivhaus UK methods. The living spaces are inside the super-insulated core of the house, and the thermal mass acts as a whole-house storage heater,

Lift-up House, Hoxton Street, London (2006), is a contemporary interpretation of weavers' lofts. The transparency of its skin of U-profile glass stands out from the corporate glass forms around it.

the contemporary equivalent of the farmhouse's central fireplace. The design of its solar 'lantern' atrium gives the scheme the benefits of solar gain, and its orientation on the masterplan plot lends flexibility and a memorable identity.

MÆ has also designed M-House (2002–2003), which was prefabricated using a volumetric steel frame and fully finished in a factory. The two halves were zipped together on-site. It has the spatial qualities of a loft or Scandinavian cabin. Simple, industrially precise and matching the environmental standards of a house, its two parts are each designed to the maximum transportable size of 3.2 x 17 metres. This is regarded in legal terms as the same as a caravan, so M-House does not need planning permission.

MÆ's Dunroamin' house concept for the Royal Institute of British Architects' Make Me a Home competition for Stockton-on-Tees (2008) is 'the last house you will ever need'. Potentially any size you please, it is a basic unit that can be extended to suit changing family requirements. Laying out the houses in terraces with shared surfaces for pedestrians, cycling, playing and 'maybe occasionally cars', MÆ shifts emphasis away from the usual dominance by the car towards a greater sense of community, with gardens opening on to residents' allotments within the spaces of neighbourhood blocks.

Creating socially engaging, characterful places that delight the senses is vital to MÆ, which has long been interested in the way architecture, cities and towns are shaped by government policies. The practice draws on the many memories that have been embedded into the urban environment over time, finding patterns and parameters that help it create an innovative and sympathetic landscape of spaces and enclosures.

This manifests itself both in MÆ's language and in its urbanist strategies, which are closely integrated. Hyllen (Strata), a proposal for a building for Oslo's National Museum of Art, Architecture and Design, employs organizational and landscape devices of ascending terraces and courtyards. The articulation of 'strata', or shelves, on the facade resonates with the topography of the area and the notion of 'storage'.

For the Nordhavnen scheme in Copenhagen's old port, a new district consisting of 4,000,000 square metres of housing for 40,000 inhabitants, MÆ focused on polycentric urbanism, creating a matrix of design principles coalesced as a simple masterplan based on the notion that facilities must be easily accessible, something Cedric Price called 'propinquity'. In its entry for the open competition, MÆ proposed that each phase be planted before development, to help generate its identity, and suggested a set of sustainable construction

and management strategies. The practice also outlined a delivery strategy that encouraged citizens' sense of ownership of what will be a socially diverse place that will grow in an environmentally responsible way, policed by a local group. These aspects were included in a Citizens' Charter devised by MÆ, encouraging residents to 'act locally and think globally', and a Design Code of building and public-realm types. Together they constitute a sound framework for governance and design management, and a model for how to respond to the localism agenda of the current United Kingdom government.

Finding ways to advance projects of this complexity as communicative and analytic platforms is central to MÆ's ways of working. For the North Prospect estate area of Plymouth in Devon, it was appointed to carry out consultation and develop a spatial framework for regeneration. 'Prospectopolis' was the game MÆ devised to help consult with key stakeholders in order to communicate the need for better, higher-density development. The different game scenarios were evolved into a spatial framework using parametric modelling techniques, which have an advanced analytic capacity, giving MÆ insight into a number of design options by allowing them to be tested and refined.

The edge of Letchworth Garden City in Hertfordshire, one of the United Kingdom's first New Towns and the world's first Garden City, founded in 1903 by the urban planner Ebenezer Howard, is the site of MÆ's Wilbury Hills non-denominational chapel, mausoleum and cemetery (2007). Constituting a transitional area between the city and the countryside, it has a range of types of space: some forested; others with meadows and lawns; and a hard landscaped area. MÆ, which campaigns for better-designed cemeteries, enabled it to become a social environment by making it a threshold to nearby amenity spaces. What MÆ calls the 'relaxed geometry' of the chapel is redolent of the way agricultural barns in nearby Bedfordshire are grouped.

MÆ believes there are certain universal conditions of a city, for example connected streetscapes, that are 'inflected by their local and social contexts'. If codified – not strictly, but as a set of simple rules – these conditions can help architects and planners, with sufficient freedom, to a successful outcome. Such a stance has to be seen in the context of MÆ's agreement with the sociologist Richard Sennett's definition of urbanity: that making use of density and differences in a city, and understanding the risks involved, helps people achieve a balanced sense of identification with place.

M-House is a prefabricated, factory-produced mobile home designed to have the environmental standards of a house and the spatial qualities of a loft (2002–2003).

Interview with Alex Ely

Can you recount a few architectural memories from childhood?

My memories range from the architecturally expedient to the poetic. I loved making simple retreats or wigwams by spanning blankets between chairs or making a clearing in a copse of trees. I enjoyed the economy of making space and enclosure out of what was around me.

By contrast I was inspired on family outings to such country houses as Chatsworth, Castle Howard or Hardwick Hall. While I found it hard to reconcile the grandeur of these houses with meaningful inhabitation or social justice, I was in awe of their scale, their splendour and the sheer conviction of the presence of architecture. They intricately combine architecture and landscape, offering planned journeys through the grounds with glimpsed, then revealed, views towards the house or out to managed topography.

How would you describe your architectural background?

MÆ emerged from teaching practice. The partners ran a studio at the University of Greenwich where we asked questions about the city and how we engage with it. We studied such issues as how London is shaped by framework, for example the protected viewing corridors; how we deal with the fact that we are running out of burial space; how the river can be intensified in use. We questioned means of representation, forms of fabrication and typology. This engagement in making, in presenting, in questioning typology and in influencing policy continues in our practice.

What are your greatest influences, architectural or otherwise?

Our influences are diverse. The city around us continues to be an endless source of inspiration. We try to respond to its idiosyncrasies and, to rephrase Louis Kahn (who famously asked, 'What do you want, Brick?'), we ask, 'What do you want, City?' Architecturally, I'm drawn to the work of Álvaro Siza. His housing expresses ideas of inhabitation; the morphology of his buildings grows out of their context and is full of character. I'm also interested in the urban and typological investigations of Aldo Rossi, particularly in relation to 'projective typologies', which reflect our thoughts on buildings being able to change over time.

Clay Country Eco-House St Austell, Cornwall I competition, 2010

Dunroamin' competition entry, 2008

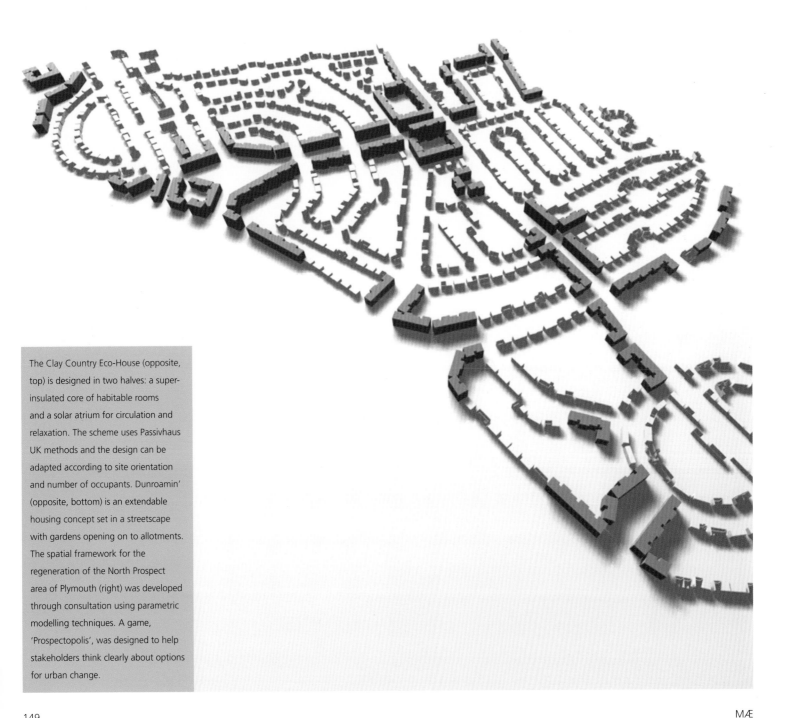

The Clay Country Eco-House (opposite, top) is designed in two halves: a super-insulated core of habitable rooms and a solar atrium for circulation and relaxation. The scheme uses Passivhaus UK methods and the design can be adapted according to site orientation and number of occupants. Dunroamin' (opposite, bottom) is an extendable housing concept set in a streetscape with gardens opening on to allotments. The spatial framework for the regeneration of the North Prospect area of Plymouth (right) was developed through consultation using parametric modelling techniques. A game, 'Prospectopolis', was designed to help stakeholders think clearly about options for urban change.

Closer to home, I've worked with really inspiring people, from architects such as Pierre d'Avoine to mentors such as Sir Stuart Lipton and Jon Rouse.[1]

Give one example of the way in which your architecture communicates effectively with people.

We try to produce culturally recognizable and socially legible buildings. Projects follow well-established rules and have a level of familiarity, but seek to be inventive at the same time. Our New Islington houses [in Manchester], for example, follow the archetype of a 'home', with its association with the form of a pitched-roof house.

Are you a maker or a thinker?

MÆ is made up of both.

Do you prefer bespoke or standardized?

Both are relevant to our work. We're interested in systems, repeat patterns and other principles of organization in planning, which are particularly relevant to our work in housing, as well as in modern methods of construction, which may have standardized components. However, we try to tailor these to the characteristics of the site and the brief.

What theories lie behind your design methods and practice?

We research the characteristics and history of the site and the opportunities presented by the brief to find original work. We try to reflect cultural and political contexts and design collaboratively with the aim to innovate, creating places with meaningful character and which delight the senses.

Do you strive to create new architectural typologies? If so, please give an example.

In the majority of our projects we try to create a new model or evolve a type that, while related to a specific situation, appears part of a more comprehensive identity. Architectural typology helps us make cities legible and meaningful. Our Hammond Court housing project in north-east London proposes a new form of mansion block, while our New Islington housing in Manchester reinvents the semi-detached house; the side-by-side houses are conjoined across the depth of the block.

M-House

M-House feels like a Scandinavian cabin inside. It is constructed in two parts, each of which is designed to a maximum transportable size of 3.2 × 17 metres, classifying it as a caravan.

What are the most challenging aspects of your architectural practice today?
Managing growth and maintaining quality.

What impact do you hope your architecture has on the public realm?
Our work switches between architecture and urban design, and we approach the design of public space in the same way as that of our buildings: a topology of spaces and enclosures where routes and views are planned to enhance people's experience of the place.

What personal significance do you give to architectural precedent?
Referring to precedent helps us in the process of communicating to colleagues and clients, although we are wary of referring to recent buildings where the lessons are still not clear.

Which technical advances excite you the most for exploitation?
We use computational methodologies or parametric modelling to develop codes or signs and patterns for housing and urban plans. It helps manage complexity while freeing up our time to concentrate on design. We also use BIM (Building Information Modelling) to ensure integrated and coordinated projects.

Do you practise a transdisciplinary approach to architecture, and if so, what is especially important to you right now?
We have two strands to our business: architecture and urban design; and policy development, guidance and training. They are hugely complementary to each other, and each adds credibility and authority to the other.

How do you go about generating the best possible relationship with your clients?
By being nice to them.

Can you give an example of your participatory methods?
For our project to regenerate the North Prospect area of Plymouth, we designed a game, 'Prospectopolis', to aid consultation. Game scenarios were then developed into a spatial framework using parametric modelling techniques. Games ask simple questions but can have complex outcomes. Prospectopolis

The Guts
New Islington Millennium Village, Manchester I 2009–

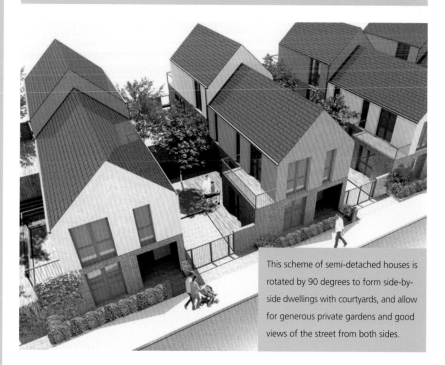

This scheme of semi-detached houses is rotated by 90 degrees to form side-by-side dwellings with courtyards, and allow for generous private gardens and good views of the street from both sides.

Hammond Court
Waltham Forest, London I 2007–

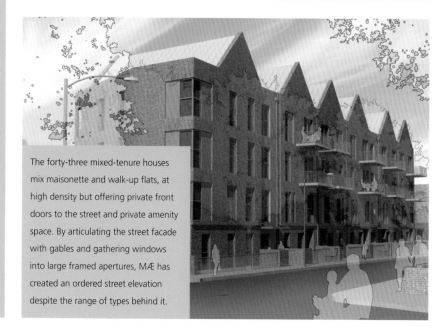

The forty-three mixed-tenure houses mix maisonette and walk-up flats, at high density but offering private front doors to the street and private amenity space. By articulating the street facade with gables and gathering windows into large framed apertures, MÆ has created an ordered street elevation despite the range of types behind it.

This building for the National Museum of Art, Architecture and Design in Oslo is organized by way of ascending terraces and courtyards. 'Strata' or shelves on the facade resonate with the local topography and with the notion of 'storage'.

was a tool masquerading as a game; it enabled a group to think clearly about urban options for change in North Prospect, and proved hugely successful.

How do you communicate your architecture?
Architecture is a language, so we draw on memory and familiarity.

What do you aim to achieve with your practice (in a single sentence)?
Respect.

What advice would you give to a young architect embarking on their career?
Do an MBA (Master of Business Administration) course.

What single improvement to the procurement of architecture in the United Kingdom would you recommend? More competitions, different planning system, legislation affecting developers, etc.?
We need to move away from using the design-and-build form of contract. Clients are becoming more aware of the importance of design and yet are obsessed by fixed time and cost contracts that are adversarial in their nature and don't recognize the value of design.

[1] Sir Stuart Lipton is founding chairman of CABE (Commission for Architecture and the Built Environment) and co-founder, with Elliott Bernerd, of Chelsfield Partners; Jon Rouse is a former chief executive of CABE, and chief executive of the London Borough of Croydon.

Wilbury Hills Chapel and Cemetery

The non-denominational Wilbury Hills Chapel and Cemetery in Letchworth Garden City is set in parkland. The chapel has a distinctive top-lit roof that orientates people and a generous-sized porch in which they can gather. The design signals a return to the civic values of the great Victorian burial-grounds, when cemeteries were not simply for burying the dead but also a central part of the community. The series of external rooms includes eco-plots and areas for different religious groups.

NORD

NORD (Northern Office for Research & Design) was founded in 2002 by Alan Pert, now Professor and Director of Research at the Department of Architecture at the University of Strathclyde, and Robin Lee, who since 2011 has directed Robin Lee Architecture from offices in London and Dublin. Yet another multidisciplinary practice, NORD, which is based in Glasgow and has an office in London, takes an approach to architectural practice that influences and shapes future development not only environmentally, but also in a way that is economically and socially sustainable. NORD approaches its work with great maturity and a sense of architectural refinement that is wholly compatible with the needs of landscape and the ecology of sites today, and of the vast varieties of context found across the United Kingdom. Through Pert's activities in academia, he has been instrumental in setting up the Centre for Community Practice in the impoverished Govanhill area of Glasgow, driving forwards community projects and local research, which further informs and encourages NORD in its many community consultation projects.

All NORD's project work includes significant analysis of landscape and site; researching materials, precedent and typological references; and producing sketches and diagrams, physical models, computer models, graphic representation and detailed drawings. This is, of course, true of every practice in this book, and besides buildings and masterplans, NORD – in common with many other practices featured – also operates in areas beyond the more traditional boundaries of architecture, including exhibition design, renewable energy, product design, policy-making, curating, sociology, publishing and graphic design.

Shingle House (2010) in Dungeness, Kent, is a straightforward house evoking the appearance of functional buildings near by. It began life when NORD was selected by the not-for-profit organization Living Architecture (founded by philosopher Alain de Botton) to design a holiday let dwelling on the site, one of a number of similar affordable and beautifully designed buildings around the United Kingdom. (Other architectural practices that have so far participated in the scheme are Peter Zumthor, Hopkins Architects and MVRDV.) It is usually hard to get planning permission for new buildings in Dungeness, so NORD's house was agreed to as a replacement structure. Its design is geared to a simple lifestyle of daily rituals, especially preparing meals and dining. The south-east-facing kitchen, dining room and bathhouse build the house's close relationship with nature, and the small existing smokehouse was retained. On an oblong plan, the two-storey house incorporates one single and three double bedrooms as well as a mezzanine living room.

Dungeness has one of the largest expanses of shingle in the world, and NORD wrapped the pitched-roof house with tarred shingles, a material that is used widely there. Sitting comfortably alongside the local vernacular, Shingle House has a vivid silhouette at night. When closed, the shutters of the carefully positioned windows give it a seamless appearance, but when they are open the interior is strongly connected to views of the natural surroundings, giving the occupants a bigger, yet sheltered experience of the landscape.

NORD's bespoke furniture complements the stained oak and white concrete used inside the house. Inspired by the theme of the sensations of time in a holiday 'home from home', NORD also designed a series of light fittings, seating and ceramic wall tiles, which were exhibited at the Milan Furniture Fair in 2010, in the *Handmade* exhibition staged by *Wallpaper** magazine to examine the marriage between craftsmanship and design.

Another house, Linthills (2008) in Lochwinnoch, south-western Scotland, has a very different rural context, next to agricultural land with 360-degree views. NORD had to fit it into the contained footprint of the cottage and chicken shed that previously occupied the hillside site. Instead of interrelated rooms, the interior is treated as a series of linked spaces; floor-to-ceiling windows 'pull' the landscape view into the house. The main block is clad with vertical larch boards and set on an expressed Portland stone base course

The Primary Substation (2009), the first utility building to be realized in London's Olympic Park, and intended to inspire the design of others, has carefully modulated proportions. Applied in a black lattice-bond design, the brick refers to warehouses in the local post-industrial environment, and gives visual weight and a sense of dignity. It requires little external maintenance.

with extensive flush glazing, contrasting with the more solid element above it. As do all NORD's commissions, Linthills benefits from the practice's strong track record in the management of interior environments, manifesting itself also in exhibition design, including the Victoria and Albert Museum's Furniture Galleries, to be finished in autumn 2012.

In 2009 NORD completed the Primary Substation for the 2012 Olympic Games, in east London, the first Olympics utility building to get detailed planning permission and to be finished. It took two years from commission, and Graeme Williamson, who previously co-directed the award-winning London-based firm Block Architecture, joined NORD as Senior Architect to deliver the project. It is not meant to be an event building, but one of a number that constitute the fabric of the Olympics site itself, with a sense of permanence, weight and dignity. Standing on the eastern side of the site, next to the King's Yard Energy Centre by John McAslan + Partners, the Primary Substation provides London and the Olympic Park with a permanent asset containing essential infrastructure as part of a wider network of utilities. It is not open to the public, but, rather, visible from afar. NORD chose dark brick to refer to the post-industrial context and to give the building weight and density, and because it is a very durable material that requires little maintenance. The functional requirements led to carefully modulated proportions but did not deter NORD from arranging the brick forms so that they appear intriguingly like black lace screens against the sky.

When it comes to the role of architecture in defining entire residential districts, Pert puts forward a strong case, which is all the better for not being unrealistically overstated: good urban design is not, in itself, sufficient to determine the quality of life of a neighbourhood, because of other factors, such as the economic climate, educational provision and safety, but he feels strongly that it 'can be a catalyst for the development of economic and social benefits'. NORD's masterplan for RENEW North Staffordshire and developer Urban Splash (resulting from a competition win) for the Canal Quarter in Hanley, Stoke-on-Trent, demonstrates this intention. Its architectural tactics respond to a need for a sustainable mix of residential and commercial buildings, and in early research and development two priorities emerged: for the Bridgewater Bridge (2009) over the Caldon Canal; and for a new building to replace a pottery, which had been ready to move to the outskirts of town. NORD successfully argued for it to keep its central site, and through the practice's proposed design interventions, the richness of the locality will be retained; at the same time, the travel times of staff and visitors who would otherwise be commuting back and forth will be reduced. The plan is that the new building will harness the waste heat from the kilns, feeding it into rooftop greenhouses to help produce food for the canteen and the local community.

The architect made a strategy for the landscape and public realm the framework for the phasing of the development. The new landscape creates an ecologically grounded basis for development throughout the whole site. Its series of edges, terraces and secondary routes lay out a structure for built form, rather than the other way round, with the buildings determining everything else, as is the norm. NORD's approach reinterprets the character of older canal buildings and terraced housing without being nostalgic, and the new landscaped routes give the pottery a new identity as well as uniting the town and the canal so that people have new ways of reaching the water.

NORD knew that the site, on a junction between the canal and a principal road into the city, presented a challenge in terms of connecting successfully with existing transport infrastructure, and squarely addressed that as part of its work. The practice's researchers also examined typological and historical patterns in the local context to make sure that the strategies they developed responded to local conditions and embraced the town's cultural life and ambitions.

NORD's capacity for smaller projects is galvanized by its interest in designs that are deeply rooted in their surroundings. It has a wide and incisive understanding of typology and local vernacular, which are studied afresh for each commission, and the resulting insight and inspiration are absorbed into the architect's holistic approach to urban, rural, semi-rural, maritime and other contexts.

Three other major projects commissioned from NORD and now completed are the Bell House, Strathblane (2004); Destiny Church, Glasgow (2004); and the Wexford County Council headquarters in Ireland (2011). The last, for which Robin Lee was Principal in Charge, was an international competition win for NORD in 2006. All three are schemes for which Lee was jointly responsible before the partners separated, and he took them to completion; they are discussed on pp. 210–21.

The simple, modest form of Shingle House for Living Architecture in Dungeness, Kent (2010), cloaked in tarred shingles, achieves a close relationship with its poetic context, a nature reserve. Shutters link such interior spaces as the kitchen and dining room, which have a south-east aspect (maximizing natural light), to the outside.

Interview with Alan Pert

Can you recount a few architectural memories from childhood?

I have a few distinctive memories, which are often triggered by the day-to-day experiences of architectural practice: trips to a number of Scottish castles from a very young age, but, most notably, Crichton Castle and its sculpted, kaleidoscopic northern courtyard walls; the sculpted roof form of Gillespie, Kidd & Coia's St Benedict's Church in Drumchapel Road, Glasgow, framed by my grandmother's window, but now demolished; the incredible production lines of the Singer sewing-machine factory in Clydebank, where I grew up, in particular the japanning room, where everything was coated in black; the smell of freshly cut lignum vitae from my father's workshop.

How would you describe your architectural background?

Strongly rooted in the landscape of Scotland but specifically rooted in the social and historical context of Glasgow. Glasgow has become our architecture laboratory, a place where we have invented projects, tested ideas and gained our architectural apprenticeship. We have shaped our techniques of observation by studying the richness and variety of Glasgow's townscape over a prolonged period of time. We have become fascinated by the city's rich layering, both physical and social. We find inspiration in the familiar yet uncelebrated because it is so embedded in the everyday life of the city.

From domestic life to civic life we come across a richness of pattern and craft, texture and treatment in the streets and buildings we use. From the tenements' gable-end paintings and wall tiles to park railings and bronze statues, from the floors of churches to the fronts and backs of buildings, we see a rich array of patterned surfaces – sometimes in stone, sometimes in ceramics – cast, carved, moulded and crafted to create a layer to the city that is both functional and decorative. The city's preoccupation with detail and pattern stands as a testament to the enduring significance of meticulous craft-based skill synonymous with the people working in the city.

What are your greatest influences, architectural or otherwise?

I am influenced by anyone who applies rigour to his or her craft.

Linthills

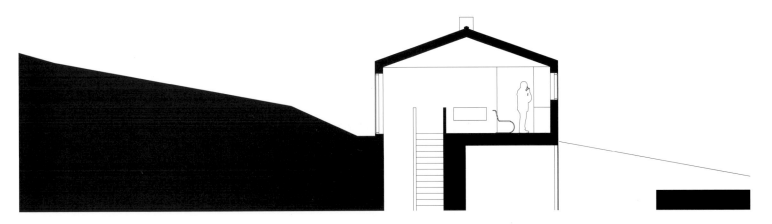

Linthills is a private house with a base of Portland stone below larch cladding. It fulfills planning requirements by occupying the footprint of a former cottage and chicken shed. Bordered by agricultural land, it has panoramic views from floor-to-ceiling windows at ground and basement levels, creating a strong connection with the landscape.

Richard Sennett describes the craftsman in his book of that name (2009):

> The carpenter, lab technician and conductor are all craftsmen because they are dedicated to good work for its own sake. Theirs is practical activity, but their labour is not simply a means to another end. The carpenter might sell more furniture if he worked faster; the technician might make do by passing the problem back to her boss; the visiting conductor might be more likely to be rehired if he watched the clock. It's certainly possible to get by in life without dedication, but the craftsman exemplifies the special human condition of being engaged.

Give one example of the way in which your architecture communicates effectively with people.
We would like to think that each of NORD's projects tells the story of a place. We would also like each project to be examined as if it narrated a number of stories: stories about everyday living (houses), stories about works of art (galleries), stories about working and stories about making things.

Are you a maker or a thinker?
Both. Research = thinking. Design = making.

Do you prefer bespoke or standardized?
That depends on scale and context. Each project is bespoke and responds uniquely to its social and physical context.

What theories lie behind your design methods and practice?
Architectural practice is a process of constantly refining our technical skills and scientific knowledge. As a practice we simply want to improve our skills with every project we undertake, but to do so also requires a good measure of experiment and questioning. We don't believe that there is a single correct solution for each project, but we strive for the best possible solution.

Do you strive to create new architectural typologies? If so, please give an example.
At NORD we are interested in architectural tradition and the history of places, but we are very much engaging with the modern world. Through exploring a place we can often arrive at a choice of material, a form or a construction technique, but each place, community, tradition and way of observing things

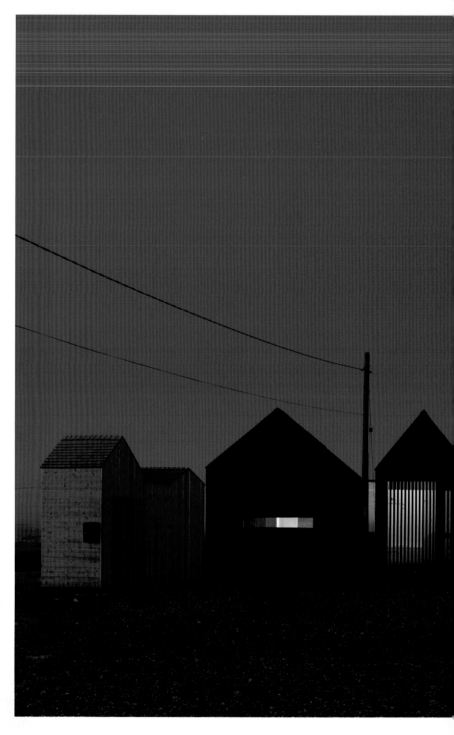

Shingle House

The house is wrapped in a continuous skin of tarred shingle, concealing the prefabricated system beneath. Its shutters are a series of punctuations in this seamless yet adjustable facade, carefully positioned to allow views of the landscape and out to sea. When closed, they give the impression of an introverted, defensive form, but when they are pulled back, the house opens up to the surrounding flat shingle landscape. A sense of remoteness and escape pervades the interior.

implies a different architectural solution. Every project is a constant process of evolution and we would not restrict ourselves to the reworking of one particular theme.

At Dungeness we took time to understand the place before making any architectural proposition. We inquisitively studied the history, the traditions of the fishing community and people's stories about Dungeness, but we also meticulously studied weather patterns, regional detailing, planning policy, built form and the continuously changing shingle landscape to understand how to build in such a specific context. Dungeness is an unfamiliar landscape: a power station next to a lighthouse on a shingle beach with a fishing community, a miniature steam railway, an assortment of sheds, bird-watchers and rare plant species. The act of designing is often led by an intuitive response to a site or a brief, but at Dungeness we found ourselves metaphorically dismantling the place in order to understand why and how things came to exist, then rebuilding them as thoughts and ideas. The dismantling begins with observations and assumptions, records of personal experience, drawings, notes and photographs; like archaeologists collecting fragments of the past for clues to a previous life, we try to unravel the story of Dungeness with the anticipation of adding to that story.

Dungeness challenged us to design, in a rural setting of historic sensitivity, a contemporary dwelling that in some way can be seen and felt to 'belong' to that context, while still being an object of authentic architectural character. If it needs the skills of a good researcher and archaeologist to document the existing structures, objects, history and cultural context of Dungeness, it needs an artistic eye to be creatively moved by the sight of ruins, discarded shelters and old stones, and to turn that prompt into an architectural idea that will inform a new creation. The resulting architecture tells a story of our time in Dungeness; it is undeniably new but also strangely familiar.

What are the most challenging aspects of your architectural practice today?
The desire to spend more time on something balanced against economic value. In today's labour market, doing good work is no guarantee of good fortune.

Shingle House

The calm, robust interior of the four-bedroom holiday house reflects NORD's desire to create a bespoke environment in concrete and timber, attuned to nature and a simple way of living, with coordinated lighting, materials, furniture and ironmongery.

What impact do you hope your architecture has on the public realm?

NORD is made up of architects who demonstrate the continued desire to engage with the world outwith our own discipline. We take great inspiration from Glasgow's legacy of 'making things'. Streets have become generic, and we face the danger of having every city in Britain look all too familiar. But in Victorian Glasgow there was a true sense of collective pride and craftsmanship about what came out of factories and workshops. This understanding of and passion for materials, detail, craftsmanship, texture and pattern underpin our work. NORD is often provoked and inspired by social and cultural issues inherent in the contemporary city, and this awareness also allows a response in form and materials. Such an approach has led to the development of a series of public-realm products or objects. An example of this is NORD's ceramic ashtrays in response to the smoking ban [in Scotland] of 2006.

What personal significance do you give to architectural precedent?

Great significance. The challenge is deciphering what is relevant.

Which technical advances excite you the most for exploitation?

We are interested in the simplest product with longevity. We are still getting to grips with bricks!

Do you practise a transdisciplinary approach to architecture, and if so, what is especially important to you right now?

NORD emphasizes research within every project as a tool for testing, analysing and questioning preconceived ideas. See my answer to the question about participatory methods below.

How do you go about generating the best possible relationship with your clients?

With an honest and open approach: work in progress is continuously on show, enabling clients to critique projects. Also by understanding different clients' approaches and ambitions.

Can you give an example of your participatory methods?

Most of NORD's projects involve academic input from a variety of disciplines. We recently established the Centre for Community Practice (CCP) to focus on the redevelopment of a community

Canal Quarter

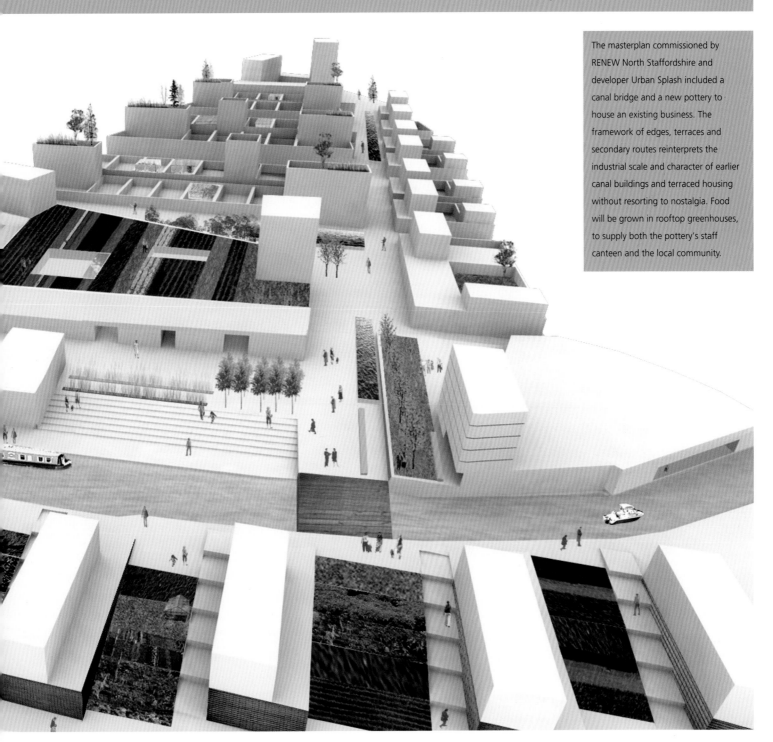

The masterplan commissioned by RENEW North Staffordshire and developer Urban Splash included a canal bridge and a new pottery to house an existing business. The framework of edges, terraces and secondary routes reinterprets the industrial scale and character of earlier canal buildings and terraced housing without resorting to nostalgia. Food will be grown in rooftop greenhouses, to supply both the pottery's staff canteen and the local community.

swimming pool. This is a joint initiative between architects, sociologists and a local community trust. The CCP brings together partners from the fields of design, sociology and education to enable a rounded understanding of development processes that engage the physical and social environment.

How do you communicate your architecture?

Through clarity in the execution of an idea, filtering information through a constant editing process until we are left with the distinctive thing that details the project. A great writer is efficient with his words. We are also a practice that relies heavily on the use of architectural models to explain an architectural idea. We employ an in-house model-maker to work through the early stages of every idea, and these models become an important communication tool.

What do you aim to achieve with your practice (in a single sentence)?

To shorten the distance between research and construction.

What advice would you give to a young architect embarking on their career?

Invent projects. We did this for the first three years until some became a reality. Do not wait around for projects to find you: go out and find them, no matter how small. Also be aware of the commercial opportunities and disadvantages of what we do.

What single improvement to the procurement of architecture in the United Kingdom would you recommend? More competitions, different planning system, legislation affecting developers, etc.?

It took the profession a very long time to recalibrate the weighting between design quality and cost, and overnight we have allowed it to swing back to a cost-driven procurement process. Changing this back has to be our priority.

Primary Substation

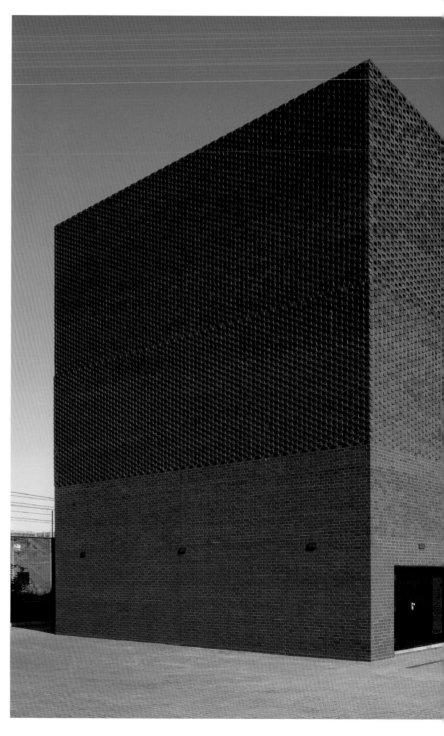

Most people will view the substation, with its black lattice-bonded brick design, from a distance, so it was important that it worked as a sculptural form. The open pattern of the bricks allows ventilation across the cooling towers, and illumination at night.

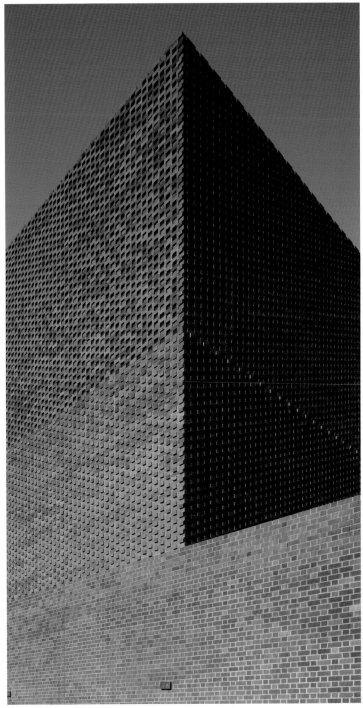

OSA

Not everyone likes to work in 'in-between' spaces, but the architectural collective OSA (Office for Subversive Architecture) forges 'untraditional approaches' to reinterpret the concept of urban architecture in its own spirit of place-making. Using guerilla tactics, evoking everyone from the Situationists to Cedric Price, and from Kurt Schwitters to Constant Nieuwenhuys, the European collective has self-confessedly 'taken more risk' in England than in its native Germany, its installations defying rules as well as being embraced by commissioning bodies. Its members see OSA as a 'research lab' for the growing possibilities between art and architecture; it is a niche market still, maybe, but in this tinkering with the interfaces between public and private – some playfully transgressive – valuable meanings are unearthed.

For the Urban Oasis, a family of furniture and markings were laid out as if in a community hall on a field of astroturf at Broadgate in the City of London, a nature–culture hybrid that challenges the relationship between urban and natural environments. Kölnisch Wasser (Eau de Cologne; 2010), meanwhile, a temporary water surface in the somewhat shabby square in front of the city's Schauspiel theatre, sidesteps the classical motif of a water fountain for a new identity with its own experiential frisson: a mundane puddle and branded rubber boots. OSA's reprogramming of space commands urban leftovers: for Anwohnerpark (Residents' Park; 2006), on the site of the car park for the Cologne fairground, OSA extrapolates the modest graphic of the car park's function (the marked spaces) on to the huge firewall of a neighbouring studio complex.

OSA partners, who tend to do everything themselves, relish courting illegality if it means they can add a resource in the city where none existed before. Point of View (2008), the first viewing platform for the 2012 Olympic Games, set against the perimeter fence of the main site in east London, lasted sixty hours before being removed, but managed to flag up the distancing from the Olympics spirit of this barrier. The project's twin, Intact (2004), an

For one month in spring 2008, in the empty Leeds International Pool, built in the 1960s and fallen into disrepair, OSA (commissioned by Leeds City Council) developed a lit, funnel-shaped work – Accumulator – that initially looked like a computer-generated model but was a real, crafted construction and water collector. It transformed the 45-degree angle of the roof and carried shifting shadows of metalwork and walkways.

illegal makeover of a redundant railway signal box in Shoreditch into a cute little house, was later rendered uninhabitable through being damaged by the authorities.

Art, but always habitable as far as possible, is OSA's domain. A beacon amid Liverpool's local industrial heritage – a new roof for the Blade Factory, jokily named Kunsthülle ('Art Wrapping'; 2006) – offers new views of the River Mersey and the city centre, and a place for discussions on the relationship between art and architecture. Such installations as the Accumulator (2008) in Leeds effect more profound transformations: that project concerned an important public swimming bath dating from the Swinging Sixties, deemed to lack energy efficiency and hence scheduled for demolition. Taking its cue from that era, the gigantic funnel ('a virtual water collector') symbolizes architecture's yearning to be sustainable as a fitting adieu to the building. Some 700 people attended the opening. In Frankfurt in 2006, the cake and candles on the rotunda of the Schirn Kunsthalle, set out 'on' a table draped with a lacy cloth, merged into their context on the occasion of the museum's twentieth anniversary, in an 'inside taken outside' kind of way. OSA's work operates as a mobile decoy in the city. Its mobile periscope for Architecture Week in Bristol in 2005, for example, moved around the centre of the city, surfacing and tracking the architectural environment at four locations. Legacy Trail, the architect's network of waypoints within a new urban route for Weymouth in Dorset, encourages people to explore the area and the natural environment.

Sheer practicality also seems to surface in the office of OSA and its associated firm, KHBT, in Berlin. Sober and awkwardly shaped, it has a sleeping space in the back – but in fact it is 'a floating sculpture' with a corridor like a cutout. KHBT's conversion of a 1970s building in Offenbach, near Frankfurt (Haus B, 2012), updates the timber facade by using strips of wood and glass, much of it recycled, over a black waterproof barrier. Conceptually this links to OSA's recent Merzen project in homage to Kurt Schwitters in the CUBE Gallery, Manchester (2011), where a collection of materials – old bins, timber and newspaper taken from a six-week forage around the city – forms, without cutting anything up, OSA's own brand of assemblage architecture. Schwitters called for 'a detoxification of materials' to change our perception of them, while OSA, as architects, are playing their own game – as usual. 'We really lived sustainability', says Karsten Huneck.

Urban Oasis, a temporary outdoor installation (London, 2005) in association with the Belgian beer Hoegaarden and Cow PR, challenged the relationship between urban and natural environments with an array of turf-covered furniture. Visitors and onlookers were encouraged to reflect on the impact such spatial manipulation had on their reading of the context and how they behaved there.

Interview with Karsten Huneck, Bernd Trümpler and Ulrich Beckefeld

Can you recount a few architectural memories from childhood?

KH The building of a new petrol station opposite our flat fascinated me, and I wanted to become a builder.

BT My mum was pregnant with me at the time my parents built their own house.

UB At that time I wasn't at all interested in architecture. But perhaps most influential, as memories are what you remember today, were my school buildings, which I loved, and later the university building where we studied, all from the 1970s.

How would you describe your architectural background?

Very classical: an academic education at the university in Darmstadt, a technical university that provided 'universal studies', in which a conceptual approach was required, while social, environmental and technical aspects had to be considered as well. More importantly, most of us in OSA have had another education before, in business, craftsmanship or whatever; we are very diverse.

What are your greatest influences, architectural or otherwise?

A close relationship to the art world is key to our architectural approach. But within the group the interests in artistic topics are very different: music, visual arts, theatre, cooking – and architecture! Bernd and Karsten were both assistants to the renowned artist Ottmar Hörl during their studies, and that significantly influenced their work. Anja [Ohliger] and Ulrich worked in architectural offices before studying architecture.

Give one example of the way in which your architecture communicates effectively with people.

The project Kölnisch Wasser [Eau de Cologne], from 2010, shows how a simple idea can interact and communicate with people. In general, our projects give people leads to follow, rather like a manual: we are not 'animating' situations or spaces; people have to do and see things for themselves.

Kunsthülle Liverpool

A temporary pavilion inhabiting the roof of the Blade Factory on Greenland Street acted as a playful beacon, drawing people to the area and giving visitors spectacular views of the River Mersey and the city centre. It was used by A Foundation and Liverpool Culture Company's Cities in Transition programme for talks as part of the Liverpool Art Biennale. A cross-section of the light superstructure is shown opposite, bottom.

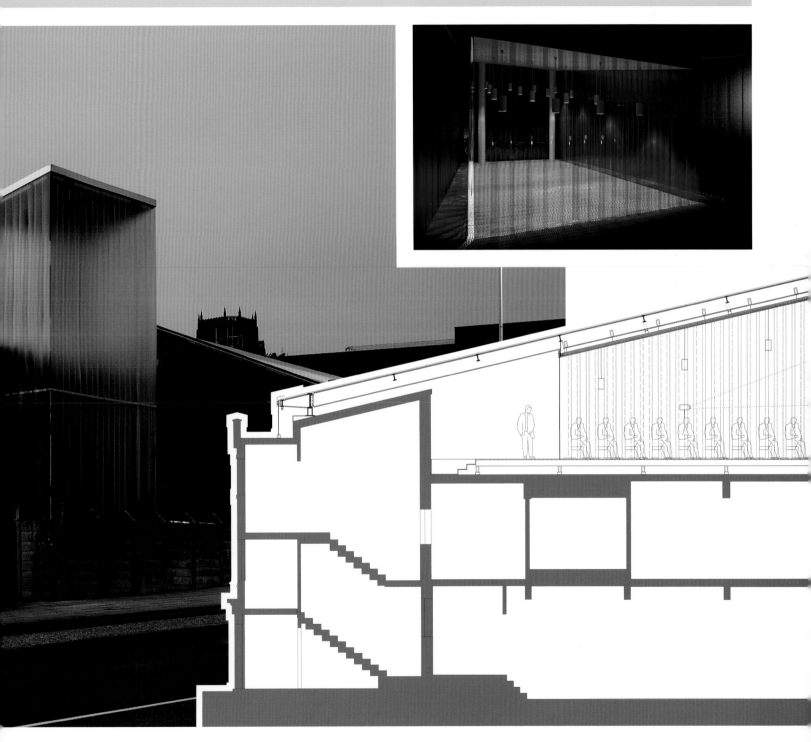

Are you a maker or a thinker?

OSA as a group clearly embodies both thinking and making. A strong concept, often addressing many different layers, usually leads to a realized project. In many cases these even get physically built by us. Bernd and Karsten are both trained cabinetmakers and carpenters. On the other hand, Ulrich writes essays on theory for various architectural publications, and the fact that most of us teach or taught at one point at universities underlines this hybrid approach. Perhaps all of us are both, and OSA is the chance to express this mentality fully.

Do you prefer bespoke or standardized?

As our projects work with the inherent nature of a space or site and pursue a specific demand or theme, they are bespoke per se. However, a standardized or repeated method can be useful and adapted to certain projects.

What theories lie behind your design methods and practice?

We do not work with a specific theory but follow a form of OSA rules. The first step is a very precise analysis of the situation, the site and the task or demands. The second – which really comes first – is a general curiosity. And the third is a positive view of changes as chances. All this applies to the urban context as well as to the details of a building or space.

Do you strive to create new architectural typologies? If so, please give an example.

No. A typology means the repetition of an old answer. We try to find specific answers and sometimes a new one could be the right one. So traditional methods are part of our approach as well as new ideas. We don't believe in reinventing the wheel constantly; however, the way we make public space interact with the people is new, and we believe we are certainly at the forefront of this contemporary movement. The idea of subverting common views on architecture, and what architecture is, is our driving force.

What are the most challenging aspects of your architectural practice today?

We have to be inventive and cost-effective and find new ecological solutions, but at the same time the legislation is so bureaucratic and ludicrous that it is very difficult. Perhaps most challenging is to fight anxiety.

Weymouth and Portland Legacy Trail 2012

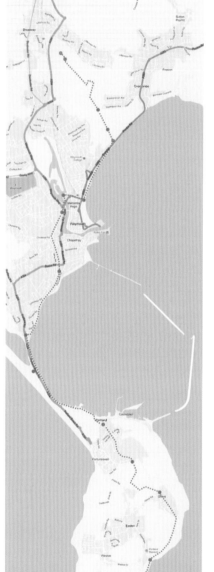

A design for a wayfinding system engaging with local communities and visitors, introducing variously sized three-dimensional red rings as single elements of a long chain.

Intact involved the illegal makeover of a redundant railway signal box near Shoreditch Tube station as a miniature house, adorned with artificial geraniums and installed with a light run on a car battery. A director's chair on artificial grass sat on the converted balcony.

What impact do you hope your architecture has on the public realm?

As mentioned above, a lot of our work deals with the public realm, so it is one of our main objectives to have a real impact. In fact, our very first project as a collective was the transformation of an abandoned subway into a flat, which left passers-by speechless as well as triggering a thinking process.

What personal significance do you give to architectural precedent?

In the era of digital communication and the Internet, precedents automatically influence any creative thinker. However, this can be problematic, as we often lose sight of the 'normal', which is sometimes much more exciting. In the end it is important for us to concentrate on a specific project regardless of any precedents around.

Which technical advances excite you the most for exploitation?

New and recycled materials and the potential in the virtual world, as we are interested in implementing the 'imaginative' in reality.

Do you practise a transdisciplinary approach to architecture, and if so, what is especially important to you right now?

Our practice is based on transdisciplinary thinking, as our work moves between art and architecture depending on the specific task. This includes all kinds of collaboration with different practitioners, including artists, musicians and film-makers, and – last but not least – our clients on the one hand and the craftsmen with whom we work on the other.

How do you go about generating the best possible relationship with your clients?

We are very proactive on all levels and always aim for a result that not only stands out in a spatial, aesthetic or functional way but also creates a process of dealing with a specific topic where the client takes part as well. In a way our clients know at the beginning that they will be taken on a specific journey, and we try to create an atmosphere of trust: not so much in the result, but in the corporate process. They enjoy the process as it generates great pleasure beside the serious and hard work involved.

Point of View
Stratford, London | 2008

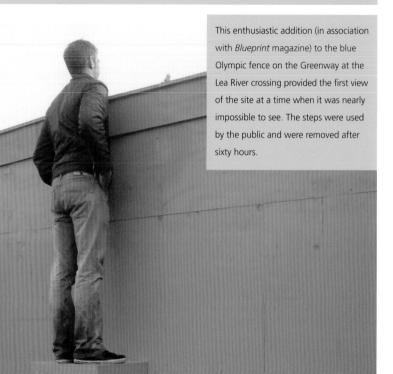

This enthusiastic addition (in association with *Blueprint* magazine) to the blue Olympic fence on the Greenway at the Lea River crossing provided the first view of the site at a time when it was nearly impossible to see. The steps were used by the public and were removed after sixty hours.

Signs around the installation at the Arena at Broadgate Circle in the City of London read 'keep on the grass'. Turf furniture formed a temporary pub on a carpet of grass.

Can you give an example of your participatory methods?

We aim to get people involved on different levels, depending on the nature of the project. Projects like Intact, Accumulator, Point of View or Volksbühne, for example, arrive out of the blue and create a surprise moment in which people can participate. For a project in Oldham we are creating a street market and festival using the front gardens of abandoned, boarded-up houses. Different user groups, such as school classes and voluntary performing groups, are involved throughout the process. In this sense we provide the framework for the actual activities.

How do you communicate your architecture?

Our projects themselves communicate architecture to all kinds of people: that is one of our main objectives. As a lot of our projects are temporary, the media of photography and film are very important to us, and we use them to spread news of our projects, as well as giving lectures or participating in exhibitions or film festivals. Discussing our projects is part of our work. Teaching is another tool for us to communicate our approach and encourage young people.

What do you aim to achieve with your practice (in a single sentence)?

To touch people and make them think about space and its potential – and their own potential.

What advice would you give to a young architect embarking on their career?

We used the following statement in our manifesto some years ago. This still stands and also acts as advice:

> Passivity can't go wrong – it's safe. How can we interact directly with our environment and implement our ideas without losing the drive, the energy and continuity? OSA is trying to overcome the usual obstacles in order to be able to realize ideas that have an impact on our public and urban spaces, buildings, systems and authorities, and on people. A major part of our work focuses on areas of the city that tend to be overlooked, forgotten or abandoned but have enormous potential and need to be treated. The methods are simple, ranging from soft (performative) to hard (materialized), and the projects are often on a very low budget but yet still very powerful and effective, in fact almost more than 'highly sophisticated'

Accumulator

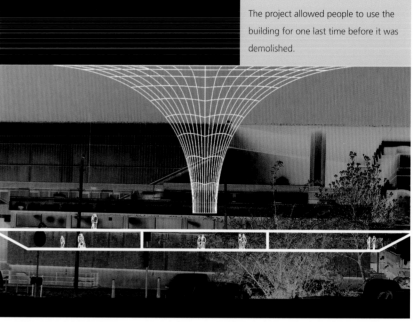

The project allowed people to use the building for one last time before it was demolished.

London Roof

London | 2002

The umbrella, that practical and utilitarian object used by about eight million people in the City, can be an architectural module. This fluid roof was created by 250 umbrellas in the midst of one of the busiest streets in London.

This temporary installation reflected on the work of the artist Kurt Schwitters and his Merz ('sensing without knowing') collage technique, which rearranged paper, timber, wire, paint and fragments of text. OSA gathered materials from the streets and invited visitors to add their own to the process, creating shifting relationships.

and 'complex' structures. In some instances formal and official procedures ('fences') literally have to be jumped in order to realize the ideas. Intact, the illegal makeover of a redundant signal box in Shoreditch, proved to be the most radical and impressive form of this approach.

The message to everyone is clear: It is possible – get on with it. Do what you believe in! But do believe in it! And be curious about what you don't believe in!

What single improvement to the procurement of architecture in the United Kingdom would you recommend? More competitions, different planning system, legislation affecting developers, etc.?
It is difficult to highlight a single improvement; in fact, all the ones mentioned in your question are exactly what need to be improved. Therefore we will all need much more courage – sometimes even audacity. The way legislation and planning work in the United Kingdom (and some other countries) is ludicrous and also totally counter-productive to the aims and targets set out by government. At a time when inventiveness is needed on all levels, for instance economically as well as technically and environmentally, this needs to change.

OSA/KHBT Studio

Part of the ground floor of a listed factory building (1908) in the former East Berlin was converted into the practices' studio and living area. A single 'floating' form with full-height doors divides the large room from the more intimate space at the rear, helping to limit interventions in the studio, which is also used as a gallery, workshop and seminar space. The kitchen (seen on the left) is also sober.

Piercy Conner Architects

'In an attempt to humanize and fragment prescriptive living we try to explore the reality of space, texture, light, flexibility and interactivity', wrote the architect Stuart Piercy in 2001. In 1999 he and his fellow architect Richard Conner, who had met while working together at Nicholas Grimshaw & Partners, had founded Piercy Conner Architects. Together they also incubated a digital communications company, Smoothe, to breathe life into architectural concepts – theirs and other people's – through film and image. The fluid relationship between practices they set in motion opened up a stimulating environment of sharing ideas, evolving applications of computer software and of graphics, architecture and communications strategies.

Much of the duo's previous experience came from large international transportation projects, and this spurred their conviction that industrial architecture had much to offer low-budget construction, through the prefabrication of large building elements, thick wall construction and high-performance materials. Piercy today remains committed to the affinity that British architecture has with making, craft and form. The practice's responsive buildings respect context, and are borne out of initial analysis considering the immediate physical surroundings of a site but also its cultural and social influences, environmental status, vernacular cues and historical narratives.

Piercy Conner Architects is now run by Piercy after Conner branched out to set up his own firm, but the approach remains consistent. Concepts are not celebrations of technology or construction detail but relate much more to 'how technology can set us free to live, work and play'. From the first, the practice has been concerned with simplifying the essentials of living, in the belief that a radical rethink of dwelling typologies and intelligent construction could draw essential life back into city centres.

The practice's Martello Tower Y (2010) in Suffolk won the support of English Heritage, which heralds it as an exemplar of how to convert a significant historic building. Built in 1808, the Napoleonic defence tower was a Scheduled Monument on the At Risk register, and the challenging brief entailed complex planning negotiations and on-site logistics. Standing out in the landscape, its massive form with 3-metre-thick solid-bonded brick walls is a simple, bold one that hides its inner complexity as well as the beauty of the plan and geometry of the space. The walls, designed to resist direct cannon fire from the North Sea, create a base to which to tether the new roof, which follows many of the curves inside the original building. It also recesses gently, protecting the house from views from the footpath along the sea-defence wall. Below, the first floor was replaced by a gallery, allowing light deep into the masonry shell.

The success of Martello Tower Y was followed with a four-bedroom family house (2012) in the historic townscape of Kew, west London, next to the Royal Botanic Gardens. With a strong roofscape and weathering-steel shell perforated with a leaf pattern that creates dappled shadows in the spaces below, the house interprets the vernacular rather than imposing a new language. Traditional and modern, conservative and contemporary are not treated as separate entities; rather, the lines between them are blurred. The steel sheet was made in a factory and the interior and furniture fabricated on-site with a CNC (computer numerical control) machine.

Piercy has long wanted to create a building for Clerkenwell, a district of London with many robust and restrained industrial warehouses that have served as a good framework for its ongoing reinvention. He appreciates the fact that, while they are rationally planned, their facades have been highly articulated and animated, contributing to a varied and rich townscape. The refurbishment for Derwent London of 63 Clerkenwell Road (2014) on the site of Turnmills nightclub was inspired by Barbara Hepworth's sculpture comparing ancient and modern Greece, with its dark, articulated skins and pure white interior. A ribbon of masonry, suitably dark, heavily articulated and textured, wraps a light and flexible interior, celebrating with its reveals and voids the contrast between the materials.

Martello Tower Y (2010), Suffolk, in the mist. The project converted the Napoleonic defence tower of 1808 into a private residence with a new roof following many of the curves of the original building.

Piercy Conner Architects

In a similar way, for Wakefield Street (2012) in Bloomsbury, central London, a contextually sensitive brick skin wraps a flexible open-plan interior. These are new town houses – some of the first to be built in this Conservation Area for more than 100 years. Avoiding pastiche or kitsch, they respect neighbouring listed buildings and gardens, and have gone through lengthy consultation with the local community group. With grand interior proportions and gallery-quality finishes, the houses can be configured to have two, three or four bedrooms, with living spaces on ground and basement floors.

In 2005 Piercy Conner won the Living Steel International Architecture Competition for sustainable multifamily housing for the planned Rajarhat New Town at Kolkata in India, showing how steel could be used for residential housing in a country traditionally reliant on concrete for constructing apartment blocks. The practice used it not just for the internal structure but also for the cladding. 'Western architecture is dominated by the sealed environment, whereas architecture in India is much more open and expressive', Piercy explained. 'We wanted to create something that draws on the permeability of subtropical architecture, which historically uses shade, sun-paths and wind-channelling to control environmental factors with minimal impact on the planet.'

The twelve boutique apartments of the resulting Restello scheme (2012) mix elements of traditional Eastern architecture with innovative sustainable practices, creating flowing living spaces and private rooms. The skin has one permeable outer layer of perforated steel screens and an inner layer of floor-to-ceiling glazing. Between the two are double-storey terraces at the front of the flats, facilitating flow between the outside world and the internal domestic environment. Although permeable, the outer screens offer protection from sun and rain, while maximizing natural light and maintaining external views. This creates dappled patterning and an airy effect in counterpoint to the strength of the steel.

An early project of Piercy Conner's, one that propelled the practice into the limelight, was the speculative, prefabricated Microflat apartments, first displayed in the windows of Selfridge's in London in 2002, complete with a couple living there for two weeks. Designed for a range of inner-city sites, including on top of supermarkets, it was a brave attempt to open the door to a new solution for inner-city living for young people. Some 200,000 people expressed interest in purchasing a Microflat. Now, Piercy's ability to rethink essentials fundamentally resurfaces with the Van for the Great Outdoors (ongoing), a reimagining of that 'wobbly, cramped and whiffy plastic box': the caravan. The Van with its poetic form is a more subtle version of the white plastic cube, and gently merges into the landscape. Inspired by the Anglo-Saxon long barn with its intimate eaves and recognizable form, and its functional open space that might even be co-opted for inhabitation, and also by the coaches of the Orient Express, the Van has a gently faceted oak frame – and aims to be more than a home from home.

In its exploration of each project's scope for reconsidering, reworking, reinforming and redesigning, Piercy Conner has consistently been one of the most conceptually advanced practices of its generation. Its work has extended the theory and practice of architecture in a way that demonstrates a profound understanding of its cultural and communicational possibilities. Testing ideas is an essential step.

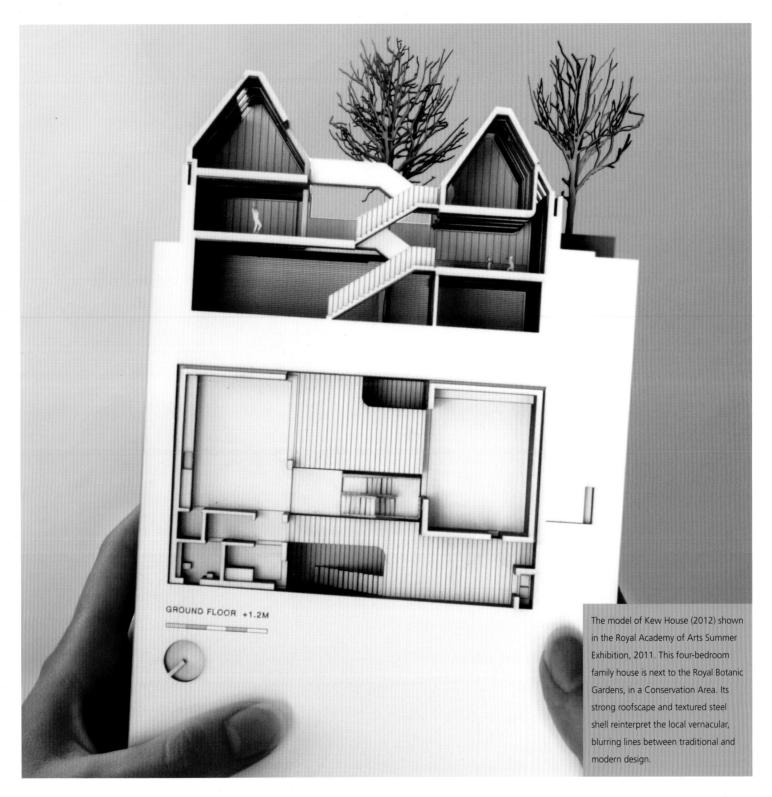

GROUND FLOOR +1.2M

The model of Kew House (2012) shown in the Royal Academy of Arts Summer Exhibition, 2011. This four-bedroom family house is next to the Royal Botanic Gardens, in a Conservation Area. Its strong roofscape and textured steel shell reinterpret the local vernacular, blurring lines between traditional and modern design.

Piercy Conner Architects

Interview with Stuart Piercy

Can you recount a few architectural memories from childhood?

I spent my childhood in a rural part of Yorkshire. The landscapes there have a brooding kind of beauty, and the sky feels as though it is hovering just above the ground. I still love the brutal beauty and ruggedness of Yorkshire, and I often think about its colours, textures and materials. Another very strong memory is of the taxidermy room and skeletons of animals in a small collection at a museum called Cliffe Castle in Keighley, where I used to spend every Sunday with my parents. I could never understand why the animals were all so different; this idea of evolving a nature particular to circumstance has been a very strong influence on me recently.

How would you describe your architectural background?

Richard Conner and I were very lucky to win a few early competitions we entered jointly, and we set up Piercy Conner [in 1999] on the back of these. We were still relatively young – in our twenties – and we were working on Zurich Airport for Grimshaw Architects, which gave us a real confidence about scale and how things go together. When you spend as long as six or seven years with a practice, you start to align your thinking with the studio. We spent the first few years of our new practice trying to explore a broader field and develop our own ethos. Grimshaw has been a strong influence, even if the language and approach of our own studio are different, and we are still very process-based – searching for the poetic within the pragmatic. Competitions have played a huge role within the office, and I think we are on number 87 or 88. This is the testing ground: the best work won in the hardest possible way!

What are your greatest influences, architectural or otherwise?

My father for his work ethic; the sculptors Lynn Chadwick and Barbara Hepworth for form and materials; Steven Holl for genuine originality; Toyo Ito for lightness; and Louis Kahn for junctions. The artists Francis Bacon and Polly Morgan disturb me in a good way.

SymHomes MK1 'Restello' housing

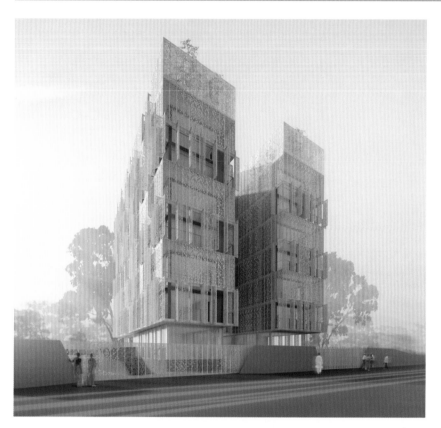

This development of twelve flats (opposite, top) draws on elements of traditional Eastern architecture, yet at the same time deploys innovative sustainable practices. Its steel structure creates a mix of open living spaces; the facade of perforated steel screens over glazing filters sunlight for an airy effect that belies the strength of the steel (right). It lies in front of permeable two-storey terraces in front of the flats, and provides natural ventilation. A typical living room is pictured opposite, bottom.

Piercy Conner Architects

Martello Tower Y

Give one example of the way in which your architecture communicates effectively with people.

I hope through a reading of the forms and materials. Martello Tower Y, for example, tries to tell the story of a form derived entirely from the existing building. The clearly new element floating above the massive base has a natural affinity with the existing proportions and curves, even though it is of an entirely different language, one based on a double-curved surface made up entirely of flat, two-dimensional curves. Something odd happened with the heritage bodies: they grew to like the proposal from an initial outright refusal.

Are you a maker or a thinker?

We are definitely 'makers', but I'd like to add another category: 'talkers'. London has lots of talkers.

Do you prefer bespoke or standardized?

I don't think there is enough space to discuss this here! The original ethos of Piercy Conner Architects was to apply what we had learned at Grimshaw about commercial and industrial architecture to providing efficient mass housing. The Microflat project was the embodiment of this idea: a factory-made one-bed apartment that can be arranged in four ways to provide the necessary variation to the streetscape. We have held on to our belief in the efficiency of component architecture and off-site manufacture, but our ideas on standardization have changed to developing efficient digital craft-based processes that retain the economic benefits, but allow more freedom in expression and more ability to respond to the local.

What theories lie behind your design methods and practice?

It is difficult to define an 'ethos' or theory. We don't have an academic platform as such, but we do believe in process and evolution. We believe there is a nature to every project, one that needs to evolve out of the conditions of the physical and historical environment. The programme or problem grounds the work, and from that point we are searching for the poetic within the constraints of the real issue. I think our ideas are work in progress: we have a strong process of making but our theories are shaped constantly through exposure to new problems.

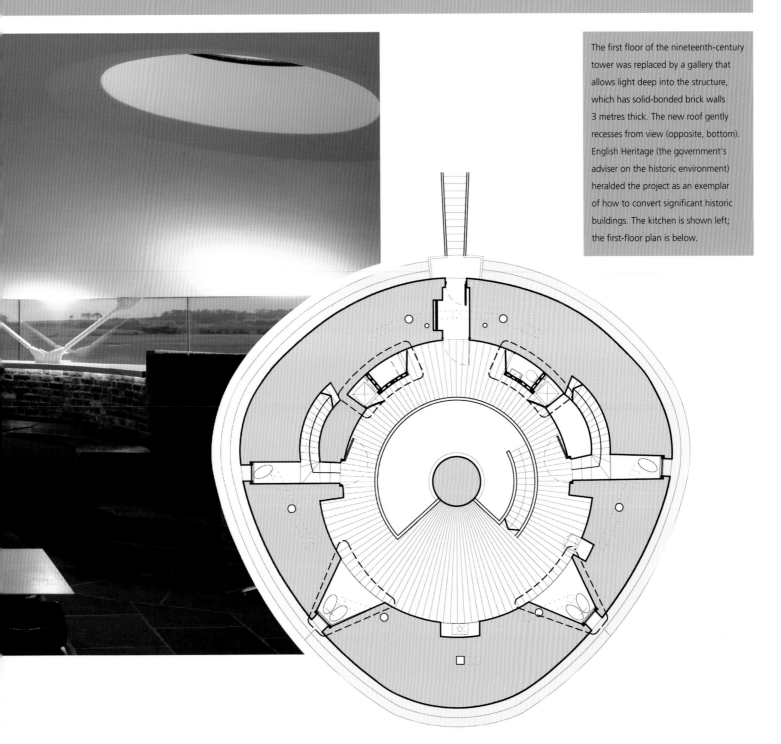

The first floor of the nineteenth-century tower was replaced by a gallery that allows light deep into the structure, which has solid-bonded brick walls 3 metres thick. The new roof gently recesses from view (opposite, bottom). English Heritage (the government's adviser on the historic environment) heralded the project as an exemplar of how to convert significant historic buildings. The kitchen is shown left; the first-floor plan is below.

Piercy Conner Architects

Do you strive to create new architectural typologies? If so, please give an example.

At the Athletes' Village for the 2012 Olympic Games we had the problem of how to deal with the requirement for traditional town houses with front gardens in a site where the general massing was about ten floors. We created three-storey town houses articulated very clearly as independent dwellings. At the house parapet level there is a deep recess and then a further five floors of apartments sitting quite happily on top – a kind of residential typology stack.

What are the most challenging aspects of your architectural practice today?

We are part of a generation that had witnessed only economic prosperity, and when things turned ugly in the United Kingdom suddenly the whole process of renewal just stopped. At times like this there is a lot of reflection on the value of architecture, and I am afraid the new government has made it very clear that it sees design as a luxury. Thankfully, not all clients are as short-sighted, and we have experienced a renewed interest in young practices as people who can offer a fresh look at old problems.

What impact do you hope your architecture has on the public realm?

Our clients are predominantly private, so we rarely have a chance to cross the site's curtilage literally into the public realm, which is frustrating. So we hope that through materials, transparency and programme we can improve the experience of people who rub up against our buildings. In townscape terms, our work is often heavily articulated, so we hope that brings some joy and animation to the street.

What personal significance do you give to architectural precedent?

It would be more of a challenge to ignore precedent – why would you? We are collectors, like magpies: if it's shiny, it goes in the sketchbook.

Which technical advances excite you the most for exploitation?

Digital craft – rediscovering an expression that would be technically and economically difficult to produce without machines.

Wakefield Street

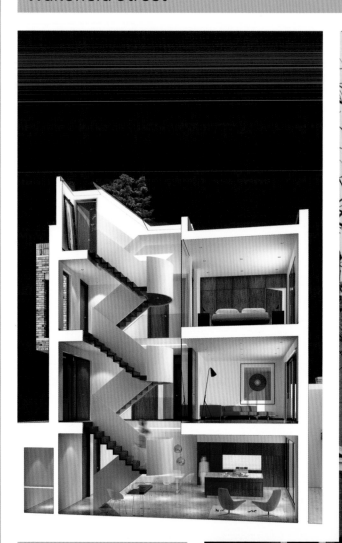

These new town houses in the Bloomsbury Conservation Area have flexible open plans and grandly proportioned interiors wrapped in a contextually sensitive brick skin.

Piercy Conner Architects

Do you practise a transdisciplinary approach to architecture, and if so, what is especially important to you right now?

We have always had a close relationship with structural engineers. Often the poetic comes out of reduction and simplicity; this is hard to test without many iterations and models shared with somebody who deals with the reality of making things stand up. We have also been very closely linked to CG (computer-generated) illustration and film, and in fact until 2009 had a studio of sixty people, Smoothe, producing beautiful CG film work for other designers all around the world. We can rarely afford to explore our ideas in film at the moment, but I hope to bring those techniques back into use to tell the story of our work.

How do you go about generating the best possible relationship with your clients?

We try to make our ideas easy to envisage.

Can you give an example of your participatory methods?

More than half of our studio space is dedicated to model-making: models usually form the centrepiece of meetings. We use models to explore physical relationships and form. We also use CG illustration to explore the qualities of light, texture and materials.

How do you communicate your architecture?

As above, and by whichever tools best explain the ideas.

What do you aim to achieve with your practice (in a single sentence)?

To produce work that has a visceral quality, like that of Anish Kapoor, Antony Gormley or Barbara Hepworth.

What advice would you give to a young architect embarking on their career?

Get some experience in a top studio for a few years. Don't wait to be discovered: it just doesn't seem to happen that way any more.

Van for the Great Outdoors

A fundamental rethink of the static caravan, depicted above in the snow. Inspired by the Anglo-Saxon long barn with its functional open space, and also by the fittings of the Orient Express train carriages, the oak-framed caravan has more intimate spaces at the eaves for sitting and sleeping.

Piercy Conner Architects

What single improvement to the procurement of architecture in the United Kingdom would you recommend? More competitions, different planning system, legislation affecting developers, etc.?

The quality threshold for architecture in the United Kingdom is very low indeed (look around at the work in Europe and Japan!). Because of the way the planning system is set up, the dumb and mundane slip through the net while the genuinely interesting work has to fight all the way through. It is called the Banana mentality: 'Build absolutely nothing anywhere near anyone.' The newly formed Design Council CABE (the Commission for Architecture and the Built Environment in its reformed guise) has done excellent work in training planning officers in design, and we now have such champions of design as Paul Finch[1] and Peter Rees[2].

1 OBE, former CABE chair and now deputy chair of the Design Council, director of the World Architecture Festival and editorial director of the *Architects' Journal* and *Architectural Review*.

2 City Planning Officer, Planning and Transportation Department, City of London.

63 Clerkenwell Road

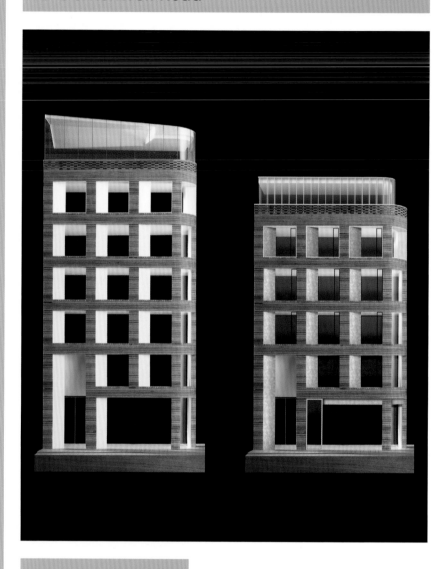

Model of the converted warehouses. The proposal is a tribute to the historic fabric of Clerkenwell and its present-day incarnation as the centre of London's creative media industry. Ribbons of dark, heavily articulated and textured masonry wrap a light and flexible interior; the reveals and voids celebrate the contrasts between materials.

Model of the four-bedroom family house. Its weathering-steel shell is a perforated interpretation of a leaf pattern, creating dappled shadows in the spaces below.

Plasma Studio | GroundLab

The plasma, or fourth, state of matter is a unique condition that arises when there is a complex overlay of external forces. The practices Plasma Studio and GroundLab are themselves overlaid globally in cultural and operational terms, and this complexity produces dynamic results. Intrinsically part of the same 'family', they are designed to do wholly complementary things. Architects Eva Castro and Holger Kehne founded Plasma Studio in London in 1999, working on small but challenging refurbishment projects in the city, and the practice has since grown to become one of the leading emergent architecture and design practices with a worldwide scope and outlook, engaged at all scales with furniture, installations, buildings, urbanism and masterplanning.

Combining academic research at the Architectural Association (AA), London (Diploma Unit 12 and the Landscape Urbanism Masters programme, of which Castro is director), with their professional work allows a high degree of cross-fertilization. They are uncompromising in their approach. The point is to create coherent and holistic 'ambiences', resulting from an integrated vision of the built environment that is fully sustainable, high-performing and closely related to the realities and challenges of today and tomorrow.

GroundLab emerged later from the converging interests of Castro, Kehne and architects Alfredo Ramirez and Eduardo Rico, a constellation of talents who developed their methodologies in the Landscape Urbanism Masters programme at the AA. Architects, urban designers, engineers and landscape architects pool their expertise on projects in which architecture, landscape and ecological processes entwine. They use parametric modelling to develop innovative urban models that produce flowing yet differentiated space, rather than basing their work on old codes.

In this sense there is an obvious kinship with Zaha Hadid Architects' design approach, transcendence of modernist paradigms and multidisciplinarity, and the practices obviously share many interests, processes and tools. But Plasma Studio and GroundLab have their own specific phenomenological concerns and distinct language of drawing landscapes into buildings, born of the partners' histories and the specific contexts with which they have grappled, lending each project its own unique set of qualities – seen, for example, in their evolution of the Alpine vernacular.

The two practices create unique architecture and landscapes by 'calibrating the dynamic and fluid nature of flows, events and ephemera on the one hand, and the rational, structural and systemic parameters of material, organization and resistance on the other'. This ambition has so far been realized most singularly in northern Italy and in China, and it has huge validity today. In response to cities, and landscapes in between urban environments, as constantly changing natural processes, GroundLab in particular creates flexible and adaptable mechanisms and designs that can configure and reconfigure different contexts. By closely analysing and responding to the existing and potential conditions of a site, using the forces that shape cities – social, economic, environmental and infrastructural – they can continue to research and develop innovative urban models and techniques.

Since 2002 Plasma Studio's work has extended to new residential and hospitality projects in northern Italy, in Sexten and San Candido (both in the Dolomites); its local office at Sexten is run by Ulla Hell. Such projects as D_Cube (2007), a private residence, Hotel Rainer (2008) and Cube House (2008), all in Sexten, and Esker House (2008) in San Candido, combine complex geometry with local materials, employing digital processes and fabrication techniques. It has been a high priority to develop a fresh take on the local Alpine vernacular building tradition, to engage with the landscape. Cube House, for example, on a steep site, is inserted into the ground, with two covered parking spaces at the front and a stair leading up to the main living spaces. Esker House sits on top of a 1960s house, and is formed by a series of steel and timber frames that deform to evoke the hillsides of the Dolomites. Its angular, dynamic planes produce

An extension to Residenz Königswarte, Strata Hotel (Sexten, Italy, 2007) is a block of rented 'wellness' apartments on a steep hillside in the Dolomites. This unique Alpine design of family suites interweaves a topography of timber strips, their shifting planes appearing like strata, responding to the natural environment.

the impression of an ever-changing perspective and spatial arrangement adhering to the soft, fluid morphology of the roofscape. Throughout the whole is a loop of contrasting spaces at different gradients, going from the most private spaces to the more public terraces.

Plasma Studio's dynamic design language also manifests itself strongly at the Hotel Puerta América in Madrid (2005). Each of the twelve drastically different floors was created by a different architect or designer, including Zaha Hadid Architects, Jean Nouvel, Norman Foster and John Pawson. Plasma Studio's was clearly one of the most challenging to realize, with walls treated as deformative forces distorting the corridor, and a colour gradient as a seam of LED lights. A huge step away from repetitive units and anonymous, undifferentiated circulation spaces, it encouraged an intuitive sense of place.

The majority of Plasma's projects question the boundary between public and private spheres, with strategies to unify disparate elements formally and programmatically. Furthermore, 'configuring space and activities elastically, we arrive at forms that are fine-tuned around specific requirements and express the multiple aspects that informed them'. The practice believes that architecture should be felt and interpreted on a purely phenomenological basis, and it frees physical space and events from society's dependence on historic, linguistic, cultural and intellectual knowledge and interpretation. For this architect, most new buildings and structures are exchangeable, detached from life, simply monuments to media culture, and so – while acknowledging that it is impossible to avoid iconography – it tries to produce unusual and exotic ambiences: 'What appears abstract at first becomes part of a larger story through the active experience and discovery of the space.'

Winning the commission for the Xi'an International Horticultural Expo 2011 in China, a joint entry by Plasma Studio, GroundLab and LAUR Studio (the landscape practice run by Plasma's Chinese partner, Dongyun Liu), has been pivotal to their adventurous further development. Coming after the Beijing Olympics and the Shanghai Expo, the event received more than 200,000 visitors in the first weekend. It is sited on a former sandpit, and addresses the issues of sustainable urbanism. The intervention includes Flowing Gardens, the 37-hectare centre of the Expo, which features flowing paths as part of a sustainable landscape with three striking yet fully integrated buildings: the Guangyun Entrance, a landbridge with a tensegrity trellis structure; Chang-Ba Flower Valley, inspired by a river delta, with its many sinuous paths; and the Creativity Pavilion,

which links the landscape with the lake. Visitor paths flow across a landscape that runs in between these three 'finger' buildings, above the level of the lake and leaning towards the shoreline. On the other side of the water, a greenhouse, like a crystal sunk into the hillside, can be seen. The architects' designs are permanent, not temporary, and form a central park for a new district. The architects have sketched out an economical, low-maintenance legacy strategy for the park, using local plants and maximizing usable green surfaces, for example trees for extensive shading. They envision the buildings evolving in the future with a fluid, looping circulation connecting the ground and first floors in a single gesture, a path that connects their internal terraces and enables views out. There is an idea to turn one of the Creativity Pavilion buildings into a church.

This project is grounded in a wish to make an authentic, contemporary expression for Chinese society, free of typological and historical references to Xi'an's past. It does this by modifying the convention of buildings dominating in order to balance urbanism and landscape.

Some sixteen million visitors came to the 37-hectare Flowing Gardens of the Xi'an International Horticultural Expo in China in 2011. The exhibition building – its cantilevering elevations seen here framing views of the lake – entrance bridge, greenhouse and gardens were designed with LAUR Studio, following success in an invited international competition.

Plasma Studio I GroundLab

Interview with Holger Kehne

Can you recount a few architectural memories from childhood?
I can still recall a particular dream: it was a Felliniesque space with symbolic artefacts and various doors and curtains; otherwise, I come from an area of Germany that is low on architecture, and thus most of my spatial memories are of landscapes.

How would you describe your architectural background?
A mix of different places with different cultural influences and architectural education, from Germany to Italy and Latin America, with architectural training based on phenomenology, German rationality and functionalism, Dutch realism and the theorist Jeff Kipnis.

What are your greatest influences, architectural or otherwise?
The whole of architectural and cultural history, with particular sections from Latin American modernism, organic modernism, and constructivist and kinetic artwork.

Give one example of the way in which your architecture communicates effectively with people.
I could mention function or iconicity, but let's be less obvious and say: architecture can make otherwise hidden systems and networks visible.

Are you a maker or a thinker?
We make to think.

Do you prefer bespoke or standardized?
It's got to be both; the skill is how to combine them.

What theories lie behind your design methods and practice?
We are influenced by Kant, the philosopher, in that we work on a synthesis of abstract and concrete parameters. We work out architecture as this interface between the abstract and the concrete, between time and space, between temporary and permanent, between the individual and the communal, between history and the future. Material language is the medium through which we attempt to choreograph this complexity.

Cube House

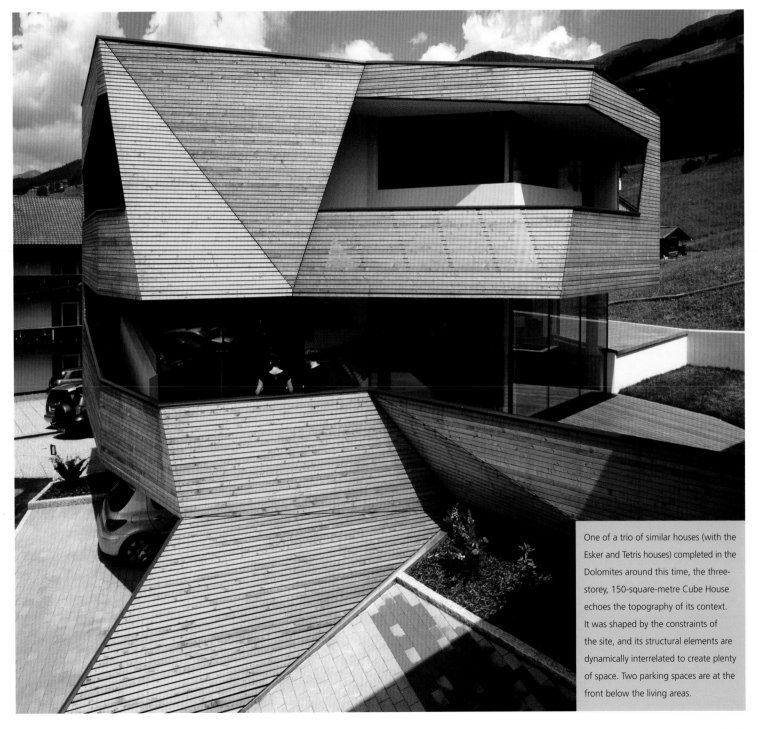

One of a trio of similar houses (with the Esker and Tetris houses) completed in the Dolomites around this time, the three-storey, 150-square-metre Cube House echoes the topography of its context. It was shaped by the constraints of the site, and its structural elements are dynamically interrelated to create plenty of space. Two parking spaces are at the front below the living areas.

Plasma Studio | GroundLab

The philosophers Gilles Deleuze and Félix Guattari's thoughts on materialism have been a great influence on how we develop architecture through the concept of a 'material system': it means that everything in architecture is material, including thought and abstract concepts. In reverse, material is not just 'stuff', but has an embodied intelligence and diagrammatic scope.

Another more direct bearing on our work comes from the theories of the architect Claude Parent and the philosopher Paul Virilio on the function of the oblique. Their critical stance towards the vacuousness of modernist rationality and the subsequent vision of (re)connecting body and space through inclined planes has been instrumental to the formation of our design intentions and repertoire.

Do you strive to create new architectural typologies? If so, please give an example.

Our work is somewhat anti-typological, in that we foster decoded abstract forms that avoid taxonomies and normative reference systems, but demand to be explored actively through time, movement and multiple senses. We have, however, developed a range of diagrams that we apply to a variety of projects where they induce similar functions, patterns and effects. One example is the arrangement of multiple floors as split levels connected by ramps in various configurations: for instance, as a loop around a central void to form a continuous helix. Obviously we did not invent this system, by any means, but it realizes in many ways our vision of fluid, boundless yet systemic spaces, and we hope to be able to explore the potential in future projects.

What are the most challenging aspects of your architectural practice today?

The biggest challenge is that we have an ever-decreasing amount of time and also too little information available to work out meaningful and solid design responses. There is a general precariousness to practice, with projects increasingly uncertain and dependent on a broad range of shifting parameters. While we are embracing relational and parametric processes and developing robustness and resilience in relation to these blurry settings, tradeoffs cannot be avoided, mostly in terms of specificity and depth.

Xi'an International Horticultural Expo

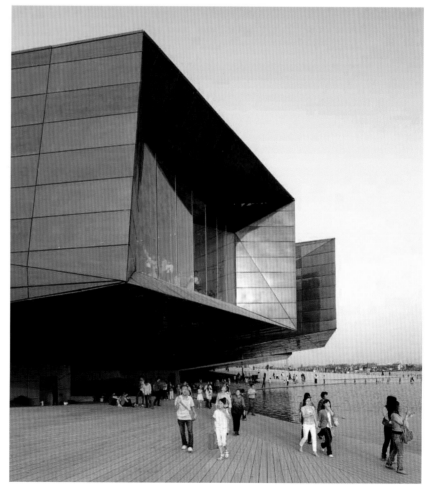

Xi'an, China | 2011

The Flowing Gardens (opposite, top) are network of sinuous paths and waterscapes, a mix of semi-enclosed and open plazas stretching over 37 hectares, creating a legacy for the city. The 5000-square-metre Creativity Pavilion exhibition building (opposite, bottom, and left) cantilevers over the lake. Elsewhere in the gardens are a greenhouse and entrance building.

Plasma Studio | GroundLab

What impact do you hope your architecture has on the public realm?

First and foremost through giving the public a tangible expression of its location in time and space. Furthermore, through aiming at creating civic spaces, transparency and openness – essential expressions of optimism, humanism and trust to counter the general disintegration of the public sphere.

What personal significance do you give to architectural precedent?

It's vitally important to be aware of what precedents already exist and can be used as a starting point, but at the same time our work strives to transcend at least partially these references and achieve something genuinely new.

Which technical advances excite you the most for exploitation?

The ability to introduce real-world parameters into complex design models, allowing feedback and subsequent optimization. Ironically I feel that this might even strengthen the designers' conscious and subjective capacities.

Do you practise a transdisciplinary approach to architecture, and if so, what is especially important to you right now?

Architecture has always been a beacon of transdisciplinarity. Like many architects before and among us, we are designing, planning, calculating, writing, estimating and coordinating projects but also teaching, lecturing on, writing about and discussing a wide range of related issues and fields. At Plasma Studio we are specifically extending into object design, furniture and installations where our architectural experience and interest in landscape and systems can produce different results from those of specialists.

The hand-in-hand collaboration between Plasma Studio and GroundLab is most pertinently breaking disciplinary moulds, and rakes in new, unforeseen results in terms of integration and consistency. GroundLab in particular was formed to integrate expertise, knowledge and sensibilities from other fields, such as engineering, urbanism and landscape design.

How do you go about generating the best possible relationship with your clients?

Our clients have all been very idiosyncratic, so you have to play it by ear in each case. We strive to make the work accessible at all

Xi'an International Horticultural Expo

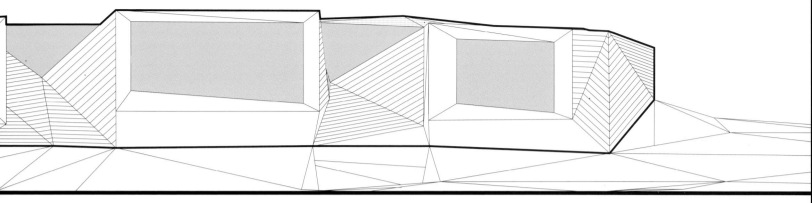

The three structures of the Expo: the Creativity Pavilion (elevation seen top) manifests itself as an extension of the ground, and is massed as three parallel volumes cantilevering over the lake; Guangyun Entrance (opposite) bridges the site's main road, in three lanes conceived as braids; the greenhouse (above) is sunk into the hill.

stages – for instance through the use of 3D models and diagrams – and try where possible to be clear, transparent and numerical.

Can you give an example of your participatory methods?
I cannot comment on this as we have not had much opportunity to explore these tools. I see the users as the real client, and would welcome direct feedback from them to assist in the design process. I am, however, critical of any blanket usage of participation in design as it may lead to bland and streamlined results.

How do you communicate your architecture?
Ideally through the immediate experience it offers to users, which for us is central. At the same time, we have to use a combination of media to present surrogates to the majority of our audience. We are getting better at creating captivating imagery and have become interested in exploring moving images to incorporate movement and time, which are essential to our work.

What do you aim to achieve with your practice (in a single sentence)?
To contribute to culture manifold contemporary, authentic and mind-opening experiences of what it means to live now, physically, with all the senses.

What advice would you give to a young architect embarking on their career?
Make sure that you are really in love with architecture because it is not worth it otherwise. For us it has been an incredibly hard endeavour, but also incredibly rewarding. I just don't understand why so many bother to try to do it as a mere job.

What single improvement to the procurement of architecture in the United Kingdom would you recommend? More competitions, different planning system, legislation affecting developers, etc.?
I think they are all in dire need of improvement. A single improvement would be at odds with the others, so any real progress would have to be based on a gradual shift of all factors and processes, with the underlying cultural acceptance that environmental quality is an asset, not just a luxury.

Strata Hotel

Inside the rental apartment building set on a steep hillside are 40- and 50-square-metre two-storey apartments fitted out with larchwood, leather, loden (an Austrian waterproof fabric) and Dolomitic rock.

Plasma Studio | GroundLab

Robin Lee Architecture

In 2011, nearly a decade after co-founding NORD with Alan Pert in Glasgow in 2002 (see pp. 156–69), Robin Lee renamed his practice and relocated to London. Sharing Pert's commitment to creating buildings and spaces that respond to specific needs, Lee's latest venture promises to add another substantial and mature practice to the local and international scene. Lee played a key role in all NORD's projects, including the Primary Substation for the 2012 Olympics (2009); Bridgewater Bridge, Stoke-on-Trent (2009); Linthills, Lochwinnoch (2008); Destiny Church, Glasgow (2004); and the Bell House, Strathblane (2004). The completion of the Wexford County Council headquarters (2011) is a fresh and insightful interpretation of the twenty-first-century civic building.

The Bell House is an extension of a 1950s brick bungalow, the Bell-Simpson House, between Strathblane and Milton of Campsie in Stirlingshire, with two large living spaces and a study. Positioned in the sloping back garden to the north of the original dwelling, it is stripped of surface articulation, and treated in a homogeneous manner to give the idea of a uniform skin that looks familiar and yet strikingly new at the same time. Walls, roof, windows and doors are all pulled flush to its outer face, so that there is no sense of hierarchy between elements. 'This is an attempt to create an architecture that is stripped of articulation and expression, appearing generic in its language', says Lee of his approach, which is consistent with his preference for architecture as a backdrop to people and their activities.

Destiny Church, in the southern inner suburbs of Glasgow, is a relaxed and informal place, with leaders and ministers called by their first names. Its 1970s annex needed to be refurbished as it detracted from the fine character of the non-denominational church, which is listed Grade B, and from its ethos, which is to encourage everyone to feel at home. The practice used the limited budget strategically to reline the existing spaces with oak lining board, reflecting the character of the church in a way that could be read clearly. Externally, black cement cladding panels wrap the annex, closing off all existing

Wexford County Council's new headquarters (2011, with executive architect Arthur Gibney & Partners) on the outskirts of Wexford town, overlooking the Slaney Estuary, is a new civic landmark. It signals its presence with a unifying double-skin, low-iron glazed facade over Kilkenny Blue limestone, and is surrounded by a landscaped public space.

Robin Lee Architecture

windows while emphasizing the new illuminated entrance, through which the church can also be accessed. The new wayfinding strategy of the aptly named church (everyone has a destiny) clarified the circulation routes through the church hall and its ancillary spaces. Stripped of signifiers, the project creates a neutral setting mediating between the church and the wider community. The scheme demonstrates the architect's ability to work on a minimal budget with maximum impact.

In 2011 Lee's practice, in association with executive architect Arthur Gibney & Partners, completed Wexford County Council's new 11,500-square-metre headquarters in Ireland, and the first council meeting was held there in July. Overlooking the Slaney Estuary, the building responds to the steep topography of the site. This is a project that was won in an international competition staged in 2006 by the Royal Institute of the Architects of Ireland, beating 100 entries. It marks out its civic presence with a unifying double-skin, low-iron glazed facade and an entrance area consisting of a stepped public space with landscaped gardens. Here the architect's unifying impulse has been used strategically to communicate the ideas of democracy, openness and status, with a piece of public realm at its heart, rather than a closed set of spaces with amenity but no sense of intimacy.

The building contains six departments, each housed in its own block, separated by transparent courtyards with pools of water and planting, which act as intermediaries between the enclosed spaces and the landscape beyond. The intention is to 'give identity to the collective endeavour of the council as a unified organization while giving individual expression to the separate departments and their unique activities', explains Lee.

Each block is accessed from a high-ceilinged 'street' with cantilevered concrete soffits. Cladding is of Kilkenny Blue limestone, a material often used in civic buildings in Ireland for its sense of solidity and dignity without stuffiness. The outer glazed skin protects the building on its exposed site but also regulates the interior temperature through the control of air around the building, cooling it in summer and creating an insulating layer in winter. The low-iron glass sits on anodized aluminium mullions, giving it a uniform, sheer appearance.

The large third-floor Council Chamber with its circular oak desk has an intimate character, and is reached by an oak stair. Its elevated position gives it a dramatic panorama of the river and town to the east, and the mountains on the Carlow and Wicklow borders to the north and west. Facilities on the second floor include the staff canteen, an important social space with broad refectory-style tables and room for informal meetings inside a pavilion-style structure filled with light, from which users can enjoy views of the river. There, too, bespoke acoustic panelling in oak ensures an intimate environment, while generously planted roof terraces to the south and north constitute spill-out space from the canteen for use in fine weather. Lee's clear organization of function, form and space, including individual meeting rooms on the fourth and fifth (top) floors for deciding policy, matches the ethos of Wexford County Council as an open and responsive organization, and gives it a distinct identity reflecting its democratic and civic purpose and status.

With his new practice located in London, after many years in Glasgow, Lee intends to maintain his longstanding connections with Scotland and Ireland. He plans to continue building architecture and spaces that are coherent as a family of projects, each one enduring and engaging in its language, not as instantly stimulating visual icons but for more sustained impact.

The beautifully crafted, tactile Wexford County Council Headquarters contains two public staircases in oak.

Interview with Robin Lee

Can you recount a few architectural memories from childhood?

From the age of seven until I left school at eighteen, I attended drawing and painting classes in the Mackintosh building at Glasgow School of Art, so that particular building is linked with my memory of childhood. I loved the darkness of the corridors and the dark timbers. There is virtually no colour in the building, which I recall, as a child, being a strange and powerful thing.

How would you describe your architectural background?

I studied architecture and then sculpture. I think this background informed my approach to making buildings. When I studied sculpture I learned to focus on one material at a time, so, although the approach was ideas-based, there was always an underlying need to understand the material and the craft of how materials are processed and put together.

What are your greatest influences, architectural or otherwise?

Mies van der Rohe would be a clear influence on a project like Wexford County Council Headquarters. His work is often used as a shorthand for a kind of openness in architecture. This is interesting, of course, but it's the sculptural qualities of his work that constantly fascinate us, along with its qualities of weight and density, particularly in his final building, the powerfully tectonic Neue Nationalgalerie in Berlin.

Give one example of the way in which your architecture communicates effectively with people.

We are interested in architecture that exists as a backdrop to people and their activities. There is enough information in the world without the need for architecture to be another foreground.

Are you a maker or a thinker?

To make the kind of architecture we're interested in, we don't believe one activity can happen without the support of the other; it's a reciprocal process. Certainly the early stages of a project require the processing of ideas more intensely, but in architecture, compared to some forms of art practice, there is an inevitability

Destiny Church

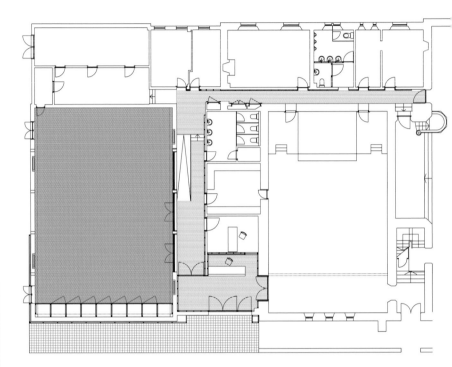

In refurbishing the 1970s extension to this Grade B-listed church in Glasgow, the architect gave the interiors an oak lining (opposite, top right) and wrapped the exterior in black cement cladding panels (opposite, top left), closing off all existing windows while illuminating the new entrance. The floor plan is above; the front elevation (right) shows the church and its refurbished extension.

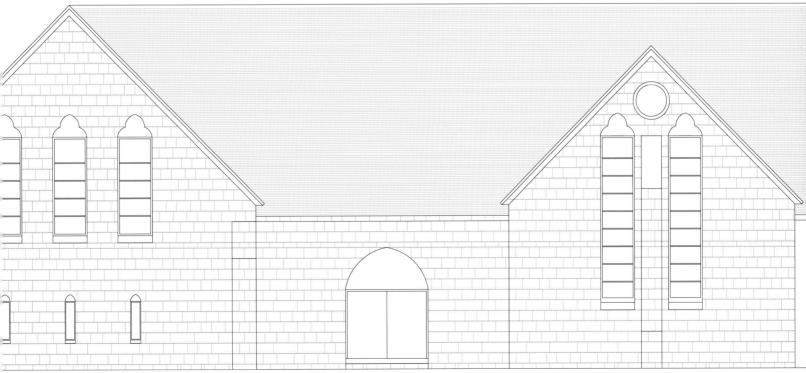

Robin Lee Architecture

that the ideas need to be channelled and communicated through physical built form and spaces.

Do you prefer bespoke or standardized?

When building at scale it's not possible to limit the process to bespoke elements or components. Repetition and standardization have economic and practical benefits in terms of the control of quality, and this is extremely important in making enduring buildings. Architecture is inextricably linked to construction processes, and our experience is that engagement with manufacturing and production companies can lead to very specific solutions using standard technology.

What theories lie behind your design methods and practice?

Theory implies a critical position that exists independently of the project or the place. We believe that design ideas should emerge from an understanding of places and uses, so different strategies apply to different projects. Each project is treated as a unique opportunity to create buildings and spaces that respond to the specific requirements of context. Context is certainly one of the things we're most interested in, and that interest drives our approach.

Do you strive to create new architectural typologies? If so, please give an example.

Sometimes it's appropriate to work with typologies that exist in a particular context; in other instances, the setting might suggest a more strongly autonomous approach. Wexford County Council Headquarters is an example of the latter: there, we made a building informed by many contextual ideas, but the resulting structure has an autonomous identity.

What are the most challenging aspects of your architectural practice today?

Working at a range of scales is challenging but also one of the most rewarding aspects of the practice.

What impact do you hope your architecture has on the public realm?

At Wexford County Council Headquarters we turned the building in on itself and placed the public realm at the heart of the building. The idea of internalizing and enveloping the public realm allowed a space to be created of a scale appropriate

Bell House

This extension to a brick bungalow between Strathblane and Milton of Campsie has uninterrupted views of the Campsie Hills. The upper level is a full storey and a half in height, with two large gable walls and large areas of glazing. It has the technical innovations of a 'folded' window, wrapping from the roof to the hip and down to the lower level (right), and an apex roof light (opposite). The envelope is treated in a homogeneous manner, with all components pulled flush to its outer face to reinforce the notion of a uniform skin.

to its civic status but with a certain intimacy, allowing experience at an individual level.

What personal significance do you give to architectural precedent?

We give a great deal of consideration to precedent. We're interested in the history of architecture and established typologies, and in making work that extends or deviates from these existing patterns.

Which technical advances excite you the most for exploitation?

We're interested in established technology and the developments occurring in those areas. Pre-cast technology, for example, has a rich history in architecture and is being developed to guarantee a high degree of quality with effective cost. In our practice technical advances are useful to us; they do not drive the expression of the architecture but they allow us to make buildings that perform well.

Do you practise a transdisciplinary approach to architecture, and if so, what is especially important to you right now?

There needs to be a very strong focus when making buildings because there are so many demands on the architect to make spaces that work, and to make buildings that engage with their setting and perform technically. The potential for architecture to perform as social engineering, autonomous works of art, technological prototypes or philosophical manifestos is beyond the scope of what we believe is valid. It is inevitable, though, that the influence of these disciplines should directly or indirectly inform the way we think about architecture.

How do you go about generating the best possible relationship with your clients?

The best client/architect relationships we have had were when both parties had a shared commitment to a project and a shared aspiration. Without this being established at the beginning of a project, there will always be imbalance in the process.

Can you give an example of your participatory methods?

We designed a multipurpose hall for a local church that had a small community programme. The church organization was very effective in engaging with its own community and was

Wexford County Council Headquarters

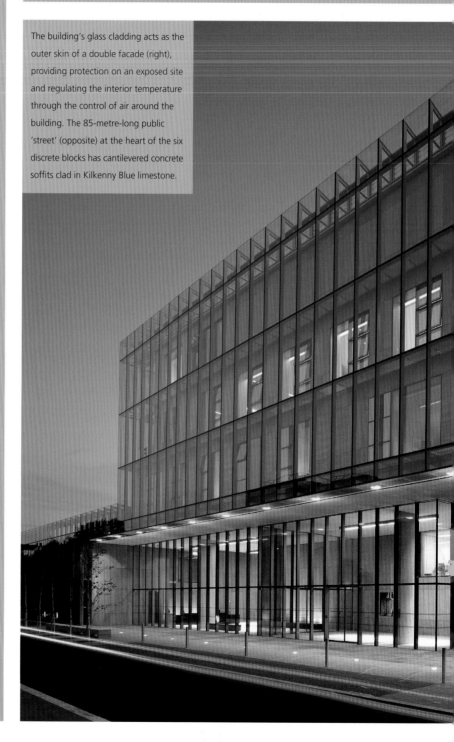

The building's glass cladding acts as the outer skin of a double facade (right), providing protection on an exposed site and regulating the interior temperature through the control of air around the building. The 85-metre-long public 'street' (opposite) at the heart of the six discrete blocks has cantilevered concrete soffits clad in Kilkenny Blue limestone.

Robin Lee Architecture

interested in broadening this appeal through communication. Through discussion we encouraged the church to consider the building project as an opportunity to communicate at a number of levels and to a broader audience. It was clear that the image of the building was the key to creating a neutral setting, a meeting ground, that mediated between the church and the wider community. This resulted in a building stripped of colour and elemental in form. Devoid of signifiers, the building was open to all groups and the sense of ownership was shared.

How do you communicate your architecture?

Architecture is very much about the experience of space and the physical presence of built form in a setting, so communicating it is difficult. But we experience the world through images more than ever before, so we can't escape the fact that our experiences are increasingly mediated. At Robin Lee Architecture we understand the need to make architecture that can be assimilated clearly and directly, but we are generally interested in architecture that is enduring and engaging in a more sustained way.

What do you aim to achieve with your practice (in a single sentence)?

To make buildings and spaces that can be understood as a coherent body of work.

What advice would you give to a young architect embarking on their career?

I think that, for an architect, the period between college and being established is a critical time to make important decisions about your own individual position. It is important to understand that there are skills that need to be acquired in order to practise but not to lose sight of the opportunity to make work that has intellectual or creative rigour.

What single improvement to the procurement of architecture in the United Kingdom would you recommend? More competitions, different planning system, legislation affecting developers, etc.?

A more open and expansive competition system to increase design quality and encourage ambition.

Wexford County Council Headquarters

The central public spaces are punctuated with planted courtyards. These bring light to the deeper parts of the building and connect the interior with the surroundings, endowing the building with a strong sense of place.

Robin Lee Architecture

Serie

In the short time since they co-founded Serie in London, Mumbai and Beijing in 2006, Christopher C.M. Lee and Kapil Gupta have built up a unique reputation for their critically profound and relevant approach to architecture as a language that enriches cultural contexts. The three offices are currently advancing a diverse range of projects, from residential and commercial buildings to hotels, schools and masterplans – each one a revelation in its lightness of touch and response to its surroundings.

Serie's lucid mix of poetry and prose certainly gained impetus from Lee's eight years of academic involvement as Unit Master at the Architectural Association in London. The partners' teaching (Gupta as a guest lecturer there), writing and design mean that – in common with that of many of the other architects in this book – Serie's work is constantly being examined and discussed. Being based on two continents – Lee in London, Gupta in Mumbai – the duo communicate virtually much of the time, but meet to discuss and work together as much as they can.

Serie (so named because it works in series) analyses precedents not in isolation but in their urban and historical context, inventing new types as a conscious, ongoing process. 'The first project informs even the most recent ones', says Lee, and there are a lot of intriguing ideas to be gleaned from the practice's mutually engaged nature. Its work transcends not just scale and use, but also programme, context and geographic challenges, as its first built works, in the United States and in India, on site in Slovakia, and soon in China, attest. Through these means and over time, Serie can evolve fresh readings that it can connect back to the body of work. The consistency in this process further accrues through its focus on the development of three 'deep structures' it has identified: plans/circles, ceilings/vaults and facades/grids.

Lee and Gupta firmly believe that architectural meaning can be derived only from convention and tradition. Building typologies are usually independent of function, and can possess cultural relevance only if related to the wider urban context in which architecture has a role. It is their organizational potential that gives them power, gaining meaningful embodiment through Serie's 'deep structures' of type.

The deep structure used by Serie for the Blue Frog Acoustic Lounge in Mumbai (2008), a recording studio, restaurant, bar, lounge and performance stage in an old industrial warehouse, is a rhythmic cellular environment, with a variety of circles like horseshoes in plan, within an undulating surface of acrylic resin. Punctuated by cylindrical mahogany seating booths for up to ten diners, the space is arranged in one big horseshoe shape around an open centre, so that, whether seated or standing, the audience has sight lines at varying heights. This central point can function either as a stage or as space for onlookers standing up, gathered close to the action. The multiple programmes of Blue Frog retain their individuality and quality within a visually stimulating and resonant, rather than repetitive, formal whole.

The dynamic variegation of nature comes to the fore at the Tote (2009), a set of disused colonial buildings at the Mumbai Racecourse converted into a banqueting hall, restaurant and wine bar. Needing to conserve the roof structure, Serie evolved its design inspired by the large leaves of the rain trees on the site, creating a continuously differentiated space with a set of arches and vaulted ceiling. The Tote's deep structure, a variegated branching construction, defines the space and holds up the roof in such a way that the wine bar, bar/lounge (as immersive as the other spaces, yet the darkest of all), restaurant and light, foliaged banqueting hall each have a spatial volume of a markedly different character. In order to imitate nature's patterning logic, the accuracy of the welding of the steel branches, in total more than 7 kilometres long, was of great concern to Serie, and the welders made many mock-ups to find a way to control the final forms of the trusses.

A single undulating 'carpet' of one million four-coloured light threads becomes a mesmerizing suspended ceiling at the otherwise

One million four-coloured threads are arranged in an otherwise white space to create a suspended ceiling inspired by the traditional dhurrie or heavy Indian rug. It holds all the technical equipment for Serie's Monsoon Club in Washington D.C. (2011).

totally white Monsoon Club at the Kennedy Center, Washington D.C. (2011). Borrowed from the traditional dhurrie or heavy Indian rug, it looks a bit like an unfolding loom across the ceiling of the room. Serie converted the club into a live music venue and gallery for the Maximum India Festival in such a way that the bold carpet as a defining element is wholly compatible with the various activities taking place.

The year 2011 saw the start of many projects, including Serie's Bohacky-Zahorska Bystrica residential masterplan in Bratislava, Slovakia (begun in 2009), which went on site. In order to achieve a sense of privacy within this development of villas, Serie conceived the site as a forest, with the buildings set in clearings. Instead of hard, impermeable boundaries, an undulating web of hedges and manicured trees demarcates each plot in a soft, natural way. Not only is this a more cost-effective solution, but also the timber for the guide fence is local and can be recycled.

The villas are high-end. So often such a motivation results in a chaotic gaggle of novelty houses seemingly taken from a reproduction-style catalogue without any connection to innovative architecture. To achieve that quality of diversity hand-in-hand with coherence across the masterplan – an approach from which all cultural contexts can benefit – Serie developed a courtyard house as a semi-outdoor room set in the outdoor room of its individual naturally enclosed plot. Circular courtyards facilitate circulation, spiralling into rooms like fingers with ample outdoor views and framing the plot's open spaces. This allows for villas of varying sizes and permutations, all sharing a typological grammar.

The conversion and design of XianTian Di Factory H, one of four for a new urban core north-east of Hangzhou, China (2010–), has employed the same deep structure as that for Blue Frog, with a mat building with a layered, differentiated ground rethought on the lines of a plinth structure. Instead of filling the hall, facilities are positioned within the surrounding plinth, the top surface of which undulates and is punctured by green patios and pools of water. This enables the central, 16-metre-high volume, given a newly glazed lantern and restored concrete truss structure, to retain its spatial drama.

In 2010 Serie won second prize in the competition for the Xi'an International Horticultural Expo masterplan on the periphery of the city, ceding first prize to GroundLab (see pp. 198–209). With its Five Climates Crossing proposal, Serie challenged the idea of architecture looking like landscape and also the notion that the city is antithetical to landscape and nature. Instead, the historic city walls were the starting point as relevant elements for a horticultural exposition park. Unfolded to a clear and legible structure 1 kilometre long, geometrically pure and made up of five greenhouses each with its own climate, and with parabolic vaults, the walls complement nature. Meanwhile, for the Yan Zhenqing Calligraphy Museum in Linyi, China, Serie also created a structure with a bold identity within its landscape, not merging into it but set on a series of terraces reminiscent of a traditional Chinese scholars' garden.

Driven by a strong commitment to the transformative powers of architecture through a deep engagement with serialism as an instrumental cultural force as well as an ethical, locality-based construction logic, Serie strives to work with clients who are committed to their projects. The agenda of a serial dialogue set in motion globally by the practice's inventive architecture – delicate yet robust, culturally grounded yet globally networked – is too important as an active societal practice for anything less.

In the Tote, Mumbai (2009), tree-column structures of mild steel plate finished with coats of epoxy paint branch upwards to meet the punctured ceiling plane of patterned gypsum board.

Interview with Christopher C.M. Lee

Can you recount a few architectural memories from childhood?

I grew up in a tiny village in Malaysia with only one-storey houses, and I remember trying obsessively to draw the staircase of a house from different views and getting annoyed that it wasn't looking quite right. I was probably five or six years old then.

How would you describe your architectural background?

The Architectural Association (AA) in London is our spiritual home. Kapil Gupta, my co-founding principal of Serie, and I studied in the same unit at the AA, and I continue to teach there, first as Unit Master for Diploma Unit 6 and now leading the Projective Cities MPhil course. My associates Bolam Lee and Martin Jameson, and my Beijing director, Stephie Qin Sun, were all students of mine. Martin also now teaches at the AA.

What are your greatest influences, architectural or otherwise?

Works and writing by other architects. In his writings, Aldo Rossi shows us the importance of the city and its history, and that to be meaningful, architecture must contribute to the idea of the city. In their architecture, Kazuyo Sejima and Ryue Nishizawa of SANAA show us the poetry of organizational intelligence and formal restraint.

Give one example of the way in which your architecture communicates effectively with people.

Serie works typologically. We begin with precedents and project their intelligence and delight into new or different architectural solutions. For instance, with Blue Frog [in Mumbai], we have been told people not only appreciate the beauty of the project but also understand its organizational conceit – that we have embedded a restaurant into a theatre plan and linked the two organizations stylistically with an undulating, lit surface. This reminds me of the archaeologist and theorist Quatremère de Quincy's account of how we recognize beauty: partly with the eye and partly with the mind.

Are you a maker or a thinker?

It has to be both in this field of ours.

Monsoon Club
Washington D.C. I 2011

The club was created from the converted Terrace Gallery for the duration of the Maximum India Festival, and hosted art and live performance events.

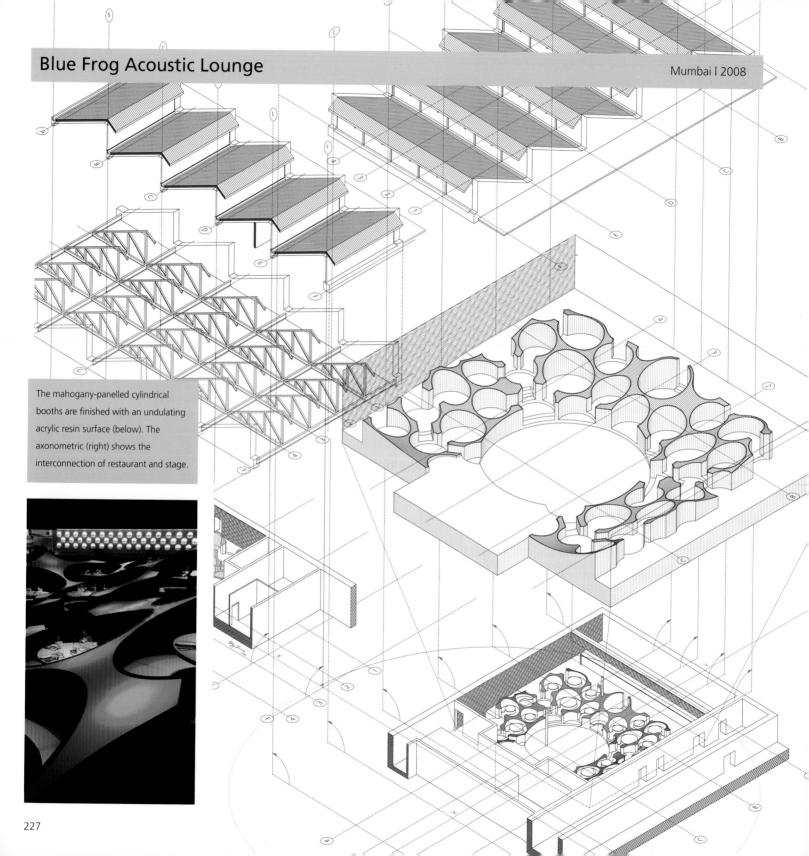

The mahogany-panelled cylindrical booths are finished with an undulating acrylic resin surface (below). The axonometric (right) shows the interconnection of restaurant and stage.

Do you prefer bespoke or standardized?

Both united: bespoke standard.

What theories lie behind your design methods and practice?

Our interest lies in the potential offered by dominant types and the ideas of the city. The word 'dominant' means ruling, governing or having an influence over something; it also means 'prevailing'. Thus, for a 'type' to be dominant, it has to prevail. The prevailing is also the most typical, and what is most typical is also common to all. And no sphere is more common to all than the city. Thus, a 'dominant type' can be understood as the typical element that constitutes the city and is the embodiment of the common. Our architecture tends to rethink notions of the city as a place that accommodates multiple and often conflicting demands, and it is governed by the deep structures of the dominant types. I have written about this at length in *Working in Series* (2010) as well as in 'Typological Urbanism' (*Architectural Digest*, January 2011).

Do you strive to create new architectural typologies? If so, please give an example.

Our work is deeply embedded in the history of architecture and the city. We are not interested in novelty for the sake of it. Thus we treat so-called new architecture with great suspicion. To work typologically is to draw on past solutions that have been tempered by history and convention. These lessons and solutions should not be seen as further formal variations or the re-creation of the image of the past, but rather as guiding principles that rule over the precedents: a shared and accepted principle that will produce an architecture common and, we hope, of interest and value to all.

What are the most challenging aspects of your architectural practice today?

We have grown from three people to thirty in the short span of two years, with offices in London, Mumbai and Beijing. The challenge I see now is to realize our larger projects the way we want them to be, as the construction industry in China and India is very different to that in the United Kingdom.

What impact do you hope your architecture has on the public realm?

We hope our architecture will turn out to be one that is generous to the city and that speaks the common language of the context in which it sits, making it truly public.

Bohacky-Zahorska Bystrica

Bratislava | 2009–

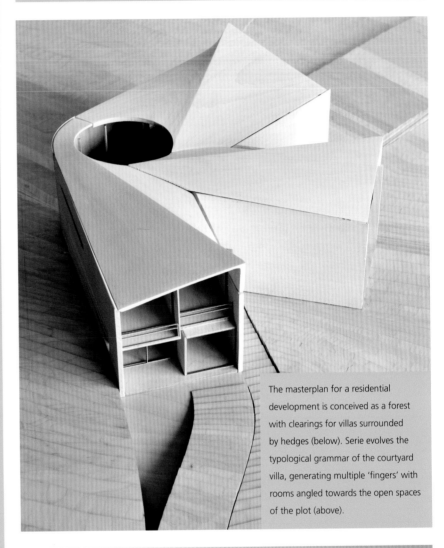

The masterplan for a residential development is conceived as a forest with clearings for villas surrounded by hedges (below). Serie evolves the typological grammar of the courtyard villa, generating multiple 'fingers' with rooms angled towards the open spaces of the plot (above).

new arcadians

The Tote is the conversion of disused buildings on the Mumbai Racecourse into a banqueting hall, restaurant and bar. From the immersive bar/lounge space (left) clad in plywood on an articulated frame, to the airy articulated arches introduced into the banqueting hall (far left and above), its spaces are differentiated yet interconnected.

What personal significance do you give to architectural precedent?

It is the very essence of doing architecture. As architect and academic Alan Colquhoun said, 'The object of architectural knowledge is architecture itself, as it has been historically constituted. It does not consist of abstract functions but of concrete forms.'

Which technical advances excite you the most for exploitation?

I always approach 'new' technology with much scepticism.

Do you practise a transdisciplinary approach to architecture, and if so, what is especially important to you right now?

What the idea of the city will be in the next ten years.

How do you go about generating the best possible relationship with your clients?

We work with our clients and other consultants as equals. We have been blessed that they have all been consistently excited about the work we bring to the table.

Can you give an example of your participatory methods?

Listen. Listen. Listen.

How do you communicate your architecture?

Rationally, with beauty and dignity.

What do you aim to achieve with your practice (in a single sentence)?

To maintain that architecture is first and foremost a cultural discourse that must involve the wider milieu in which it is produced; it is not pop-arch or techno-utopian.

What advice would you give to a young architect embarking on their career?

Don't be too arrogant to look to history for lessons and to the everyday for inspiration.

What single improvement to the procurement of architecture in the United Kingdom would you recommend? More competitions, different planning system, legislation affecting developers, etc.?

Don't shut out young architects by insisting on built work.

XianTian Di Factory H

Hangzhou, China I 2010–

Renders show the converted factory, which, with three others, will generate a new urban core. Serie is restoring the concrete-truss roof structure and other original elements, and adding a glazed lantern, maintaining the spatial quality of the huge interiors. Restaurants, bars, offices and shops will be on a punctuated, undulating plinth.

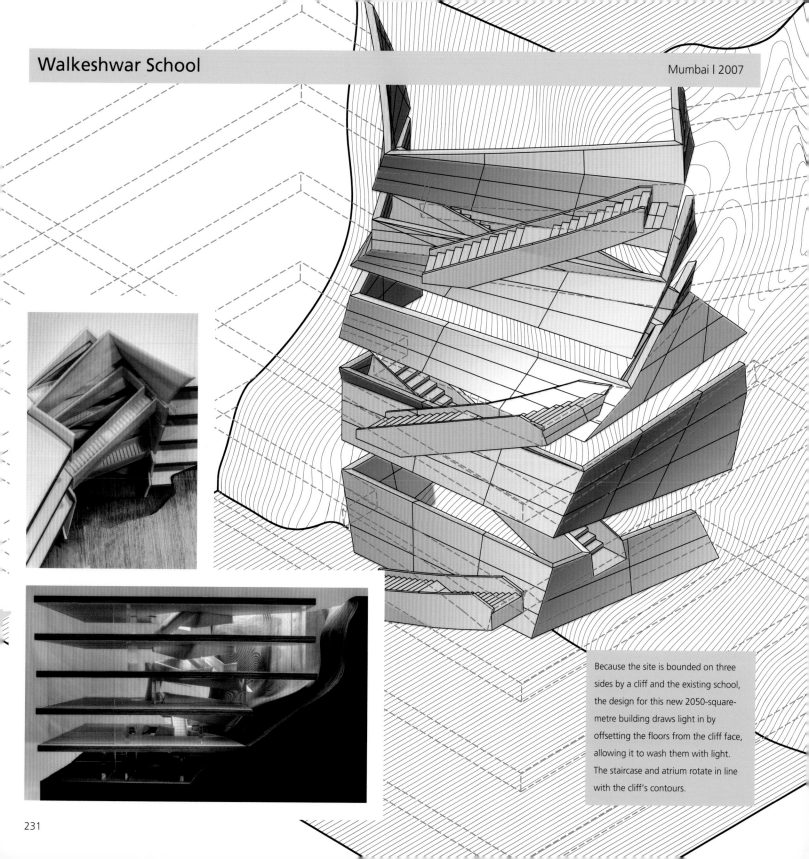

Because the site is bounded on three sides by a cliff and the existing school, the design for this new 2050-square-metre building draws light in by offsetting the floors from the cliff face, allowing it to wash them with light. The staircase and atrium rotate in line with the cliff's contours.

231

Studio Weave

Studio Weave 'creates places through playing into and exploring their hidden stories'. The practice's projects evolve out of the unique aspects of a place and through its physical and geographical qualities, its uses past and present, and even its myths and legends. Co-founders Je Ahn and Maria Smith are remarkable agents for creative change: they reveal hidden gestures and evolve engaging micro-structures for public spaces. Among their many strong points are great imagination, energy, a capacity for fresh solutions in the most diverse contexts, and the ability to mobilize participation in many different ways.

They also use stories to articulate design proposals and serve as an agent for change: for example, for the Longest Bench, their public furniture on the seaside at Littlehampton, West Sussex. Occasionally they devise fictional character roles for their structures, for example Freya and Robin at Kielder Water in Northumberland.

The first phase of the Longest Bench opened on 30 July 2010. This sinuous structure travels from the harbour down the promenade at Littlehampton, overlooking the Blue Flag beach and giving definition to the promenade by connecting a series of locations, manoeuvring around lamp posts and bins. To make the structure – which has room for 300 people to sit, side by side – the architect reclaimed thousands of hardwood bars from old groynes and arrayed them so that the motley timbers are interspersed with brightly coloured ones positioned at the dips, bends and curves of the bench. Local primary-school children showed how they use the promenade, and told the architect what they thought of it. In response, Studio Weave replaced two old shelters with new Shelter Charms, where the bench loops inside two bronze-finished monocoques, creating seats and openings, and framing views. The nearby East Beach Cafe, designed by Thomas Heatherwick, is a third Charm in this unfolding series of playful spaces. Now the Longest Bench is engraved with hundreds of messages from supporters.

The modular elements of the installation 140 Boomerangs, for the London Architecture Biennale in 2006, were made with the help of 140 local primary-school children during the course of nine workshops. A version designed as more free-form play furniture was installed at Queen Street in the City of London (left) and in the playgrounds of three local schools.

Shelters for walkers and cyclists in rural places are rarely more than utilitarian, but Freya and Robin, structures on the scenic, forested banks of Kielder Water, are instead visible markers and destinations. 'We like to think of the area as a stage set or backdrop against which we can tell a story,' the architects explain. 'Made' by two fictional characters, one simple wooden cabin is clad in timber shingles, the other in interwoven branches and pressed flowers.

No other architect has designed a space for the annual Glastonbury festival, a music event set in a field in south-west England and beloved by its fans. Studio Weave's Graviton in the HUB (Hot Utopian Bliss) Space of Shangri-La, the festival within the 2010 festival, was a series of trapezoid platforms of diminishing size made of charred, reclaimed scaffolding boards. Emitting light and smoke, it evoked the embers of a building, and made the pyramidal dance platform seem to disappear amid the dancing.

An earlier foray into London's public spaces, 140 Boomerangs in Clerkenwell, for the 2006 London Architecture Biennale, was made with the help of 140 local primary-school children. The helical timber structure wrapping the 'Peace' fountain in West Smithfield had modular elements that could be reassembled in different permutations. The children made clay sculptures based on fictional characters to go inside, 'to play on and intensify the site as an urban retreat' and place of fantasy for visitors.

Invited by the Royal Hospital for Sick Children in Edinburgh to propose a design for its new site, Studio Weave experimented with ways to invent imaginary urban worlds collectively, conceiving structures for play. These could be closed or opened out into the playroom and ward or even beyond, and customized with projection, video mapping and interactive media.

New interventions in the City of London bring further psycho-spatial narratives in a mixed historic context. For an invited competition staged by Street Scene, City of London Corporation, for the churchyard of the late eleventh-century church of St Pancras Soper Lane, which was destroyed in the Great Fire of 1666 and never rebuilt, Studio Weave proposed an overgrown woodland space. This outdoor room has an irregular herringbone floor, ornate pew-like furniture and diamond-shaped beds of shrubs. Meanwhile the highwalks of Chamberlin, Powell & Bon's Barbican Estate (1982), spaces that need improving, are being given repairs and bespoke tubular benches and metal planters.

In Blackburn, Lancashire, a neglected public space is due to become a landscaped garden, framing views of landmarks with new follies. Inspired by the eighteenth-century Claude glasses used by artists and tourists to capture picturesque views, Studio Weave worked with a book illustrator to develop contemporary equivalents.

The practice's list of collaborators is extensive, but the architects themselves are ingenious in their materials and methods: the resilience of vitreous enamel features in the Longest Bench, while the structural properties of LVL (laminated veneer lumber) are exploited to realize the 140 Boomerangs helix. While galvanizing children and the rest of the public in its enlivening endeavours, Studio Weave has built up a formal client list that includes local authorities; regeneration teams; art, architecture and music festivals and foundations; residents' boards, working parties and campaign groups; and schools, hospitals, charities, teachers and play specialists. With an arsenal of inventive stories and design ideas, the practice reaches intuitively for one of architecture's democratic goals: 'shared ownership'.

The project Freya and Robin, on Kielder Water in Northumberland (2009), embraced the man-made nature of the lake and forest, which is home to more than twenty art and architecture installations by James Turrell, David Adjaye, Tania Kovats, Charles Barclay and others. The two small structures, on opposite sides of the water along the Lakeside Way, are designed as marker points for walkers and cyclists. Made of plywood with a perforated, highly reflective copper–aluminium alloy cladding, Freya's Cabin (right) responds to its extraordinary rural setting, balancing on stems set in concrete foundations and carved internally to resemble a forest.

235

Interview with Je Ahn and Maria Smith

Can you recount a few architectural memories from childhood?

JA My most vivid architectural memory from childhood must be looking at the blueprints for our new house. I grew up in South Korea, where it's considered a significant measure of success to have your own house built, and I was incredibly proud, as well as pleased, to have my own bedroom.

MS I was born to a Polish mother in Edinburgh, and one of my earliest memories is of trying to explain to my Scottish playgroup classmates, in Polish, how to build their blocks in overlapping layers (stretcher bond!) so they wouldn't fall down. Later, when I was about eight, I wrote to Jimmy Savile, the presenter of the TV programme *Jim'll Fix It*, and asked him to make me an architect. Oh dear!

How would you describe your architectural background?

Neither of us has architects in our family or among our family's friends, so we both came to the subject with little prior exposure or baggage. We studied at three different universities (University of Bath, Delft University of Technology in The Netherlands and London Metropolitan University), each with a very different ethos, and we hope these experiences have made us very open-minded as architects.

What are your greatest influences, architectural or otherwise?

We make a concerted effort to allow ourselves to be inspired by absolutely anything. We try to look at things in context and see them for what they are, rather than being clouded by absolute standards or fashions dressed up as absolute standards. We try to be flexible as to what we might like and be influenced by.

Give one example of the way in which your architecture communicates effectively with people.

We aim to make our projects meaty, with enough room for interpretation and happy misunderstanding, like the English language. For most of our projects, effective communication isn't about getting across a truth, but about building relationships

Graviton
Glastonbury, Somerset | 2010

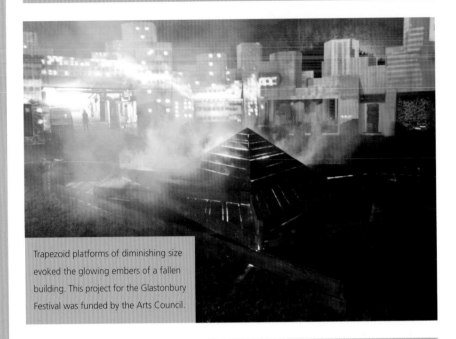

Trapezoid platforms of diminishing size evoked the glowing embers of a fallen building. This project for the Glastonbury Festival was funded by the Arts Council.

St Pancras Churchyard
Soper Lane, City of London | 2010–

Studio Weave's design respects the heritage of the location while opening it up for public enjoyment.

In summer 2011 a rare pop-up cinema was seen floating through the five Olympic host boroughs, conceived by Studio Weave with Somewhere artists Nina Pope and Karen Guthrie. Funded by the Arts Council and commissioned by the Olympic Delivery Authority, the customized narrowboat screened films on the move and moored at various locations for larger-scale screenings and events relating to waterways, including a reading by author Iain Sinclair and a DJ set by Saint Etienne. The conversion involved an array of fabricators and local craftspeople, and included a patterned, quilted canopy ('the Puff'), flip-up seats, upholstery cushions and a smocked blackout screen.

between people and other people, between people and things, or even between things and other things.

Are you a maker or a thinker?
Both. Good architects need to be a healthy balance of both, and a good practice needs to strive for an even finer balance across the team.

Do you prefer bespoke or standardized?
It's a matter of scale and situation. It's important to us to be very aware of the difference between tailoring something to suit and needlessly reinventing the wheel. We love finding bespoke, off-label uses for standardized products or processes.

What theories lie behind your design methods and practice?
We value playful, divergent thinking and a good sense of humour. We believe that play is important and functional, not merely an idle distraction, and we aim to use it throughout our work to allow the development of new ideas and solutions, and to generate good design.

Do you strive to create new architectural typologies? If so, please give an example.
This is not a goal of ours in and of itself, and we feel it's dangerous to consider this newness as a measure of success. We do strive to create something that is particular – and sometimes peculiar – to its site, situation and inhabitants. We like things to be the best possible versions of themselves, rather than poor emulations of an abstract ideal.

What are the most challenging aspects of your architectural practice today?
The roles and responsibilities of architects are currently in flux; however, we sense a lingering hierarchy of respect for different aspects of the role, which creates a lot of tension and resistance to adaptation. Such skills as entrepreneurship or management, for example, are often seen as the dirty, impolite side of practice, but they are becoming more and more important. The result seems to be a bizarrely archaic 'never talk money at the dinner table' etiquette that isn't helping the industry.

London's Largest Living Room London | 2008

Fashion designer Eley Kishimoto's outsized silkscreened furniture has a cartoon-like character. It was first staged in the courtyard of Somerset House as part of London's Largest Living Room, produced by Design for London and the London Festival of Architecture. The intention was to encourage the public to think of the city as their home and to use neglected open space. The birch plywood pieces were cut out quickly and accurately using computer numerical control (CNC) technology.

Made of hardwood bars reclaimed from old seaside groynes, the bench adapts its angle to accommodate various activities and such street furniture as lamp posts and bins. The bars at the 'wriggle', 'bend' and 'dip' points are painted in bright colours. Studio Weave worked with the children of Connaught Junior School (now River Beach Primary School), who gave insights about the site and its significance.

Studio Weave

What impact do you hope your architecture has on the public realm?

So far, almost all our projects are entirely publicly accessible, so they offer their whole selves to the public realm. As these kinds of project aren't designed for a specific group of people, or even a very specific function, the key to their success is in creating an offering that, despite its broad brief, feels particular and unique and capable of inviting strangers to fall in love with it.

What personal significance do you give to architectural precedent?

Architectural precedents are incredibly important, but can be a double-edged sword. We believe it's important to avoid the traps of attempting to emulate success by copying physical attributes out of context, and of over-emphasizing the sometimes dogmatic views of the architectural community.

Which technical advances excite you the most for exploitation?

In terms of our approach to materials, we have a lot to learn from other industries, and there are many advances, as well as established practices, that we could benefit from. In terms of the profession more broadly, 'Web 2.0' and its successors have had and will continue to have a huge impact on how we communicate, and thereby on everything else.

Do you practise a transdisciplinary approach to architecture, and if so, what is especially important to you right now?

Architecture is by its very nature a transdisciplinary enterprise, and we strongly believe that successful projects are realized only by finding others with different skill sets from your own and offering them trust and enough autonomy to allow them an effective and personal relationship with the project.

How do you go about generating the best possible relationship with your clients?

We aim to create an open, comfortable and informal conversation with our clients. Our approach is often quite playful, and while we don't belittle important issues, we try to keep things as friendly and unpretentious as possible.

Holm Hall

Dartford, Kent | 2010–

This folly for the island in Dartford's Central Park, commissioned by Artlands (North Kent), was given a fictional history encapsulating the town's past, revealing the layers of change. The timber skeleton expresses in hybridized form the inspiration behind each design iteration, from a humble tree house to a medieval hall house to the decorative structures of Victorian artisans.

140 Boomerangs

This installation exploited the structural properties of laminated veneer lumber (LVL), which is used mainly for long-span beams. The modular boomerang elements could be assembled in various permutations. Children's workshops encouraged the perception of the site as a place of play and retreat, where stories could be conceived about the 'Peace' fountain around which it was wrapped.

Studio Weave

Can you give an example of your participatory methods?

We strongly believe that the purpose of participation is not to ask for a solution, but to understand properly the nature of a situation or problem. With this in mind, our approach to participation is often quite analytical, as a way to get to the essence of a situation. We especially enjoy working with children, and have invented lots of workshops and games.

How do you communicate your architecture?

We try to put things into a meaningful context, to communicate not only the proposal but also something about how it can be evaluated. Every project is some kind of transformation, and we like to present the logic of the change in an engaging way. We often employ explicit stories that serve as analogies and offer an antidote to the very abstract and formal nature of most architectural tools.

What do you aim to achieve with your practice (in a single sentence)?

We aim to design playfully (as distinct from designing for play) and so be ambassadors for that magical quality of a great story within the built environment.

What advice would you give to a young architect embarking on their career?

Architectural education is currently in a very difficult position because there's a very big generation gap between the students and many of their teachers. We believe young architects and architects-in-training need to broaden the education offered them by architecture school and try to see it (and the profession in general) in a wider context.

What single improvement to the procurement of architecture in the United Kingdom would you recommend? More competitions, different planning system, legislation affecting developers, etc.?

We think a cultural change is needed to repair the eroded trust and respect between different players in the built environment. We suspect that legislation can't achieve this, and indeed that the bottom lines offered by regulation and guidance often lower standards.

Freya and Robin

Freya's Cabin, made of layers of CNC-cut plywood glued and held together with tension rods, with acrylic sheets in between, is clad in copper–aluminium alloy sheets perforated in a tear pattern, moving in the wind. Conceived as part of a fictional love story, with the sheets representing Freya's golden tears, it faces Robin's Cabin across the water.

Studio Weave

Biographies

6a Architects

6a Architects was founded by Tom Emerson and Stephanie Macdonald in 2001 after they met at the Royal College of Art in London. Emerson studied Architecture at the University of Bath, the Royal College of Art and the University of Cambridge, and is now Professor of Architecture at ETH Zurich, having previously taught at the Architectural Association (AA) in London and at the University of Cambridge from 2000 to 2010. He has published many articles on architecture, literature and art. Macdonald studied Fine Art at Portsmouth College of Art, and architecture at the Mackintosh School of Architecture, the Royal College of Art and the University of North London. She leads 6a's residency at the Institute of Contemporary Arts (ICA), London, and has lectured at several schools of architecture in the United Kingdom. Takeshi Hayatsu, 6a's Associate, studied architecture at the AA, and was project architect for Raven Row and the South London Gallery. He previously worked for David Chipperfield Architects and Haworth Tompkins, and has experience of working on listed buildings and high-profile arts projects.

The practice has developed a focus on contemporary arts projects, and on working in sensitive landscapes and historic environments. It completed Raven Row, a centre for contemporary art in Spitalfields, east London, in 2009 and an extension to the South London Gallery in 2010. Three major competition wins in recent years have been for a new sustainable country house and park in Cambridgeshire; the redevelopment of Offley Works, a large industrial complex in Kennington, south London, for the London Development Agency; and a new halls of residence for Churchill College, Cambridge. 6a is currently redesigning Gallery 40 for the Victoria and Albert Museum, and the Romney Studio in Hampstead (both listed buildings in London), as well as undertaking new houses in north London and a photographer's studio and archive. The practice won a Royal Institute of British Architects' Award and a New London Award (2011), was nominated twice for a Mies van der Rohe Award (2010), was a finalist in the Design Museum/Brit Insurance Designs of the Year award (2010) and won an *Architects' Journal* Corus 40 Under 40 award in 2005.
6a.co.uk

AOC

AOC is a practice of architects and urbanists established in 2003 by Tom Coward, Daisy Froud, Vincent Lacovara and Geoff Shearcroft. Tom Coward and Geoff Shearcroft studied architecture at the University of Nottingham and the Royal College of Art, London; Daisy Froud, French and Italian at the University of Cambridge, and then a Master's degree in Cultural Memory at the University of London; and Vincent Lacovara studied architecture at the University of Cambridge and the Royal College of Art. Early projects include a rural retreat for Stephen Daldry, Folly for a Film-Maker, Hertfordshire (2004), and House for a Philosopher for Alain de Botton (2006). A series of competition wins gave AOC prominence, including one for the Lift – A New Parliament (2008; touring from 2009), a demountable performance space for 200 people built in different locations in London, including Newham, Lambeth, Hackney and Barking. AOC has since redeveloped the Street for the Royal Armouries museum in Leeds (2008), and has built the Janet Summers Early Years Centre (2006) and Charles Dickens Primary School (2006–10), both in Southwark, London; Stowmarket High School, Suffolk; and private residences including Chatley Lodge, Somerset (2009), and Hearth House, London (2009). In 2007 AOC's exhibition pavilion, No. 1 Lower Carbon Drive, for the London Development Agency and the Building Centre, was realized in Trafalgar Square, and the interactive exhibit Polyopoly showed at the Venice International Architecture Biennale in 2008.

The Rodney Road mixed-use urban block at Elephant & Castle in south London was completed for Wandle Housing Association in 2010, while the nearby Crown Terrace courtyard housing, for the same client, has been in design development since 2008. Wooddene Estate, a mixed-use masterplan for 400 homes on the Peckham Estate for the London Borough of Southwark, was a competition win in 2006, as was Birnbeck Island hotel and public park at Weston-super-Mare in Somerset for Urban Splash (second prize; 2008). Building Futures, the Royal Institute of British

Architects and the Commission for Architecture and the Built Environment also commissioned AOC to design an urban regeneration game.

In 2011 AOC completed a new teaching block for secondary pupils with autistic-spectrum disorders at the Spa School, Bermondsey, as part of the London Borough of Southwark's Building Schools for the Future phase 2. The practice won an *Architects' Journal* Corus 40 Under 40 award in 2005 and was shortlisted in the *Building Design* Young Architect of the Year Award 2008. The partners, who lecture regularly in the United Kingdom and Europe and contribute to television, radio and live public debates, have taught at many leading schools of architecture and were the Louis I. Kahn Visiting Assistant Professors at the University of Yale in 2011.
theaoc.co.uk

Carmody Groarke

Kevin Carmody and Andrew Groarke set up Carmody Groarke in London in 2006. Carmody was educated at the Royal Melbourne Institute of Technology and the University of Canberra, and Groarke at the University of Sheffield before working for Haworth Tompkins. Both have worked for a number of internationally recognized architects, including David Chipperfield Architects. Since 2011 both have taught in the Department of Architecture at the Royal College of Art, London.

Carmody and Groarke decided to set up on their own after winning a competition staged by the Van Alen Institute to design the Coney Island Parachute Pavilion in New York; the previous year they had won the Burnham Award for a river transit system in Chicago. Within a few years the practice was winning further competitions, and in 2007 it won one to design the Sheffield Festival Centre, which will be the first of the practice's permanent buildings in the United Kingdom.

A commission for Portland Spa (2008), a 450-square-metre suite for exercise and relaxation beneath a house in Limerick, on the west coast of Ireland, was followed by a commission for the Fondazione Prada and the artist Carsten Höller on the hybrid space of the Double Club in Islington, London (2008, for three months).

In 2009 Carmody Groarke's 7 July Memorial was unveiled in Hyde Park, London, a permanent installation commissioned by the Royal Parks and the Department for Culture, Media and Sport to honour the fifty-two victims of the four terrorist bombings in London on 7 July 2005. It was realized in collaboration with the structural engineer Arup, graphic designer Phil Baines and landscape architect Colvin & Moggridge.

Carmody Groarke's ornamental pavilion (2010) in Regent's Place, London, for the real-estate investment trust British Land originated as a competition staged by the Architecture Foundation in London in 2007. It was followed by a pop-up restaurant, Studio East Dining (2007), in a car park overlooking the Olympics site in Stratford, east London. In 2011 the architect completed another memorial, the Indian Ocean Tsunami Memorial outside the Natural History Museum in South Kensington, London.

The firm's exhibition designs include *The Surreal House* at the Barbican Art Gallery, London (2010), supported by the graphic design of Angus Hyland, a partner at Pentagram; *Postmodernism* for the Victoria and Albert Museum, London (2011–12), and *Drawing Fashion* for the Design Museum (2010–11), both collaborations with graphic designer APFEL; the Frieze Art Fair, Regent's Park, London (2011); and *Bauhaus: Art as Life* at the Barbican Art Gallery in summer 2012.
carmodygroarke.com

David Kohn Architects

David Kohn Architects is based in London and specializes in arts and culture projects. David

Kohn studied architecture at the University of Cambridge and Columbia University, New York (as a Fulbright Scholar), and established his own office in 2007 following a decade working in leading practices in the United Kingdom and elsewhere, including Caruso St John Architects and East. He currently leads a Diploma Unit at London Metropolitan University and previously taught at the University of Cambridge and London School of Economics. He writes regularly for *Building Design* magazine on cultural topics, and has recently lectured at the Royal College of Art, London, the Glasgow School of Art and Istanbul Technical University.

Kohn's first projects included the Modern Art Gallery (2008) and Flash, a restaurant at the Royal Academy of Arts (2008–2009), followed by Skyroom, a rooftop pavilion for the Architecture Foundation (2010; all in London); *Tutti a Tavola* exhibition for the Milan Furniture Fair (2010); Carrer Avinyó, Barcelona (2011); Brit Insurance *Designs of the Year* exhibition for the Design Museum in London (2011); and *New Holland Island*, an exhibition in St Petersburg for the Architecture Foundation (2011). Current projects include several contemporary art galleries; a community arts centre adjacent to the 2012 Olympics site; and an installation in collaboration with the artist Fiona Banner, to be placed on the roof of the Queen Elizabeth Hall, Southbank Centre, during 2012 for Living Architecture and Artangel (all in London). David Kohn Architects was named *Building Design*'s Young Architect of the Year in 2009 and One-Off House Architect of the Year in 2010 for Stable Acre, a house in rural Norfolk. Kohn is a member of Newham Council's Design Review Panel.
davidkohn.co.uk

Duggan Morris Architects

Mary Duggan and Joe Morris founded Duggan Morris Architects in London in 2004. Duggan studied at the University of Brighton before spending two years teaching Architecture and Design in Penang, Malaysia, as part of a twinning scheme set up by De Montfort University, Leicester. She graduated from the Bartlett, University College London, in 1997. Morris studied at De Montfort University, the University of Greenwich and the Bartlett, graduating in 1996.

Morris is a member of the Design Review panels of the London boroughs of Southwark, Brent and Lewisham (Duggan took on this role in 2008–2010) and of the East Midlands, and – in common with many practices in this book – they have regularly taken part in charrettes (for example King's Cross, Clerkenwell Green and Design for Education/Royal Institute of British Architects (RIBA)), talks and events.

Key realized projects include Yew Tree Lodge sheltered housing in Ruislip (2009); the refurbishment of a house in Hampstead Lane, Highgate Village (2010); the renovation of two buildings on Fitzroy Street and Maple Place in Fitzrovia for Derwent London (2010); and a family dwelling at Kings Grove, Peckham (2010), all in London. Proposals for new secondary schools in Croydon as part of the Cooking Spaces Project date from 2011.

In progress in 2011 were a new sports and swimming pool complex for Alfriston School, a special-needs school for girls in Buckinghamshire (planning permission received; waiting to go out to tender); a commercial development on Curtain Road, Shoreditch, in east London (permission agreed; on site); Neptune Chemical Works, Deptford, south London (planning permission received); Phase 1, Brentford Lock West mixed-use masterplan with Karakusevic Carson and Riches Hawley Mikhail Architects, a competition win in 2011 (at an early stage of design). A New Learning Centre for the South London and Maudsley Hospital in Denmark Hill started on site in October 2011, for completion in 2013.

In 2011 the practice won the RIBA Manser Medal for Hampstead Lane, and an RIBA Award and a New London Award for Maple and Fitzroy; in 2009 it was shortlisted for *Building Design's* Young Architect of the Year Award.

dugganmorrisarchitects.com

EcoLogicStudio

EcoLogicStudio was founded in London in 2004 by Claudia Pasquero and Marco Poletto. Pasquero graduated from Turin Polytechnic in 2000, Poletto a year earlier, and they subsequently completed the Environment and Energy programme at the Architectural Association (AA) in London. Both have been Unit Masters of Intermediate Unit 10 at the AA since 2007; Poletto has also been Unit Master of Diploma 8 in the Department of Architecture and Spatial Design at London Metropolitan University.

Pasquero worked for Ushida Findlay and Erick van Egeraat, and Poletto at Battle McCarthy as an environmental designer. Pasquero has taught at the University of East London, Turin Polytechnic, Kingston University, the Universidad de las Américas (Mexico City), the Institute for Advanced Architecture of Catalonia (Barcelona), Istanbul Technical University, Istanbul Bilgi University and others.

Both partners have written extensively, including in David Littlefield, ed., *Space Craft: Developments in Architectural Computing* (2008), and Steve Hardy, ed., *Environmental Tectonics: Forming Climatic Change* (2008); and for various magazines, including *World Architecture*. In 2012 they published *Systemic Architecture: Operating Manual for the Self-organizing City*.

EcoLogicStudio's chief realized works include a prototype design of a roof light well in a shopping centre in Carosello, Italy (2009); Il Bosco della Cultura, furniture for a new public library in Ciriè, Italy (2007); a villa conversion with lightwall, Ciriè (2009); and an extensive series of installations

including Aqva Garden, Milan Furniture Fair, 2007; Fibrous Room, Garanti Gallery, Istanbul (2008, with the architect Tuspa); STEMcloud v2.0, for *YOUniverse*, Seville, Spain (2008); *EcoMachines: The Making of Artificial Ecologies*, Venice International Architecture Biennale (2008); Metropolitan Proto-Garden, video installation for Dreaming Milan, Milan Furniture Fair and the Urban Centre Milan (2009); Lightwall Apparatus, *Costruire secondo Natura* exhibition, Spazio FMG, Milan (2010); Fish&Chips Apparatus, prototype, *Spontaneous Schooling* exhibition, TEA Building, London (2010); Eco Footprint Data Grotto Machine, prototype immersive space, *AILATI* Italian Pavilion, Venice International Architecture Biennale (2010); and Biodiversity Workshop installation, ALPS Biennale, Science Museum, Trento, Italy (2011).

In 2010 the Swedish Municipality of Simrishamn invited EcoLogicStudio to design a masterplan for the coastal region of Skåne, including six prototypes, exhibited in the Marine Centre there in 2011. In 2011 the practice's scheme for North Side Copse House in Haslemere, Surrey, was in planning (2007–). In 2012 the firm stages Cyber Gardening in the City, the culmination of its AA Workshop at La Strada del Vino in Milan, and Worker City Apps, the subject of Pasquero and Poletto's AA Unit teaching linking notions of environmental design, digital technology, biomimics and biology.

ecologicstudio.com

Glowacka Rennie Architects

Glowacka Rennie Architects was founded in London in 2004 by Agnieszka Glowacka, who studied architecture at the University of Cambridge, and Eleanor Rennie, a graduate of Edinburgh College of Art. They met during postgraduate studies in architecture at the Bartlett, University College London, and while there were both nominated for the Royal Institute of British Architects (RIBA) President's Silver Medal (Rennie in 2000, Glowacka in 2002) and awarded the Sir Banister Fletcher Medal for the highest grade at Diploma (the same years), while Rennie won the RIBA Serjeant Award in 2000. Both have taught at the Bartlett since 2002, initially as Guest Critics for Diploma Unit 17 and Glowacka more recently as BSc Unit Tutor. After graduating they worked at Buschow Henley (now Henley Halebrown Rorrison) on diverse projects, ranging from housing to hotels, and from large Private Finance Initiative healthcare buildings to bespoke display cabinets.

In 2004 Glowacka and Rennie won an East of England Development Agency/RIBA design competition with a proposal for East Reef, a coastal beach destination including the Landmark Promenade, at Jaywick in Essex. It was on the basis of this win that the pair set up their practice. It was a runner-up in the international design competition for the New Islington Bridge in Manchester, with structural engineer Techniker; and it was invited by the real-estate investment trust British Land to realize a temporary pavilion next to Foster + Partners' 30 St Mary Axe (the 'Gherkin'), and by Urban Initiatives to be part of the team producing the Supplementary Planning Document and Town Centre Strategy for Sittingbourne, Kent, including advising on the bridge link north of the town.

Glowacka Rennie's invited design proposals have included the Deal Pier Cafe, Deal, Kent, and Brockholes visitor centre, Preston, Lancashire. In 2007 the practice was approached by Fingal County Council to design a visitor centre as part of a masterplan for the greening of a large landfill site on the Rogerstown Estuary in Ireland.

Further competitions resulted in the practice winning the commission for the women's lavatories off the Grand Entrance hall at the Victoria and Albert Museum, London, realized with the input of Felice Varini, a Swiss artist (2009). Glowacka Rennie is working with the Paddington Farm Trust on the refurbishment and conversion of a barn into a flexible community space at its 17.5-hectare organic farm in Glastonbury, Somerset.

In February 2010 Glowacka Rennie opened a second office, in Beirut, Lebanon, after winning the commission for Yarze, a residential development in the hills to the east of the city.

As part of the RIBA's Regent Street Windows Project in 2011, the practice was chosen to design shop windows for Hoss Intropia, the Spanish women's fashion retailer, and, on the strength of its displays, the firm commissioned Glowacka Rennie to develop its design for the Autumn/Winter Collection 2011, to be applied across the chain's international stores.

Glowacka Rennie's competition work has been advanced alongside refurbishment and extensions of houses, including those in Queens Grove, Kennington Road and Marshall Street (all in London); feasibility studies for private residences in the Park in Surrey and Middleton Road, Hackney, east London; and new build, for example Wilmer Place in Stoke Newington, east London. The practice has produced concept designs for Norway's first wetland centre, on the Dokka Delta, for the Wildfowl & Wetlands Trust. **glowacka-rennie.com**

Gort Scott

Gort Scott was founded in London in 2007 by Jay Gort and Fiona Scott. Its portfolio ranges from local community projects to urban plans and commercial developments.

Jay Gort studied sculpture and then trained as an architect at the University of Cambridge, where he is now a Design Fellow in the Architecture Department, and where he has run a design studio since 2003. He is regularly invited to be a guest critic at architecture schools around the United Kingdom, is a 'Design Surgeon' for Urban Design London and a member of the Islington Conservation and Design Panel, and has lectured at a number of venues in the United Kingdom and abroad. Before establishing Gort Scott he was a director of the architecture and urban-design practice 5th Studio (based in London and Cambridge), running projects of various scales from domestic and local community projects to large-scale urban framework plans, for example Cambridge's Southern Fringe. He also ran a large student-accommodation project for Trinity College, Cambridge, and worked on a number of award-winning projects. He has also worked for the London practice Ash Sakula, and with a house-building contractor in the north of England.

Fiona Scott trained as an architect at the University of Cambridge and the Royal College of Art, London. Before setting up the practice, she was project architect at Adjaye Associates (2002–2007), working on public projects including the Idea Stores in London, the Museum of Contemporary Art in Denver, Skolkovo School of Management in Moscow, and Wakefield Market Hall, West Yorkshire. She also ran a number of residential and private gallery projects in London and New York, and has additionally worked for MVRDV in Rotterdam and DSDHA in London. She was an Urban Design Scholar at Design for London in 2008–2009 and is currently a design adviser there. She has lectured at various institutions, including Norsk Form in Oslo, London Metropolitan University and Kingston University. She has also written a number of articles, and taught with Gort at the University of Cambridge, where she was previously a Design Fellow.

Gort Scott's George V Pavilion in Cambridge was completed in 2009. The following year the practice completed a new outdoor play area for Harlington Community School in west London, and extended and completely remodelled a three-storey Georgian town house for the Swedish fashion brand Acne's first British store, on Dover Street in London. The duo also completed Seamount, a house at Scarlett on the Isle of Man, and are tendering for a cottage in the grounds of the site. Gort Scott won the Royal Institute of British Architects' Forgotten Spaces competition for Walthamstow Reservoirs, a proposal that has been included in a funding bid for a project for Walthamstow Wetlands. Finding Flotmyr is a competition entry (2011) for a new mixed-use, high-density quarter of Haugesund, a town in western Norway. One of Gort Scott's key urban-design frameworks is for Blackhorse Lane (2010–), part of the London Borough of Waltham Forest's Area Action Plan, which is being developed by a multidisciplinary team including Maccreanor Lavington.

Gort Scott has also carried out research with University College London to help develop the High Streets Agenda of the London Development Agency, which aims to evolve a greater understanding of how high streets function in supporting London's sustainable growth and development. This work featured in the Technical University of Berlin's exhibition *City Visions 1910 | 2010* (2010), and culminated in *The London High Street Possibilities Primer*, coordinated by Design for London and with text by Kieran Long (2011). The Living Screens (ongoing), a major new residential-led mixed-use scheme in the centre of Cambridge, includes a screen devised with the artist Michael Tuck.

Gort Scott was longlisted for *Building Design*'s Young Architect of the Year Award in 2009 and was invited by the Architecture Foundation in London to be one of three emerging British practices to present their work as part of the Foundation's International Exchange programme in Oslo.
gortscott.com

Guarnieri Architects

Marco Guarnieri was born in Trieste in Italy, and trained as an architect at IUAV Venice (Istituto Universitario di Architettura Venezia). In 1996 he moved to London and worked for Zaha Hadid

Architects before graduating from the Diploma School of the Architectural Association (AA) in London in 2000, where he studied in Diploma Unit 5, run by architects Alejandro Zaera-Polo and Farshid Moussavi. He was then invited to join their practice, Foreign Office Architects, which gave him the opportunity to work on international competitions and build project experience over a number of years. In 2003 he set up his own London-based practice with AA-trained architect Lea Katz. They designed and built Pack Line, a company headquarters and production building (2006), and the FM shop (2005), both in Tel Aviv, Israel, after which Guarnieri branched off to set up Guarnieri Architects, his own architectural office, in Bermondsey, London.

In addition to carrying out residential projects for sites in Bermondsey, Kensington, Parsons Green, Fulham, Wembley and Whitechapel (all in London), and the refurbishment of the company headquarters and production unit of CMG, a major firm in Trieste, Italy (2007), Guarnieri has advanced proposals for a three-floor extension to help modernize public perception of the ESCP-EAP European School of Management on London's Finchley Road (2008–2009). He has entered several international competitions, including a proposal for the transport interchange in Oristano, Sardinia (2009), with Arup Milan; a new train station prototype for the Italian Railway Network (2007); and the National Library of the Czech Republic (with A.A. Dunkel; 2006).

Guarnieri has written articles for *Arch'it*, *D'A* and other architectural publications, and he was the curator and co-author of a special issue of *Parametro* on Italy's high-speed rail project, *Italy, High Speed: The Italian System* (258.259, 2005), with essays by him, Peter Hall (Professor of Planning and Regeneration at the Bartlett, University College London) and others. Guarnieri has also taught Intermediate Unit 6 at the Architectural Association, London, with Jonathan

Dawes (the director of Flowspace), and has lectured in Italy and the United Kingdom.
guarnieri.co.uk

IJP

George L. Legendre is a partner at IJP, a London-based architectural practice he founded in 2004 with Lluis Viu-Rebes (AADipl) and Marc Fouquet. He graduated from the Harvard University Graduate School of Design (GSD) in 1994 and worked as a lecturer and Assistant Professor of Architecture there between 1995 and 2000. Before establishing IJP he was Visiting Professor at ETH (the Swiss Federal Institute of Technology), Zurich (2001), and Princeton University (2003–2005), and Unit Master of Diploma Unit 5 at the Architectural Association, London (2002–2008). In 2011 he was appointed adjunct Associate Professor at Harvard GSD for a further five years. He lectures extensively around the world.

IJP has won a number of international competitions, principally for a bridge in Singapore, now completed: Henderson Waves (2004–2008), realized with RSP Consulting Engineers and structural engineer Adams Kara Taylor (AKT II), with which IJP has also won a competition for a roof structure over Glasshouse Street in central London (2004–2005). IJP was the delivery architect for the Berkeley Bat House at the London Wetland Centre in Barnes, west London (2009), for which Tandberg.Murata was project designer, and in 2011 he designed GhostHouse, a temporary installation for the Museum of Modern Art PS1 Young Architects Program, an invited competition for the MoMA PS1 site at Long Island City in Queens, New York.

IJP's proposals include the Seroussi Pavilion, a house in Paris (2007); the Art Fund Pavilion, Woking, Surrey (2009); the National Museum of Art, Architecture and Design in Vestbanen, Oslo (2009); PV (Photovoltaic) Dust, a selected entry to the Land Art Generator Initiative competition in 2010, exhibited at the World Future Energy Summit, Abu Dhabi, a public artwork for the outskirts of Masdar City, Abu Dhabi (a visitor centre that can harness clean renewable energy from nature, convert it into electrical power and distribute it to the utility grid of the city); and the Thematic Pavilion, Floating Island and Marine Life reef at the Yeosu 2012 World Expo in South Korea.

Legendre is a prolific writer, whose work includes *IJP: The Book of Surfaces* (2003), *Bodyline: The End of our Meta-Mechanical Body* (2006) and essays in *AA Files* 56 (2007); most recently, he guest-edited *The Mathematics of Sensible Things*, an issue of *Architectural Design* magazine (April 2011). His latest book, *Pasta By Design*, was published in 2011. In 2007 IJP was shortlisted for *Building Design*'s Young Architect of the Year Award, and Henderson Waves won a Steel Design Award from the Singapore Structural Steel Society in 2009 and a Singapore Institute of Architects Design Award in 2011.
ijpcorporation.com

MÆ

MÆ was founded by Alex Ely and Michael Howe in 2001, and is led by Ely, who is a chartered town planner as well as an architect. He graduated from the Royal College of Art and completed his professional practice at the Architectural Association (both in London), and was formerly Head of Sustainable Communities at the Commission for Architecture and the Built Environment. He has worked for Foster + Partners, Ian Simpson Architects and Pierre d'Avoine Architects. He teaches at London Metropolitan University, and lectures internationally on design and policy. Michael Howe is an adviser to the practice, assisting with research and review. A contemporary of Ely at the Royal College of Art, Howe is Senior Lecturer and Technology Coordinator at the University of Brighton School

of Architecture. He has worked for Matthew Lloyd Architects, Zaha Hadid Architects and Patel Taylor.

MÆ's realized projects include Lift-up House, Shoreditch, London (2003–2004), and the Wilbury Hills Chapel and Cemetery, Letchworth Garden City, for North Hertfordshire District Council (2007). The Guts, New Islington Millennium Village, Manchester, for Urban Splash and Great Places Housing Group (2009–) is under construction, as is Hammond Court, Waltham Forest, London, for East Thames Group (2007–), while the Colville Estate masterplan with Karakusevic Carson Architects for Hackney Borough Council in east London received planning permission in 2011. Key urban-design projects also include Pincents Hill mixed-use development with Blue Living (now Beyond Green), Greater Reading (2008–2009); a spatial framework for North Prospect for Plymouth City Council (2006–2007); M-House (2002–2003); Dunroamin' for the Royal Institute of British Architects' Make Me a Home competition, Stockton-on-Tees (2008); Nordhavnen Gateway Green Island for the City of Copenhagen (2008); National Museum of Art, Architecture and Design, Vestbanen, Oslo (2009); Clay Country Eco-House, St Austell, Cornwall, for Eco-Bos (2010); Leyton Open Spaces Investment Strategy development with Kinnear Landscape Architects, London Borough of Waltham Forest (2011–); and Hillington Square, King's Lynn, Norfolk (2011–). In 2009 MÆ prepared a patternbook of housing types for Transform South Yorkshire's Delivering Design Quality initiative, intended to raise the standard of design in the region and to be available for use by local authorities and their developer partners.

Since 2008 MÆ has developed proposals for township housing in Johannesburg, with the European Union National Institutes for Culture (EUNIC), a South African housing association and housing graduates, for the annual EUNIC Studio. MÆ developed the London Housing Design Guide (2010) with the London Development

Agency. Drafted for the Mayor of London, the guide sets out standards for improving the quality of design of new housing in the capital.

Alex Ely was instrumental in creating the Building for Life Standard, a national policy for the design of residential neighbourhoods launched in 2003. MÆ's most recent awards include a Housing Design Award in 2011 for the Guts, and in 2008 the practice was selected as one of the Architecture Foundation's Next Generation Architects.
mae-llp.co.uk

NORD

NORD (Northern Office for Research & Design) was founded in Glasgow in 2002 by Alan Pert and Robin Lee, who had established a working relationship over a number of years while at Zoo Architects in the city (1997–2002). After graduating from the University of Strathclyde, Pert worked with GMW & Partners in Berlin (1993–95), where he was involved with the refurbishment of the Hellerau theatre in Dresden. This was followed by two further years to gain his MArch from the University of Strathclyde (1995–97), after which he co-founded Zoo Architects in 1997. During his time there he was a key member of the team working on the award-winning Tramway redevelopment project in Glasgow. Pert has been a studio tutor at the University of Strathclyde since 1999, and is currently Professor of Research there. He has also been honorary lecturer at Dundee School of Art (now Duncan of Jordanstone College of Art & Design) and Visiting Professor at the Canterbury School of Architecture.

In 2008 the architect Graeme Williamson, who was director of the award-winning London firm Block Architecture, joined NORD as a Senior Architect to help deliver the Primary Substation for the London Olympic Park. He had a ten-year track record of realizing schemes for institutions including the Victoria and Albert Museum (V&A), the British Council, the Institute of Contemporary Arts, the Commission for Architecture and the Built Environment, the Design Council, the Royal Institute of British Architects, MOMA Oxford, the Glasgow Lighthouse and Magasin 3 in Stockholm. Williamson has taught the Diploma in Architecture at the Bartlett, University College London, since 2008 and has lectured extensively in the United Kingdom and elsewhere.

NORD's built projects include Destiny Church, Glasgow (2004); Bell House, Strathblane (2004); Linthills, Lochwinnoch (2008); the Primary Substation for the 2012 Olympics (2009); and the Wexford County Council headquarters on the outskirts of Wexford town, Ireland, won in an international competition run by the Royal Institute of the Architects of Ireland and completed in 2011. NORD recently completed Shingle House for Living Architecture in Dungeness, Kent (2010), and Hanley Canal Quarter in Stoke-on-Trent (2013), a masterplan for RENEW North Staffordshire and Urban Splash including a new bridge over the Caldon Canal, Bridgewater Bridge (built in 2009).

Projects currently in development include a series of buildings won in international competition, such as the Furniture Galleries of the V&A, London (2012), and three projects in Glasgow: Govanhill Baths, a community swimming pool (2015); a mixed-use scheme on Royal Exchange Square (2013); and a housing project. The practice was also recently commissioned to design a number of shops in London and Europe for Pringle of Scotland.

Pert won the Scottish Design Awards Young Architect of the Year in 2001. The Bell House and Destiny Church were both *Architects' Journal* Small Projects Award winners (in 2004 and 2005 respectively). NORD has won numerous industry accolades, including *Building Design*'s Young Architect of the Year Award in 2006, and Architect of the Year in the Scottish Design Awards (2007).

NORD LLP was established in 2002, and in 2009 a separate entity was founded, NORD Architecture Ltd. The two ran in parallel before NORD LLP was rebranded Robin Lee Architecture (see pp. 210–21), while Pert trades under the name NORD Ltd. NORD gained an excellent reputation during its evolution, and the two practices will undoubtedly build on the extensive experience and accomplishment of Pert and Lee.
nordarchitecture.com

Office for Subversive Architecture (OSA)

OSA began life in 1995, when a group of German architecture students joined forces on a project. Instead of creating a company, they formed a network and collective of like minds in the fields of architecture and public space. Now the eight partners are based in seven cities: Ulrich Beckefeld in Vienna; Anja Ohliger, Frankfurt; Britta Eiermann, Darmstadt; Oliver Langbein, Dortmund; Anke Strittmatter, Graz; and Sebastian Appl, Hamburg. Karsten Huneck and Bernd Trümpler lead the London branch of OSA.

Initially, while still working as full-time architects in different practices, Huneck and Trümpler developed their body of hybrid art–architecture projects around the country and internationally. In 2009 they began devoting their time to OSA UK, established a Berlin-based studio and simultaneously set up KHBT in London and Berlin, allowing them to develop projects as OSA partners as well as independently.

The first wave of OSA projects in the United Kingdom included London Roof (2002); Intact, Shoreditch, London (2004); the Hoegaarden Urban Oasis, London (2005); On an Island, Bristol's Spike Island (2005); Kunsthülle Liverpool (2006); Rokeby Gallery, London (2008); the Accumulator, Leeds (2008); Point of View, London Olympic Park (2008); and in Germany, Anwohnerpark (Residents' Park), Cologne (2006); Geburtstagstorte (And for

birthday – a cake), Schirn Kunsthalle, Frankfurt (2006); and the OSA/KHBT Studio, Berlin (2009). OSA's most recent British projects include Merzen at the CUBE Gallery, Manchester (2011). In 2010 OSA realized the Sleeping Policeman in Tilburg, The Netherlands, and Kölnisch Wasser (Eau de Cologne), Cologne, and in 2012 the Weymouth and Portland Legacy Trail will be completed.
khbt.eu
osa-online.net

Piercy Conner Architects

Piercy Conner Architects was founded in London in 1999 by Stuart Piercy and Richard Conner, two architects who had previously worked for Nicholas Grimshaw & Partners (1995–2002), on such schemes as the Eden Project in Cornwall, the Berlin Stock Exchange and Zurich Airport.

Piercy trained at Leicester Polytechnic (now De Montfort University), the National University of Singapore and the Architectural Association, London. From 2004 to 2009 he was Unit Master at the Bartlett, University College London. Richard Conner trained at the University of Liverpool and the Bartlett. The practice has built up a diverse portfolio of innovative, bespoke projects, especially in the fields of housing and urban design, and also runs a sister company, Smoothe, which specializes in digital communications. Conner recently set up his own firm, while Piercy Conner continues to produce high-quality affordable housing projects.

Piercy Conner hit the news with the Microflat (2002), its innovative solution to the problem of providing affordable urban housing. The practice built a fully functional prototype in the window of Selfridges department store in London, and two people lived in it for two weeks. The project created widespread interest and became the subject of several television programmes. In 2005 the practice won the Living Steel International Architecture Competition with SymHomes Mk1, which became a commission to design Restello, a development of twelve family apartments in the planned Rajarhat New Town in Kolkata, India, one of the country's fastest-growing planned new cities (2012). Other projects include Martello Tower Y, Suffolk (2010); a house in Kew, south-west London (2012); the refurbishment of 63 Clerkenwell Road, London, formerly Turnmills nightclub, for Derwent London (2014); and new town houses on Wakefield Street, London (2012); while the Van for the Great Outdoors (ongoing) is a reimagining of the caravan.

In 2006 Piercy Conner won the *Architects' Journal* Corus 40 Under 40 Steel Innovation Award and was shortlisted in the *Building Design* Young Architect of the Year Award. In 2007 it won the MIPIM *Architectural Review* Future Project Sustainability Award, and in 2010 was nominated for a Royal Institute of British Architects Regional Award and both the Stephen Lawrence Prize and the Manser Medal.

piercyconner.co.uk

Plasma Studio | GroundLab

Plasma Studio was founded by Eva Castro and Holger Kehne in London in 1999, and the practice now operates from three different locations: London, Beijing and Sexten, near Bolzano, Italy, the last run by Ulla Hell since 2002. Castro and Kehne went on to co-found GroundLab, a second design practice operating from the London and Beijing studios, which they lead with the architect Alfredo Ramirez, Eduardo Rico (a civil engineer, who also co-founded Relational Urbanism in London with Enriqueta Llabres, in 2007, and works for Arup providing strategic advice on infrastructure and transportation for urban masterplanning), the architectural engineer Sarah Majid and Dongyun Liu (a landscape architect who also runs LAUR Studio, his landscape practice, in Beijing).

The two practices regularly work in tandem and are inherently multidisciplinary. Employing architects, urban designers, engineers and landscape architects, they combine different expertise in teams to respond to contemporary social, economic and environmental conditions.

Holger Kehne studied Architecture at FH (University of Applied Sciences) Münster, Germany, and the University of East London. Eva Castro studied Architecture and Urbanism at the Universidad Central de Venezuela and then completed the Graduate Design programme under Jeff Kipnis at the Architectural Association (AA), London. She has been Director of the Master's in Landscape Urbanism at the AA since 2004. From 2003 Kehne and Castro ran Diploma Unit 12 at the AA, with Jeffrey Turko taking Castro's place in 2008–10. Their Associate Partner at Plasma Studio, Ulla Hell, studied at the University of Innsbruck, Austria, Delft University of Technology and Eindhoven University of Technology. GroundLab partners Eduardo Rico and Alfredo Ramirez gained Master's in Landscape Urbanism at the AA, while Sarah Majid studied Architectural Engineering at Jordan University of Science and Technology before taking a Master's in Landscape Urbanism at the AA. Dongyun Liu is a graduate of Beijing Forestry University.

Plasma Studio works on all scales, from furniture design and installations to urbanism and masterplanning. The practice won the *Building Design* Young Architect of the Year Award in 2002, and has since become recognized as a leading emergent architectural and design practice with a global scope and outlook. By undertaking academic research at the AA and other leading institutions, Plasma Studio is developing advanced digital tools and methodologies to analyse complex problems, responding to them by synthesizing spatial effects, functions and ergonomics. GroundLab's work is rooted in the relatively new discipline of landscape urbanism, and specifically the methodology developed in the Landscape Urbanism Master's programme at the AA.

Plasma Studio's built works include refurbishments at 186 Camden High Street (2000) and 136 Old Street (1999), London; Silversmith's Studio (2001), Musician's Home (2001) and Minerva Loft (2002), east London; Residenz Alma, the refurbishment and extension of an apartment hotel, Sexten (2004); the fit-out of one floor at Hotel Puerta América, Madrid (2005); Strata Hotel, a new wing for an apartment hotel, Sexten (2007); D_Cube, a private house in Sexten (2007); Tetris House (2007) and Esker House (2008), both family houses in San Candido, Italy; and Hotel Rainer and Cube House (both 2008), Sexten.

The practice has been invited to take part in numerous competitions, and in 2009 Plasma Studio | GroundLab, with LAUR Studio, won an international competition to develop a new masterplan for Longgang City, Shenzhen, China. The two studios, working together, completed the masterplanning, landscape and building design of the Xi'an International Horticultural Expo, China (2011), with Dongyun Liu, including the design of the Flowing Gardens at the centre of the site, the Guangyun Entrance, Chang'an Flower Valley, the Creativity Pavilion and the Greenhouse. Current projects include a series of office blocks for Ordos 20+10, Inner Mongolia, China; a street-lighting system for the lighting company EWO; several new-build residential and hospitality projects with a new take on the Alpine vernacular in the Italian Dolomites; and Drape Tower, a mixed-use tower for Tehran.

plasmastudio.com
groundlab.org

Robin Lee Architecture

Robin Lee Architecture was founded in London and Dublin in 2011 by Robin Lee, after he branched out from his former award-winning practice, NORD, established in Glasgow in 2002 with Alan Pert. NORD LLP was established in

2002, and in 2009 a separate entity was founded, NORD Architecture Ltd. The two ran in parallel before NORD LLP was rebranded Robin Lee Architecture, while Pert trades under the name NORD Ltd (see pp. 156–69). NORD gained an excellent reputation during its evolution, and the two practices look set to build further on the many accomplishments of the former business partners since 2002.

Lee trained in architecture at the Mackintosh School of Architecture, University of Glasgow (1991), and has a postgraduate diploma in Fine Art from Glasgow School of Art (Sculpture, 1993). From 1996 to 2002 he worked at Zoo Architects in Glasgow with Pert, a founding member. Lee lectures regularly in the United Kingdom and Ireland, and has taught at the Mackintosh and at University College Dublin.

Lee's projects at Zoo included the award-winning Royston Recording Studios. He also worked on the RMJM feasibility study for the Scottish Parliament building and was creative consultant on the first phase of the Homes for the Future scheme, Glasgow. He played a key role in all NORD's projects, including the Primary Substation for the 2012 Olympics (2009); Bridgewater Bridge, Stoke-on-Trent (2009); Linthills, Lochwinnoch (2008); Destiny Church, Glasgow (2004); Bell House, Strathblane (2004); and the Wexford County Council headquarters on the outskirts of Wexford town, Ireland (2011).

The Bell House and Destiny Church were both *Architects' Journal* Small Projects Winners (in 2004 and 2005 respectively). NORD won numerous industry accolades, including *Building Design*'s Young Architect of the Year Award in 2006, and Architect of the Year in the Scottish Design Awards (2007).

robinleearchitecture.com

Serie

Christopher C.M. Lee and Kapil Gupta co-founded Serie in London, Mumbai and Beijing in 2006. Lee, who runs the London office, graduated from the School of Architecture and the Built Environment at the National University of Singapore in 1995, and the Architectural Association (AA) in London in 1998, when he was awarded the Royal Institute of British Architects' President's Medal Commendation Award. He has been Director of the AA Projective Cities Programme since 2010; he was Unit Master of Diploma Unit 6 from 2004 to 2009 and of Intermediate Unit 2 from 2002 to 2004, and before that Studio Tutor for the University of Pennsylvania/AA Exchange Programme. He is a Design Critic in Architecture at Harvard University Graduate School of Design (2011–).

Gupta, who runs the Mumbai office, graduated from the Sir J.J. College of Architecture, University of Mumbai, in 1996 and from the AA in 1998. He was a director of the Urban Design Research Institute (UDRI), Mumbai, between 1998 and 2003. He lectures widely, and curated, on behalf of the UDRI, India's first-ever entry to the Venice International Architecture Biennale, in 2006: 'Bombay's Land: Between the Relic and the Void'. That became the exhibition *Reading ^ the Lines* at Project 88, Mumbai (2007), and an essay, 'Abandon Mumbai', for *Art India* (vol. XII, no. 4, 2007).

The three offices are currently advancing a diverse range of projects, from residential and commercial buildings to hotels, schools and masterplans. Their built projects include the Sprüth Magers London gallery (2007); Blue Frog Acoustic Lounge, Mumbai, a recording studio, restaurant, bar, lounge and performance stage (2008); the Tote, Mumbai, a banqueting hall, restaurant and wine bar (2009); and the Monsoon Club at the Kennedy Center, Washington D.C. (2011).

In 2010 Serie came second in the competition to design the Xi'an International Horticultural Expo masterplan, won by Plasma Studio, GroundLab and LAUR Studio (see pp. 204–207), and won the commission for the Shrimad Rajachandra Ashram masterplan in Dharampur, India. The practice was commissioned to convert XianTian Di Factory H in Hangzhou, China (2010–). The year 2011 saw the start on site of the Bohacky-Zahorska Bystrica residential masterplan in Bratislava, Slovakia (won in competition in 2009), and new commissions for Yan Zhenqing Calligraphy Museum in Linyi, China; Wuxi XiShan Civic Centre in Wuxi, China; Napean Sea School, Mumbai; and An'ren Culture Centre and Museum (by invited competition) in Sichuan, China.

Serie's publications include *Typological Urbanism* (a guest-edited issue of *Architectural Design*, vol. 81, no. 1, January/February 2011) and *Working in Series* (2010). In 2010 Serie won *Building Design*'s Young Architect of the Year Award.

serie.co.uk

Studio Weave

Je Ahn and Maria Smith founded Studio Weave in London in 2006. Their portfolio of projects includes public spaces and landscapes; private houses and public buildings; shelters, follies and cabins; play spaces, furniture and structures; and art installations. They write stories as part of their design process.

Je Ahn was born near Busan, South Korea, and moved to England when he was thirteen. He went to school in West Sussex before moving to study architecture at the University of Bath, where he met Maria Smith. Together they studied at Delft University of Technology in The Netherlands and at London Metropolitan University (LMU). Before founding Studio Weave Ahn worked in London for Carmody Groarke (see pp. 40–51), Bennetts Associates and Nash Parker. He is also a director of MUSARC, an independent research and event platform based at LMU's Faculty of

Picture credits

Architecture and Spatial Design, exploring the relationship between architecture, music and sound. Maria Smith is a member of the Southwark Design Review Panel, has taught at LMU and organized a linked academic programme for schools of architecture to develop school design exemplars for what is now the Department for Education. Before founding Studio Weave she worked for Carmody Groarke, David Morley Architects and Aaron Evans Architects. Both directors lecture extensively.

Studio Weave's major completed projects include the Longest Bench, Littlehampton, West Sussex (2010), a recipient of Commission for Architecture and the Built Environment Sea Change funding and a donation from Gordon Roddick as a tribute to his late wife, Anita Roddick; Graviton, Shangri-La Field, an installation for the Glastonbury festival (2010); Fire Folly, Studio in the Woods, Isle of Wight (2010); Tourist Information Centre, Weston-super-Mare, for North Somerset Council (2009); and Freya and Robin, structures next to Kielder Water, Northumberland (2009). Ongoing activities include refurbishments and furniture for the Barbican Highwalks, and St Pancras Churchyard, with Street Scene, for the City of London Corporation; Holm Hall, a folly for Dartford's Central Park, Kent; and Blackburn's Secret Landscape Garden, Lancashire, with MESH landscape architects. Studio Weave designed Vistas, furniture for London's Largest Living Room, with a pattern by Eley Kishimoto, at the London Festival of Architecture in 2008; and 140 Boomerangs, West Smithfield, for the same festival in 2006. The Longest Bench was commended in the *Architectural Review*'s international Awards for Emerging Architecture 2010, and in 2009 Studio Weave won the prize for first-time exhibitor at the Royal Academy Summer Exhibition for Inside-Out House, its entry to the Tribeca Infobox competition.
studioweave.com

All renders, diagrams and drawings are copyright © the architect, unless otherwise stated
t = top; c = centre; b = bottom, l = left; r = right

6a Architects: 19, 20–21 (all), 24tl, r, 25; © AOC: 29, 30, 36–37 (both); © David Barbour: cover spine c, 11r, 239; © Sue Barr/VIEW: 7, 9l; © James Brittain/VIEW: 69, 78–79 (all); © David Kohn Architects: 59r, 60–61 (main), 62t, b, 64–65 (both); © Richard Davies: 47l, b, 49t, b, 50b; © Phillip Day: 171; © Duggan Morris Architects: 72; © EcoLogicStudio: 81–93; © Dominik Gigler: 15r, 32, 32–33, 33; © Glowacka Rennie Architects: 97t, b, 98–99, 100–101 (both), 103t, b, 104, 105l; © Gort Scott: 110–11 (both), 112–13 (both), 117; © David Grandorge: cover spine b, 12, 17, 22, 27, 31 (all), 38–39 (all), 67, 70b, 71tr, br, 116, 154, 155; © Stefano Graziani: 119 (all), 121, 124b, 126–27 (all), 133, 135, 139tr; © Tim Griffiths: 102; © Guarnieri Architects: 122–23 (all), 124tl, tc, tr, 125 (all), 128, 129; © Mark Hadden: 70t, 71l; © Luke Hayes/Design Museum: 55; © Luke Hayes: front cover, 43, 44t, b, 48; © Mishka Henner: 107, 109, 114, 115; © Charles Hosea: 159, 162–63 (both), 164, 165; Hufton + Crow: 14r; © IJP: 136t (photo: Stefano Graziani), 136b, 137, 138–39 (main), 139 (both) (photos: Stefano Graziani), 142–43 (both); © Ink (InkWorkshop LLP): 192l, 194–95 (both); © Andrew Lee: 157, 160, 161b, 168–69 (both), 211, 213, 215tl, tr, 216, 217, 218, 219, 220–21; © London Metropolitan Archive: 23r; © Sam Lucas: 185; © MÆ: 15l, 148t, b, 149, 152t, b, 153t, b; © Johannes Marburg: 8l, c, 173, 174, 175t, 180b, 181, 182–83; © Ioana Marinescu: 58, 60 (inset), 63; © Forbes Massie: 76–77 (all), 73t, b;

© MHJT: 131, 140, 141; © Tim Mitchell: 35l; © MUF Architecture/Art: 14l, c; © NORD: 166–67 (both); © Trenton Oldfield: 176; © OSA: 176 (all), 178, 179, 180t; © Kilian O'Sullivan/VIEW: 74, 75, 145; © Cristobal Palma: back cover t, 199, 201, 202, 203, 204 (all), 205, 206b, 207bl, br, 208–209; © Alan Pert and Robin Lee: 214t, 214–15b; © Fram Petit: back cover b, 227 (inset), 229l; © Piercy Conner Architects: 187, 188t, b, 189, 191, 193, 196, 197; © Plasma Studio/GroundLab: 206–207t; © Will Pryce: back cover c, 53, 56, 57r; © Christian Richters: 13, 41, 46t, b, 50t, 51 (all); © Daniel Schwartz: 223, 226; © Serie: 10l, r, 11l, 228t, b, 231t, b, 231 (all); © Peter Sharpe: 233, 235, 242–43; © Morley von Sternberg: cover spine t, 34, 35r, 147, 150–51 (both); © Studio Weave: 8r, 236t, b, 237t, b, 238, 240, 241; © Edmund Sumner/VIEW: 2–3, 9r, 190t, b, 225, 229tr, br; © Tandberg.Murata/IJP: 134; © Anthony Weller @ ArchImage: 95, 105r

Index

For their enthusiasm, creative input and committed cooperation, I should like to thank all the architects featured in the book. I am equally beholden to Hugh Merrell, Rosanna Lewis, Alexandre Coco and Claire Chandler for taking on this project and applying the same sterling capacities to aid its realization. My parents, Patricia and Dargan Bullivant, were ever-supportive throughout the process; Judy Dobias, Neil Byrne, Christine Styrnau, Susie Dawson, Alisa Andrasek, Theresa Simon, Kirsten Richards, Bartomeu Mari, Pati Nunez, Renata Gatti, Rowena Easton, Torsten Neeland, Edie Juniper, Aaron and Ben Bullivant-Norris were stars along the way; and a number of key people, including David Adjaye, Eelco Hooftman, Jeremy Hunt, Paul Monaghan, Deborah Saunt and Alejandro Zaera-Polo, have given me valuable advice and help.

LUCY BULLIVANT Hon. FRIBA is an architectural curator, writer, critic and guest lecturer. Born in London, she has a Master's degree in Cultural History from the Royal College of Art, London. She is the author of *Anglo Files: UK Architecture's Rising Generation* (2005) and *Responsive Environments: Architecture, Art and Design* (2006), among other books; a correspondent for *Domus*, *The Plan*, *Architectural Review* and *Indesign*; and curates and chairs the Talking Architecture events series at the Victoria and Albert Museum, London. In 2010 she was awarded an honorary fellowship of the Royal Institute of British Architects.

FRONT COVER: Carmody Groarke, Regent's Place Pavilion, London (2010; p. 48)
BACK COVER, from top: Plasma Studio | GroundLab, Xi'an International Horticultural Expo, Xi'an, China (2011, pp. 204–207); David Kohn Architects, Skyroom, London (2010, pp. 56–57); Serie, The Tote, Mumbai (2009, p. 229)
SPINE, from top: MÆ, M-House (2002–2003, pp. 150–51); Studio Weave, The Longest Bench, Littlehampton, West Sussex (2010, p. 239); 6a Architects, Raven Row, Spitalfields, London (2009, pp. 22–25) FRONTISPIECE: The Tote, Mumbai

First published 2012 by

Merrell Publishers Limited
81 Southwark Street
London SE1 0HX

merrellpublishers.com

Text copyright © 2012 Lucy Bullivant
Illustrations copyright © the copyright holders;
    see p. 253
Design and layout copyright © 2012 Merrell
    Publishers Limited

British Library Cataloguing-in-Publication data:
Bullivant, Lucy.
New arcadians : emerging UK architects.
1. Architects – Great Britain. 2. Architectural firms – Great Britain. 3. Architecture, British.
4. Architecture – Great Britain – History – 21st century.
5. Architect-designed houses – Case studies.
I. Title
720.9'22'41-dc23

ISBN 978-1-8589-4548-4

Produced by Merrell Publishers Limited
Designed by Alexandre Coco
Project-managed by Rosanna Lewis
Proof-read by Sarah Yates
Indexed by Hilary Bird
Printed and bound in China

ISBN 978-1-8589-4548-4